HANS WALTER WOLFF is emeritus professor of Old Testament at the University of Heidelberg, and the author of many widely used Old Testament studies, including *Anthropology of the Old Testament* and *Joel and Amos*. The English translation of his commentary on Micah is to be published by Augsburg.

MARGARET KOHL, who lives near Munich, has translated works by Ernst Käsemann, Wolfhart Pannenberg, Jürgen Moltmann, Klaus Koch, Willi Marxsen, and others, in addition to two other books by Hans Walter Wolff.

OBADIAH AND JONAH

Hans Walter Wolff

OBADIAH AND JONAH

A Commentary

Translated by

Margaret Kohl

AUGSBURG PUBLISHING HOUSE
MINNEAPOLIS

OBADIAH AND JONAH
A Commentary

First published 1977 by Neukirchener Verlag, Neukirchen-Vluyn, under the title *Obadja und Jona* in the Biblischer Kommentar Series.

First published in English 1986 by Augsburg Publishing House in the USA and in Great Britain by SPCK, Holy Trinity Church, Marylebone Road, London NW1 4DU.

Library of Congress Cataloging-in-Publication Data

Wolff, Hans Walter.
  OBADIAH AND JONAH.

  Translation of: Obadja und Jona.
  Bibliography: p.
  Includes indexes.
  1. Bible. O.T. Obadiah—Commentaries.
2. Bible. O.T. Jonah—Commentaries.   I. Bible.
O.T. Obadiah   II. Bible. O.T. Jonah.   III. Title.
BS1595.3.W6513   1986   224'.91077   86-22256
ISBN 0-8066-2244-X

The paper used in this publication meets the minimum requirements of American National Standard for Information Sciences—Permanence of Paper for Printed Library Materials, ANSI Z329.48-1984.

Manufactured in the U.S.A.   APH 10-4710

1   2   3   4   5   6   7   8   9   0   1   2   3   4   5   6   7   8   9

*For Jonas
and all my grandchildren
on their voyage
and their way to Nineveh
in hope*

Contents

Commentary   95

Preface

Obadiah and Jonah make strange neighbors in the Book of the Twelve Prophets. What both of them are wrestling with is the question of God's intentions towards the Gentiles. And both of them are at the same time concerned about the relationship between Israel and the Gentile world. Because of its roots in the Old Testament, the church is drawn into Israel's own unremitting tension: What is the interaction between the whole humanity which God has created and the people of God in particular?

Obadiah and Jonah answer this question in highly different ways. The contrast between them has certainly to do with the difference in their historical setting, the people who are addressed, and the commissions of the two witnesses themselves. But the very propinquity of these two little prophetic books faces the reader inexorably with some fundamental questions: What must we bear in mind here and now, when we are considering the tension between humanity in general and the people of God in particular? To whom does this or that have to be said, and how?

Obadiah speaks out against Edom, the little sister neighbor. Jonah speaks to Nineveh, the far-off center of the cruel Assyrian Empire. The book of Obadiah simply gathers together prophetic sayings. The book of Jonah chooses for its proclamation an art form, the narrative. Obadiah has in view the suffering people of God, who had been almost completely blotted out by the great power. The narrator of the book of Jonah wrestles with a selfish, sanctimonious Israelite, who begrudges God's mercy to everyone else.

With regard to the topical problems of contemporary research into the prophetic books, I hope to offer — in addition to some points of detail — two observations which may take us a little further.

In Obadiah I think I have been able to delineate more clearly than has hitherto been possible "the cult prophet," of the type that was active in the worship of the exilic period. I see him taking up sayings that had been passed down from earlier prophets, interpreting them, and giving them a topical application. We can see here a kind of "textual interpretation" which has exerted a very considerable

11

influence down to the present day. It confirms me in my view that a persevering exegetical questioning is an excellent way of discovering essential problems and finding ways towards a solution of them.

In the Jonah commentary, my eyes were opened to the widely varied types of comedy employed in the book; and here I have been stimulated by recent American work. The latter presupposed the insight that the biblical message does not merely take the form of a historical account; it also employs literary forms: fiction and poetry. For an astonishingly long time, many interpreters found it difficult to take account of the liberty and breadth in the narrative form given to the message of God's mercy in the little book of Jonah. So even today, some preachers compel their congregations to become the slaves of "historicism." To narrow down the framework in this way generally means narrowing the message as well. The Jonah commentary tries to feel its way into the biblical text so as to discern from the text itself its literary genre, and what the text wants to tell us. Even earlier, work of this kind led me to find in this story the early form of a didactic narrative, which anticipates in masterly fashion the modern literary form of the novella (see my *Studien zum Jonabuch* [1964]). But now the detailed exposition goes a step further, drawing attention to the widely varying types of humor in the book: grotesque irony and satire, in their most subtle nuances, are pressed into the service of the writer's restrained proclamation. It is through the modulations of the comedy itself that he not only delights his readers but also makes it easier for them to perceive God's loving laughter over narrow-minded piety. It is my most earnest wish that the very last "historicist" should finally discern the kindness of the God of Israel, who can clothe the message of divine goodness towards all human beings even in the form of a humorous story.

HANS WALTER WOLFF

Translator's Preface

An extended translator's preface to a commentary on these compact prophetic books would be inappropriate, but a few points may be mentioned for the reader's guidance.

The English rendering of the biblical text of Obadiah and Jonah adheres as closely as possible to Professor Wolff's own translation of the Hebrew, precision taking precedence over stylistic elegance. The Revised Standard Version of the Bible has been used for all other scriptural quotations, unless modification was required for a correct rendering of Professor Wolff's point. Names of persons and places also follow the spelling of the Revised Standard Version. In the book of Jonah, the verse numbering of the German and English text differs slightly in chapters 1 and 2. In the commentary, the German verse number (which derives from the Hebrew) is printed first, the English verse number (which follows the Septuagint) appearing afterwards between square brackets. References to this passage within the textual commentary itself, however, cite verses according to the Hebrew/German text only.

In his commentary Professor Wolff left the Hebrew, Greek, and Latin readings untranslated. Here, in order to make the work accessible to a wide circle of readers, an English translation has been added, the original reading having been retained in addition.

A comprehensive list of abbreviations is included, so that the reader may pursue bibliographical references.

I should like to express my thanks to the publishers, and more especially to the editor of academic and professional books, for the careful editing and sympathetic cooperation. Particular gratitude is also due to Professor Wolff himself for his patient help in answering questions and elucidating difficulties. Some minor corrections and modifications to the German text have been made in consultation with him, and a few explanatory phrases added.

MARGARET KOHL

THE PROPHET OBADIAH

Introduction

1. The Position of the Book in the Canon

In the Hebrew canon, the book of Obadiah is placed between Amos and Jonah. From a chronological point of view, this arrangement is incomprehensible, even if we assume that the fathers of the men who compiled the canon identified Obadiah with Ahab's steward of the same name (1 Kings 18:3ff.), just as does the Babylonian Talmud (*Sanhedrin* 39b); for in this case Obadiah would have been the 9th-century contemporary of Elijah, and would accordingly have had to be placed, not only before Jonah (who appeared on the scene in the 8th century, under Jeroboam), but also in front of Amos, and even Hosea, since they both performed their ministries under the same king as Jonah.

Now, I have already suggested elsewhere that the late book of Joel (which was relatively close in time to the compilers of the Book of the Twelve Prophets) was put before Amos because of its subject (cf. H. W. Wolff, *Joel/Amos*, BK 14/2, 2 [Eng., *Joel and Amos*, 1977]). But the thematic connections extend further still, running not only from Joel to Amos, but then on to Obadiah. The announcement of the approaching Day of Yahweh which will come upon all nations (Joel 3:2, 14) is repeated word for word in Obad. 15a, and is developed further in vv. 16f.; the particular threat presented by Edom, which is only briefly touched upon and explained in Joel 3:19, is developed at length throughout the whole book of Obadiah. In the later revision of the Amos traditions, a saying was interpolated into Amos 9:(11-)12 which now especially constitutes a bridge between Joel 3 and Obadiah; for the statement there that the fallen booth of David will ''possess the remnant of Edom and all the nations'' first of all establishes a connection between Jerusalem, Edom, and all the nations — a connection still unknown to Joel 3; and, secondly, this is a play on the very theme which is developed at length in Obadiah 16-21. (On the catchword ירש [''possess''] from Amos 9:12, cf. Obad. 17, 19f. and p. 67 below.) Broadly speaking, therefore, Obad. 1-14 would seem to be a commentary on Joel 3:19, and Obad. 15-21 a commentary on Amos 9:12.

17

The Septuagint rearranged the first half of the Book of the Twelve so that the three longer books, Hosea, Amos, and Micah, are followed by the three shorter ones, Joel, Obadiah, and Jonah. But here it was probably not the length of the books only which was the determining factor, especially since Obadiah is followed by the longer Jonah (see pp. 75 ff. below). Elsewhere, too, the Septuagint displays a certain interest in chronology (see H. W. Wolff, *Joel/Amos*, 1 [Eng., *Joel and Amos*]); so in the first half of the Book of the Twelve it will have put the three books which are dated through their superscription in front of the three that are not thus dated. Moreover, the thematic connections also retain their importance: Obadiah supplements Joel 3, and Jonah corresponds to the messenger sent to the nations according to Obad. 1.

2. The Date of Obadiah

Of the sayings in the book of Obadiah, only those in vv. 11-14 can be unequivocally dated. They talk about the days in which foreigners carried off the Jewish army and also decided to deport the civil population of Jerusalem and its ruling class (on v. 11bα see p. 53 below). During these events the Edomites looked on gloatingly. They also tried to prevent attempts to escape (v. 14). Taken as a whole, these and similar remarks can refer only to the period immediately after the Babylonian conquest of Jerusalem in 587 (on the problem of date see p. 54 below). They are confirmed by similar utterances in Lam. 4:21f.; Ps. 137:7; Ezek. 25:12-14; 35:5ff., where no one doubts that the comments refer to the events of 587. But what Obadiah says is so independent and so specific that we can only conclude that it was directly based on happenings during those catastrophic days; he cannot have fabricated this material. It would therefore seem most plausible to assign these sayings to a date not later than a few years after 587.

In the sayings that precede these verses, a reference to the behavior of Edom during and after the fall of Jerusalem in 587 can be detected, at most, in vv. 9f. (see p. 52 below). The saying in v. 3 about Edom's self-confidence is much more comprehensible if it refers to Edom's withdrawal from an anti-Babylonian alliance (cf. Jer. 27:3) between 594 and 587 (see p. 48 below); the Edomite withdrawal may perhaps have been connected with the retirement of the Egyptian army which, according to Jer. 37:5ff., had hastened to Jerusalem's help (cf. M. Noth, *Geschichte Israels* [1969[7]] 258 [Eng., *History of Israel*, 1960[2]]; S. Herrmann, *Geschichte Israels* [1973] 346f. [Eng., *History of Israel*, 1975, 1981[2]] 283]). It is therefore most probable that, apart from the sayings belonging to the period immediately after 587, and in addition to them, the book of Obadiah also contains sayings from the time immediately preceding the catastrophe. (On the form of the transmitted text and on the context of vv. 1-14, 15b, see section 3 below.)

The problems of dating the sayings in vv. 15a, 16-21 are more difficult. Some of the sentences sound like an echo of Joel, which suggests the postexilic era (on vv. 15a, 17a, cf. H. W. Wolff, *Joel/Amos*, BK 14/2, 4, 10 [Eng., *Joel and Amos*]). We can detect clear differences between this passage and the proclamation in vv. 1b-14, to which v. 15b must also be assigned (see pp. 37f. below). Edom is no longer the addressee, as she is in the earlier passage; her offenses are no longer mentioned. What is proclaimed here is merely judgment *on* Edom (v. 18; cf. v. 21), but also on "all the nations" (vv. 15a, 16f.). Whereas in vv. 1b, 7 Yahweh calls upon the nations to implement judgment on Edom, now "the house of Jacob" (i.e., Judah) is the instrument which is to be used against the nations (v. 17) and also against Edom — here, curiously enough, together with "the house of Joseph" (northern Israel; v. 18, cf. v. 20 and pp. 65f. below).

Yet, these differences do not absolutely preclude us from ascribing these sayings to Obadiah, especially since other observations show that there is a relationship between them and vv. 1-14, 15b. Thus the main subject in vv. 18, 21 is still Edom. As judicial principle, the *ius talionis* (the law of retaliation) recurs (cf. v. 16a with 15b, and vv. 17f. with 14; see also p. 63 below). And Ezekiel sayings dating from the exilic period (Ezek. 25:14; 35:10; 37:15ff.; cf. p. 65 below) already talk about Israel as Yahweh's instrument of judgment, and about the common cause of the survivors of the Northern and the Southern Kingdoms. Because of the differences mentioned, however, the sayings in vv. 15a, 16f., and 18 must belong to a later period of Obadiah's ministry than vv. 1b-14, 15b; perhaps v. 21 should follow v. 15b (see p. 62 below).

This means that it is most probably only the additions in vv. 19f., and especially v. 20, which derive from a later historical era — probably the 5th century, but certainly not from as late a period as the Maccabees (see pp. 63-64 below).

3. Obadiah's Function

We know nothing about Obadiah's life — no more than his name. (On the meaning of that name see p. 44 below.) We can only try to deduce the character of his ministry from his sayings. From what we have said up to now, it seems above all certain that he was talking about Edom's behavior during the Babylonian deportation that followed the conquest of Jerusalem (see section 2 above). In what context was he speaking, and in what capacity?

The character of his sayings and parallel events suggest that he was speaking as a cult prophet, during special services of worship. We know from Zech. 7:3, 5; 8:19 that after 587 annual services of lamentation were held in Jerusalem on the days of the year when the city had fallen and the temple had gone up in flames (see p. 42 below). What the book of Lamentations offers us is principally prayers of lament which were sung on this occasion in the ruins of the Jerusalem sanctuary (see H. J. Kraus, *Klagelieder (Threnis)*, BK 20 [1968³] 12ff.). This book also shows us that the laments did not remain unanswered, and indeed that these answers especially pronounced judgment on Edom; we can see this from Lam. 4:21f. (cf. also Ps. 60:1-5, 6-8; E. Kellermann, *Israel und Edom* [1975] 220ff.; also p. 46 below). In Obadiah we see one of the cultic prophets who gave the broken and dejected congregation on Zion the assurance that its prayers had been heard — an assurance in the form especially of a threat of judgment on its enemies.

Yet we found a reference to Jerusalem's catastrophe only in vv. 11-14 (on the special form of the indictment see p. 41 below). The words closed only with a general threat of retaliation in v. 15b (see pp. 56f. below); there is no announcement of any specific form of judgment, unless v. 21 is the original ending of this speech (see p. 62 below). This raises the question whether vv. 11ff. can be understood as a separate, isolated saying, or, if not, how it is related to the sayings that precede it. The following observations suggest that the context was originally a rhetorical one. Edom is not addressed for the first time in vv. 11-14, 15b; the second person form of address is used throughout, from v. 2 onwards, only temporally giving way to the third person in vv. 6 and 8. The preceding sentences are dominated by the specific threat missing in vv. 11ff.; we find it in varying forms in vv. 2, 4, 6f., and 8-10: here the punishments are announced which are appropriate to the misdeeds which Edom has committed, according to vv. 11-14 (see pp. 56f. below).

What is now especially remarkable is that the threatening oracles in vv. 2-4, 5f., 7, 8, and 9f., which vary considerably from each other in form and content, are not really set off against one another and against vv. 11ff. The address in the second person links nearly all of them, just as does the "I" of the Yahweh utterances (vv. 2, 4, 8, 13). Demarcating formulas are found only in the first saying, which opens with the messenger formula (v. 1b, see textual note to v. 1b) and concludes with the oracular formula in v. 4b. This saying is preceded by an unusual opening formula, with the call to battle: "We have heard tidings from Yahweh" (v. 1b). We see here an indication that the prophet joins with the congregation in listening to an earlier prophetic saying, thereby answering the prayers of complaint of the people. The parallel to Jer. 49:14-16 also makes it probable that the saying that follows (vv. 1bβ-4) is an earlier prophetic saying (see p. 46 below). With its sharply defined opening and the framework showing it to be a divine saying (a framework unique in the book of Obadiah) this traditional saying is shown to be the text, as it were, which is expounded first of all in what comes afterwards.

This exposition and development takes place by way of the adoption of traditional sayings. The fact that they are presented in the form of questions makes their interpretative function clear. A repeated "Is it not so?" in vv. 5 and 8, and "How?" in v. 6 remind the congregation of the word it had already heard earlier. In v. 5, what is passed down as a statement in Jer. 49:9 is translated into a rhetorical question. (For details, cf. p. 40 below.) The transition to the third person in vv. 6 and 8 also seems to be motivated by the appropriation of traditional sayings, with the aim of further clarification. This is clearest in v. 8, where the introductory formulas indicating a new saying are linked to the preceding threats in v. 7 through the emphatic "Is it not so?" which yet also carries the argument forward. The discourse detaches itself from traditional material more and more as it goes on, the parallel traditions from Jer. 49:7 thereby receding into the background. In vv. 9f. the speech passes from the basic text of vv. 1b-4 (which is expounded in vv. 5-8) to the detailed indictment, which follows in vv. 11-14. Now the suffering congregation learns that it is its present misery which is going to change the punishment which God had proclaimed. That is to say, we have here an oracle of assurance given by a cult prophet, affirming that a prayer has been heard; but it is here developed into a discourse in which a divine oracle uttered earlier is expounded through the reminder of other familiar sayings, and is applied to the present situation. The form of the address to Edom, which — after the opening in v. 1b — dominates the whole discourse from vv. 2-14, 15b, corresponds to an "expressive" or symbolic act (see p. 43 below), in which the prophet turns in the direction of the region in which the people who are threatened live.

In the later sayings, the address to the people of Jerusalem and Yahweh's speech in the first person in v. 16a suggest especially that what we have here is the oracle given by a cult prophet, offering the assurance that the people's prayer has been heard.

If the final formula, "for Yahweh has spoken," in v. 18b is Obadiah's own, or if this may be supposed even of v. 21 (see p. 69 below), then the writing as we have it would also derive from the prophet himself. At all events, the fact that the heading in v. 1a mentions no more than Obadiah's name, without giving any information about who he was or when he lived, shows that the writing is the work of contemporaries, at least, if it is not his own. But the question of where the original writing ends and where the additions begin can be settled only with the help of literary criteria. We cannot, at least, exclude the possibility that the cult prophet who expounded the Word of God as it had been passed down was also himself the writer.

4. The Development of the Book of Obadiah

Two-thirds of the book of Obadiah can be interpreted as a single, unified discourse, and accordingly as a self-contained writing (on vv. 1-14, 15b cf. section 3 above). Yet the little book as a whole nonetheless shows signs of a complicated process of literary development. As in Jer. 49:7, "concerning Edom" in v. 1 should be understood as a separate heading to the whole of the little book; it characterizes the book as a collection of sayings (see p. 45 below).

The first literary join can be detected in v. 15. Whereas v. 15b belongs to the preceding sentences, if only because of the second person singular form of address, v. 15a must be assigned to the saying about "all the nations" in v. 16a (see pp. 37f. below). The accidental transposition of 15b and 15a in the copying process can be more easily understood if v. 15a was initially added to v. 16 in the margin of a sheet on which vv. 1-14 and 15b had already been transcribed. The deictic (demonstrative) כִּי ("for") in v. 15a is a particle which is commonly used as link with a preceding text (see p. 62 below).

This addition probably included v. 17 at least, as well as vv. 15a and 16, since the sentences are smoothly bonded, without any visible join. Verse 18 brings a new saying — clearly so, because of the content; it is loosely connected with the preceding sentence through והיה ("then"). The final formula כי יהוה דבר ("For Yahweh has spoken") makes it plain that this verse belongs to the same literary stratum as vv. 15a and 16f. Here we have the second obvious join; for this little sentence is more frequently found at the end of literary additions (cf. Isa.

22:[24-]25; 25:[6-]8; Joel 3:[4-]8 and p. 66 below). This is the close, at least temporarily, of Obadiah's collection of sayings about Edom.

The verses that follow (19f.) have clearly been added at some later point. Unlike the preceding sayings, these verses were conceived as literary additions from the very first. With regard to the catchword וירשו, "and shall possess," from v. 17b, we can detect an interpretative process comprising three stages in all. The first two stages in v. 19 expound the areas which the remnant of the community on Zion will take into their possession for the first time; they are first of all given their geographical names and, in the additions, are described according to the peoples who occupy them, and their political affiliation (see p. 67 below). The third stage, in v. 20, says more about the people who are going to occupy the land, according to vv. 17f., talking about those exiled from the Northern and Southern Kingdoms, and about the areas which they are to be given (see pp. 67f. below).

Where v. 21 belongs remains a literary problem. The verse has a rhythmic form, and does not at all sound like a literary commentary of the kind represented by vv. 19f., even though it echoes v. 17a. Is it perhaps a later addition made by someone particularly desirous to testify to the kingship of Yahweh? We find similar examples in some postexilic texts (see p. 69 below). But for this it is too closely related to the Edom theme, and to the subject of deliverance on Zion, which is part of the message of Obadiah, the cultic prophet (see pp. 68-69 below). The mention of the mountains of Esau is especially reminiscent of Obadiah's main discourse (vv. 8f.; cf. in contrast "the house of Esau" in v. 18, but also v. 19a), while the phrase about "going up" reminds us of the call to battle in v. 1bβ ("Rise up!"). Like the opening in v. 1bβ, this final verse does not address Edom. Since vv. 1b-14, 15b do not say at all what the threat to Esau means for the community of Zion (cf. in contrast Lam. 4:21f.; Ezek. 25:13f.), it seems to me worth considering whether v. 21 may have originally been the end of Obadiah's great assurance that the people's prayer had been heard. When vv. 19f. were added as final literary stratum, this verse may perhaps have been moved from its original position after v. 15b, as an editorial measure, in order to provide the book with an impressive close.

5. Obadiah's Message

If we subject Obadiah's sayings to the moral judgment of a superior idealistic or materialistic stance, what we find is pure, primitive hate. But anyone who is prepared to enter imaginatively into the historical hour in which these sayings were written discovers a wretched people in a ruined city, in dire need of comfort. It is only if we try to picture the service of mourning in the rubble of Jerusalem after the days of catastrophe in 587 that we can begin to understand the proclamation of the prophetic spokesman.

What is being preached here is not hate of Edom; it is the punitive justice of God. Israel herself came to know this in these years (v. 16aα), and now Edom (v. 15b) and all the nations must experience it too (v. 16aβ). Edom is in the foreground of Obadiah's message. Although it did not, like Babylon, bear the main military responsibility for the fall of Jerusalem and Judah, yet — as sister nation — it was charged with guilt (vv. 10, 12). Instead of showing loyalty to its ally and readiness to help her (cf. Jer. 27:3), it collaborated with the enemy power and joined that power's auxiliary troops (v. 11). It violated those who were carried off in great treks — violated them by look, word, and act, to the point of murder (vv.12-14, 9f., 11). Its old self-confidence (v. 3) assumed vile forms. Guilt like this will be punished appropriately: the arrogant will themselves be despised (vv. 2, 4), the plunderers will be robbed (vv. 5f.), the faithless will be scorned by their friends (v. 7), and the murderers exterminated (vv. 9f.). Yahweh himself is the guarantor of this (vv. 1b, 2, 4, 8), but Israel, as well as other nations (vv. 1b, 7), can be his instrument (vv. 18, 21). In this way these defeated and broken people are encouraged to hope that the last shall be first and the first last.

What Edom will have to go through is an example to all the nations under whom God's people have to suffer (vv. 15a, 16f.). It is not only in the book of Obadiah that Edom is the prototype of the enemy world (see p. 63 below). Israel is threatened by many others, near and far, just as she is by Edom (cf. Ezek. 36:5; Ps. 60:6-8). Yahweh's cup of wrath, which Jerusalem had to drink first of all, will make the rounds of them all; and, even more than the people of God, they will have to drain it to the bitter dregs (on v. 16 cf. p. 65 below). Hard words about complete extermination are spoken (vv. 16b, 18). In these darkest of days, they underline the unbelievable truth that God's hand can utterly change everything. Other sayings suggest, rather, that though the nations will lose their (hostile) independence, they will be incorporated into the order in which the delivered people of Zion live (vv. 16b, 21). The path of help for the distraught, suffering people of God leads to the kingdom of Yahweh in its full manifestation (v. 21). At the end the great experience for Israel and all the nations will be the lordship of God: this assurance is the message that the sighing community is to hear from the prophetic lips, now, in the very midst of its sobs of despair; for it is to the prophet that God himself has entrusted this word.

On the meaning of Obadiah's message for the church today, see pp. 57, 70-71 below.

6. Literature

1. *Old Testament Prophecy: General Accounts and Investigations*: see the survey of the literature in G. Fohrer, "Neuere Literatur zur alttestamentlichen Prophetie," *ThR* 19 (1951) 277-346; 20 (1952) 193-271, 295-361; 28 (1962) 1-75, 239-297, 301-374; 40 (1975) 193-207, 337-377. R. Rendtorff, "προφήτης," *TDNT* 6:796-812. R. Meyer, J. Fichtner, and A. Jepsen, "Propheten II," *RGG*[3], 5:613-633. R. Rendtorff, "Prophetenspruch," *RGG*[3], 5:635-638. G. von Rad, *Theologie des Alten Testaments*, vol. 2: *Die Theologie der prophetischen Überlieferungen Israels* (1960, 1980[7]; Eng., *Old Testament Theology* 2, (1965). A. Heschel, *The Prophets* (1962). J. Lindblom, *Prophecy in Ancient Israel* (1963[2]). G. Fohrer, *Die Propheten des Alten Testaments* 1-5 (1974-1975).

2a. *History of Interpretation of the Minor Prophets*: W. Werbeck, "Zur Auslegungsgeschichte (des Zwölfprophetenbuches)," *RGG*[3], 6:1970. Cyril of Alexandria, *In Duodecim Minores Prophetas commentariorum*, J. P. Migne, *Patrologia Graeca* 71 (1864) 9-364.

Theodore of Mopsuestia, *Commentarius in Duodecim Prophetas Minores*, ibid. 66 (1864) 105-632. Theodoret of Cyrrhus, *Commentarius in Duodecim Prophetas Minores*, ibid. 81 (1864) 1545-1988. Hesychius of Jerusalem, *Epitome Duodecim Prophetarium*, ibid 93 (1865) 1339-1370. Bar-Hebraeus, *In Duodecim Prophetas Minores scholia*, ed. B. Moritz (1882). Jerome, *In Duodecim Minores Prophetas Commentariorum*, J. P. Migne, *Patrologia Latina* 25 (1884) 810-1578. Haimov of Halberstadt, *Enarratio in Duodecim Prophetas Minores*, ibid. 117:9-294. Rupert of Deutz, *Commentariorum in Duodecim Prophetas Minores*, ibid. 168 (1893) 9-836. G. Diettrich, "Îšô'dâdh's Stellung in der Auslegungsgeschichte des Alten Testaments an seinen Commentaren zu Hosea, Joel, Jona, Sacharja 9-14 und einigen angehängten Psalmen veranschaulicht," BZAW 6 (1902). G. Krause, *Studien zu Luthers Auslegung der kleinen Propheten*, Beiträge zur historischen Theologie 33 (1962). Îšô'dad v. Merw, "Commentaire d'Išô'dad de Merv sur l'Ancien Testament IV (ed. Cvanden Eynde)," CSCO 303/4 (1969) 92-99, 118-126.

2b. *Commentaries on the Minor Prophets*: F. Hitzig and H. Steiner, *Die zwölf kleinen Propheten*, KEH (1838, 1881[4]). H. Ewald, *Die Propheten des Alten Bundes* 1-3 (1840-1841, 1867-1868[2]). C. F. Keil, *Biblischer Commentar über die zwölf kleinen Propheten*, BC 3/4 (1866, 1888[3]). T. K. Cheyne (Hosea, 1884); S. R. Driver (Joel, Amos, 1897, 1934[2]; Micah, 1882, 1895[2]); P. T. Perowne (Obadiah, 1898; Haggai-Malachi, 1893); H. C. O. Lanchester (Jonah, 1915); A. B. Davidson (Nahum-Zephaniah, 1896, 1920[2]); W. E. Barnes (Haggai-Malachi, 1917): all Cambridge Bible for Schools and Colleges. J. Knabenbauer and M. Hagen, *Commentarius in prophetas minores* 1/2: Cursus Scripturae sacrae 2/24 and 25 (1886, 1924[2]). C. von Orelli, *Die zwölf kleinen Propheten*: Kurzgefasster Kommentar zu den heiligen Schriften (1888, 1908[3]). G. Hutcheson, *Verklaring van de twaalf kleine Propheten* (1892). J. Wellhausen, *Die kleinen Propheten: Skizzen und Vorarbeiten Nr. 5* (1892, 1898[3] = 1963[4]). H. Guthe (Hosea, Amos, Micah-Habakkuk); K. Marti (Joel, Obadiah, Haggai-Malachi); J. Rothstein (Zephaniah); E. Kautzsch and A. Bertholet (Jonah): all Die Heilige Schrift des Alten Testaments 2 (1894, 1923[4]). G. A. Smith, *The Book of the Twelve Prophets*: Expositor's Bible (1896-1898, 1928[2]). W. Nowack, *Die kleinen Propheten*: HAT (3/4 (1897, 1922[3]). M. Hirsch, *Die Zwölf Propheten* (1900). R. F. Horten (Hosea, Micah, 1904); S. R. Driver (Nahum, Malachi, 1906): all Century Bible (reprint 1922); K. Marti, *Das Dodekapropheton*: Kurzer Hand-Commentar zum Alten Testament (1904). E. B. Pusey, *The Minor Prophets* 1-8 (1906-1907). W. R. Harper (Amos, Hosea, 1905, 1953[3]); J. M. P. Smith (Micah, Zephaniah, Nahum); W. H. Ward (Habakkuk); J. A. Bewer (Obadiah, Joel, 1911, 1948[3]); H. G. Mitchell (Haggai, Zechariah); J. M. P. Smith (Malachi); J. A. Bewer (Jonah, 1912, 1951[3]): all ICC. A. van Hoonacker, *Les douze petits Prophetètes*: ÉtB (1908). H. Gressmann, *Die älteste Geschichtsschreibung und Prophetie Israels* (Amos, Hosea, 1910, 1921[2]); H. Schmidt and H. Gunkel, *Die grossen Propheten* (Micah, Zephaniah, Nahum, Jonah, 1914, 1923[2]); M. Haller, *Das Judentum* (Joel, Obadiah, Habakkuk, Haggai, Malachi, 1914, 1925[2]): all Die Schriften des Alten Testaments 2/1-3. O. Procksch, *Die kleinen prophetischen Schriften*: EzAT 1 (1910), 2 (1916, 1929[2]). B. Duhm, *Die zwölf Propheten, in den Versmassen der Urschrift übersetzt* (1910), and "Anmerkungen zu den zwölf Propheten," ZAW 31 (1911) 1-43, 81-110, 161-204. P. Riessler, *Die kleinen Propheten* (1911). E. Sellin, *Das Zwölfprophetenbuch*: KAT 12/1 and 2 (1922, 1929-1930[2,3]. F. L. Ceuppens, *De kleine Profeten*: Het Oude Testament (1924). G. W. Wade (Micah, Obadiah, Joel, Jonah, 1925); E. A. Edgehill and G. A. Cooke (Amos, 1914, 1926[2]); G. G. V. Stonehouse (Zephaniah, Nahum, 1929); G. W. Wade (Habakkuk, 1929); S. L. Brown (Hosea, 1932): all Westminster Commentaries. G. L. Robinson, *The Twelve Minor Prophets* (1926). L. H. K. Bleeker (Hosea-Amos, 1932; Joel-Micah, 1934); G. Smit (Habakkuk-Malachi, 1926; Nahum, 1934): all Text en Uitleg. H. Wheeler Robinson (Hosea, Amos); W. G. Watson (Joel, Obadiah); W. C. Graham (Jonah, Nahum, Zephaniah); J. E. McFadyen (Micah, Habakkuk, Haggai, Zechariah, Malachi): all Abingdon Biblical Commentaries, ed. F. C. Eiselen, E. Lewis, and D. G. Downey (1929). J. Ridderbos, *Die kleine Profeten* 1 (Hosea-Amos, 1932, 1952[2]), 2 (Obadiah-Zephaniah, 1935, 1950[2]), 3

(Haggai-Malachi, 1930, 1952[2]): Korte verklaring der Heilige Schrift. J. Kroeker, *Die Propheten oder das Reden Gottes: Das lebendige Wort* (1932). T. H. Robinson (Hosea-Micah, 1936); F. Horst (Nahum-Malachi, 1938): HAT, ed. O. Eissfeldt, 1/14 (1964[3]). A. Jepsen, *Das Zwölfprophetenbuch*: Bibelhefte für die Gemeinde (1937). J. Lippl (Hosea, Jonah, Micah, 1937); J. Theis (Joel-Obadiah, 1937); H. Junker (Nahum-Malachi, 1938): Die Heilige Schrift des Alten Testaments, ed. F. Feldmann and H. Herkenne, 8/3, 1/2. H. Frey (Amos, 1958; Hosea, 1958, 1961[2]); R. von Ungern-Sternberg (Micah, 1958); R. von Ungern-Sternberg and H. Lamparter (Habakkuk, Zephaniah, Jonah, Nahum, 1960); H. Frey (Haggai-Malachi, Obadiah, Joel, 1941, 1963[5]): Botschaft des Alten Testaments 13/1-3, 14/4. S. Mowinckel and N. Messel, *De Senere Profeter oversatt*: De Gamle Testamente (1944). B. M. Vellas, EPMHNEIA 1 (Amos, 1947), 2 (Hosea, 1947), 3 (Micah, Joel, Obadiah, 1948), 4 (Jonah, Nahum, Habakkuk, Zephaniah, 1949), 5 (Haggai-Malachi, 1950). S. M. Lehrman (Hosea-Zephaniah); S. Goldman (Obadiah-Micah); E. Cashdan (Haggai-Malachi): The Soncino Books of the Bible (1948, 1952[2]). F. Nötscher, *Zwölfprophetenbuch oder Kleine Propheten*: Echter Bibel (1948). J. A. Bewer, *The Book of the Twelve Prophets* 1/2: Harper's Annotated Bible (1949). A. Weiser (Hosea-Micah, 1949, 1967[5]); K. Elliger (Nahum-Malachi, 1950, 1967[6]): ATD 24, 25. J. Coppens, *Les douze petits Prophètes* (1950). G. A. F. Knight (Jonah, Ruth, 1950, 1956[2]; Hosea, 1960); J. Marsh (Amos, Micah, 1959); J. H. Eaton (Obadiah, Nahum, Habakkuk, Zephaniah, 1961); D. R. Jones (Haggai, Zechariah, Malachi, 1962): Torch Bible Commentaries. M. Schumpp, *Das Buch der zwölf Propheten*: Herders Bibelkommentar 10/2 (1950). E. Osty (Amos, Hosea, 1952, 1960[2]); A. George (Micah, Zephaniah, Nahum, 1952, 1958[2]); J. Trinquet (Habakkuk, Obadiah, Joel, 1953, 1959[2]); A. Feuillet (Jonah, 1951, 1957[2]); A. Gelin (Haggai, Zechariah, Malachi, 1948, 1960[3]): all in Sainte bible traduite en français sous la direction de l'École Biblique de Jérusalem. S. Bullough (Obadiah, Micah, Zephaniah, Haggai, Zechariah): *The Westminster Version of the Sacred Scriptures* (1953). D. Ryan (Amos, Hosea, Zechariah, Micah); S. Bullough (Obadiah, Nahum, Habakkuk); M. N. L. Couve de Murville (Joel); N. Arbuckle (Jonah, Zephaniah); A. Marsh (Haggai, Malachi): all Catholic Commentary on Holy Scripture (1953, 1969[2]), ed. R. C. Fuller, L. Johnston, and C. Kearns. D. Deden, *De kleine Profeten* 1 (Hosea-Micah, 1953), 2 (Nahum-Malachi, 1956): De Bocken van het Oude Testament. C. van Gelderen and W. H. Gispen (Hosea, 1953); G. A. Aalders (Obadiah, Jonah, 1958); J. L. Koole (Haggai, 1967): Commentar op het Oude Testament. G. Rinaldi (Amos, 1953; Hosea-Jonah, 1960); G. Rinaldi and F. Luciani (Micah-Malachi, 1969): Sacra bibbia Torino. J. Bergdolt (Hosea-Amos, 1955); J. Fichtner (Obadiah-Micah, 1957); E. Weissenstein (Nahum-Zephaniah, 1957); K. D. Buchholtz (Haggai-Malachi, 1960): all Stuttgarter Bibelhefte. A. Vaccari (Amos-Zephaniah); G. Bernini (Haggai-Malachi): Sacra bibbia Firenze 7 (1955). N. H. Snaith (Amos, Hosea, Micah, 1956); S. L. Edgar (Joel, Obadiah, Jonah, Nahum-Malachi, 1962): Epworth Preachers' Commentaries, K. F. T. Laetsch, *The Minor Prophets* (1956). J. Mauchline and H. C. Phillips (Hosea); J. A. Thompson and N. F. Langford (Joel, Obadiah); H. E. W. Fosbroke and S. Lovet (Amos); J. D. Smart and W. Scarlett (Joel); R. E. Wolfe and H. A. Bosley (Micah) ; C. L. Taylor Jr. and J. T. Cleland (Nahum); C. L. Taylor Jr. and H. Thurman (Habakkuk, Zephaniah); D. W. Thomas and W. L. Sperry (Haggai); D. W. Thomas and T. C. Speers (Zechariah 1-8); R. C. Dentan and J. T. Cleland (Zechariah 9-14); R. C. Dentan and W. L. Sperry (Malachi): all IB 6 (1956). R. Augé, *Profetes menors*: La Bíblia, versió dels textos originals i commentari Montserrat 16 (1957). T. Henshaw, *The Latter Prophets* (1958). É. Dhorme, *La Bible, L'Ancien Testament* 2: Bibliothèque de la Pléiade (1959). G. C. Morgan, *The Minor Prophets* (1960). M. G. Cordero, Biblia comentada 3: Biblioteca de autores cristianos (1961). J. Myers (Hosea-Jonah, 1960); J. H. Gailey (Micah-Malachi, 1962): Layman's Bible Commentary. L. A. Schökel and J. M. Valverde, *Doce Profetas menores*: Los Libros Sagrados (1966). A. Deissler (Hosea, Obadiah, 1961); M. Delcor (Joel, Jonah, 1961). A. Deissler (Zephaniah, Haggai, Malachi, 1964); M. Delcor (Micah, Habakkuk, Zechariah, 1964): Sainte Bible (Pirot/Clamer) 8/1 and 2. H. W. Wolff, Dodekapropheton 1 (Hosea, 1961, 1976[3], Eng.

1974 [Hermeneia]), 2 (Joel-Amos, 1969, 1975[2], Eng. 1977 [Hermeneia]): BK, ed. M. Noth and H. W. Wolff. P. R. Ackroyd (Hosea, Haggai, Zechariah); L. H. Brockington (Joel, Obadiah, Jonah, Malachi); J. P. Hyatt (Amos, Nahum-Zephaniah); D. I. W. von Thomas (Micah): *Peake's Commentary on the Bible*, ed. M. Black and H. H. Rowley (1962). J. Steinmann and A. Hanon (Micah, Zephaniah, Joel, Nahum, Habakkuk): Connaître la Bible (1962). E. Jacob (Hosea, 1965); C. A. Keller (Joel, Obadiah, Jonah, 1965); S. Amsler (Amos, 1965); R. Vuilleumier (Micah, 1971); C. A. Keller (Nahum, Habakkuk, Zephaniah, 1971) all Commentaire de l'Ancien Testament 11/a and b. J. Marsh (Amos, Micah, 1965); G. A. F. Knight (Hosea, 1966): Torch Bible Paperback (= Torch Bible Commentaries, 1959, 1960). J. P. Lewis, *The Minor Prophets* (1966). W. Rudolph (Hosea, 1966; Joel-Jonah, 1971; Micah-Zephaniah, 1975): Kommentar zum Alten Testament 13/1-3. P. J. King (Amos, Micah); D. J. McCarthy (Hosea); R. T. A. Murphy (Nahum-Zephaniah); C. Stuhlmueller (Haggai-Malachi); G. F. Wood (Joel, Obadiah); J. C. M. McGowan (Jonah): all *Jerome Biblical Commentary*, ed. R. E. Brown, J. A. Fitzmyer, and R. E. Murphy (1968). S. M. Gozzo (Micah, Habakkuk, 1968; Zechariah, 1969; Obadiah, Haggai, Malachi, 1970): Verba Vitae 25, 29, 33. Starý Zákon/překlad s vykladem: 14. Dvanáct prorokų (The O.T., trans. with Commentary: 14. The Twelve Prophets) (1968). C. Hauret, Amos et Osée: Verbum Salutis (OT) 5 (1970). J. A. Motyer (Amos); J. B. Hindley (Hosea); D. W. B. Robinson (Obadiah, Jonah); R. A. Cole (Joel); G. L. Archer (Micah); A. Fraser (Nahum); L. E. H. Stephens-Hodge (Habakkuk); D. J. Wiseman (Haggai); J. T. Carson (Zephaniah): all New Bible Commentary, ed. D. Guthrie (1970[3]). H. McKeating, *The Book of Amos, Hosea and Micah* (1971): Cambridge Bible Commentary 10. E. Osty and J. Trinquet, *Les Petits Prophètes* (1972).

3. *The Text of the Minor Prophets*: *(a) Hebrew*: M. Rahmer, "Die hebräische Tradition in den Werken des Hieronymus. Zweiter Teil: Die Commentarien zu den XII kleinen Propheten. I Hosea," *MGWJ* (1865) 216-224, 460-470; (1867) 103-106; (1868) 413-427. F. Buhl, "Einige textkritische Bemerkungen zu den kleinen Propheten," *ZAW* 5 (1885) 179-184. A. B. Ehrlich, *Randglossen zur Hebräischen Bibel* 5 (1912) 163-363. S. B. Freehoff, "Some Text Rearrangements in the Minor Prophets," *JQR* 32 (1941-42) 303-308. E. V(ogt), "Fragmenta Prophetarum Minorum Deserti Iuda," *Biblica* 34 (1953) 423-426. H. Gese, "Die hebräischen Bibelhandschriften zum Dodekapropheton nach der Variantensammlung des Kennicott," *ZAW* 69 (1957) 55-69. J. T. Milik, *Discoveries in the Judean Desert* 2 (1961).

(b) Greek: K. Vollers, "Das Dodekapropheton der Alexandriner," *ZAW* 3 (1883) 219-272; 4 (1884) 1-20. L. Z. Schuurmans-Stekhoven, *De Alexandrijnsche Vertaling van het Dodekapropheton* (1887). L. Treitel, "Die Septuaginta zu Hosea," *MGWJ* 41 (1897) 433-454. O. Procksch, "Die Septuaginta Hieronymi im Dodekapropheton," *Fests. Univ. Greifswald* (1914). A. Kaminka, *Studien zur Septuaginta an der Hand der zwölf kleinen Propheten*, Schriften der Gesellschaft zur Förderung der Wissenschaft des Judentums 33 (1928). J. Ziegler, "Die Einheit der Septuaginta zum Zwölfprophetenbuch," Beilage zum Vorlesungsverzeichnis der Staatlichen Akademie zu Braunsberg im Wintersemester 1934-35; *Beiträge zum griechischen Dodekapropheton* (1942); *Duodecim prophetae*, Septuaginta Vetus Testamentum Graecum 13 (1943); "Studien zur Verwertung der Septuaginta im Zwölfprophetenbuch," *ZAW* 60 (1944) 107-131; "Der griechische Dodekapropheton-Text der Complutenser Polyglotte," *Biblica* 25 (1944) 297-310; "Der Text der Aldina im Dodekapropheton," *Biblica* 26 (1945) 37-51. F. Dingermann, "Massora-Septuaginta der kleinen Propheton," diss. Würzburg (1948). D. Barthélemy, "Redécouverte d'un chaînon manquant de l'histoire de la Septante," *RB* 60 (1953) 18-29. P. Kahle, "Die im August 1952 entdeckte Lederrolle mit dem griechischen Text der kleinen Propheten und das Problem der Septuaginta," *ThL* 79 (1954) 81-94. D. Barthélemy, *Les devanciers d'Aquila: Première publication intégrale du texte des fragments du Dodécaprophéton*, *VT* Suppl. 10 (1963).

(c) Latin: A. Panyik, "A Critical and Comparative Study of the Old Latin Texts of the Book of Ezekiel and the Minor Prophets," diss. Princeton (1938). M. Stenzel, "Das Dodekapropheton der lateinischen Septuaginta, Untersuchungen über die Herkunft und die geschichtliche Entwicklung der lateinischen Textgestalt des nichthieronymianischen Dodekapropheton," diss. Würzburg (1949); "Das Dodekapropheton in Übersetzungwerken lateinischer Schriftsteller des Altertums," *ThZ* 9 (1953) 81-92 (= part 5 of the aforementioned thesis); "Die Konstanzer und St. Galler Fragmente zum altlateinischen Dodekapropheton," *Sacris Erudiri* 5 (1953) 27-85; "Altlateinische Canticatexte im Dodekapropheton," *ZNW* 46 (1955) 31-60.

(d) Syrian: M. Sebök (Schönberger), "Die syrische Übersetzung der zwölf kleinen Propheten," diss. Leipzig (1887).

(e) Coptic: E. Quatremere, "Daniel et les douze petits prophètes," *Notices et extraits de la Bibl. impér* 8 (1810) 220-290. H. Tattam, *Duodecim prophetarum minorum libros in lingua aegyptiaca vulgo coptica seu memphitica* (1836). A. Schulte, "Die koptische Übersetzung der kleinen Propheten," *ThQ* 76 (1894) 605-642; 77 (1895) 209-229. C. Wesseley, *Duodecim prophetarum minorum versionis Achimimicae* (1915). W. Till, *Die achmîmische Version der zwölf Kleinen Propheten*, Coptica 4 (1927). W. Grossouw, *The Coptic Versions of the Minor Prophets*, Monumenta biblica et ecclesiastica 3 (1938). J. Ziegler, "Beiträge zur koptischen Dodekapropheton-Übersetzung," Biblica 25 (1944) 105-142.

(f) Ethiopian: J. Bachmann, *Dodekapropheton Aethiopum*, 1: *Der Prophet Obadia*; 2: *Der Prophet Maleachi* (1892). O. Löfgren, *Jona, Nahum, Habakuk, Zephanja, Haggai, Sacharja und Maleachi äthiopisch*, Arbeten utgivna med understöd av Vilhelm Ekmans Universitetsfond 38 (1930).

4. *Some Individual Investigations Relating to the Minor Prophets*: G. Richter, *Erläuterungen zu dunklen Stellen in den kleinen Propheten*, Beiträge zur Förderung christlicher Theologie 18, 3-4 (1914). K. Budde, "Eine folgenschwere Redaktion des Zwölfprophetenbuchs," *ZAW* 39 (1921) 218-229. R. E. Wolfe, "The Editing of the Book of the Twelve," *ZAW* 53 (1935) 90-130. T. H. Gaster, "Notes on the Minor Prophets," *JTS* 39 (1937) 163-165. G. R. Driver, "Linguistic and Textual Problems: Minor Prophets," *JTS* 39 (1938) 154-166, 260-273, 393-405. A. Jepsen, "Kleine Beiträge zum Zwölfprophetenbuch," *ZAW* 56 (1938) 85-100; 57 (1939) 242-255; 61 (1945-48) 95-114. A. Bruno, *Das Buch der Zwölf (eine rhythmische und textkritische Untersuchung)* (1957).

5. *Commentaries on Obadiah*: C. P. Caspari, *Der Prophet Obadja* (1842). C. A. W. Seydel, "Vaticinium Obadjae," diss. Leipzig (1869). J. Bachmann, *Der Prophet Obadja* (1892). J. Halévy, "Le Livre d'Obadia," *Revue sémitique d'épigraphie et d'histoire ancienne* 15 (1907) 165-183. S. O. Jsopescul, "Übersetzung und Auslegung des Buches Abdias," *Wiener Zeitschrift für die Kunde des Morgenlandes* (1914) 149-181. H. C. O. Lanchester, *Obadiah and Jona* (1918). B. Kutal, *Liber Prophetarum Amos et Abdiae* (1933). U. Masing, *Der Prophet Obadja I: Einleitung in das Buch des Propheten Obadja* (Tartu, Estonia, 1937; proofs). J. M. Rinaldi, "In librum Abdiae," *Verbum Domini* (1939) 148-154, 174-179, 201-206. H. Veldcamp, *Het gezicht van Obadja* (1957). J. W. Watts, *Obadiah: A Critical Exegetical Commentary* (1969).

6. *General Studies on Obadiah*: E. Philippe, "Abdias," DB(V) 1 (1895) 20-23. H. Winckler, "Obadja," *Altorientalische Forschungen* 2/3 (1901) 425-432. W. Volck, "Obadja, Prophet," *Realencyclopädie für protestantische Theologie und Kirche* 14 (1904) 246-248. M. Haller, "Obadja und Obadjabuch," RGG[1] 4 (1913) 853-854. G. A. Barton, "Obadiah," *Jewish Encyclopaedia* 9 (1925[2]) 369f. W. W. Cannon, "Israel and Edom: The Oracle of Obadiah," *Theology* 15 (1927) 129-140, 191-200. M. Haller, "Obadja," RGG[2] 4 (1930) 613. J. A. Selbie, "Obadiah," DB(H) 3 (1950[11]) 577-580. W. Vollhorn,

"Obadjabuch," *RGG*³ 4 (1960) 1547-1548. J. Muilenburg, "Obadiah," *IDB* 3 (1962) 578f. A. S. Herbert, "Obadja. Obadjabuch," *Biblisch-Historisches Handwörterbuch* 2 (1964) 1323-1325. É. Bonnard, "Abdias," *DBS* 8 (1969) 693-701. E. Lipiński, "Obadiah," *EJ* 12 (1971) 1304-1306.

7. *Problems of Date*: B. C. Cresson, "Israel and Edom: A Study of the Anti-Edom Bias in Old Testament Religion," diss. Duke (1963). B. Diebner and H. Schult, "Edom in alttestamentlichen Texten der Makkabäerzeit," *Diehlheimer Blätter zum Alten Testament* 8 (1975) 11-17.

8. *Literary Problems*: A. Condamin, "L'Unité d'Abdias," *RB* 9 (1900) 261-268. J. M. P. Smith, "The Structure of Obadiah," *AJSLL* (1905/6) 131-138. H. Bekel, "Ein vorexilisches Orakel über Edom in der Klageliederstrophe: Die gemeinsame Quelle von Obadja 1-9 und Jeremia 49,7-22," *Theologische Studien und Kritiken* 80 (1907) 315-343. G. A. Peckham, *An Introduction to the Study of Obadiah* (1910). S. O. Jsopescul, "Historisch-kritische Einleitung zur Weissagung des Abdias," *Wiener Zeitschrift für die Kunde des Morgenlandes* (1913) 141-162. W. Rudolph, "Obadja," *ZAW* 49 (1931) 222-231. A. J. Freeman, "The Obadiah Problem," diss. Southern Baptist Seminary, Louisville (1950). M. Bič, "Zur Problematik des Buches Obadja," *VT* Suppl. 1 (1953) 11-25. E. Olávarri, "Cronologia y estructura literaria del oráculo escatológico de Abdias," *EstBíb* (1963) 303-313.

9. *The Form and Transmission of the Text*: T. H. Robinson, "The Structure of the Book Obadiah," *JTS* 17 (1916) 402-408. G. Fohrer, "Die Sprüche Obadjas," *Studia biblica et semitica Theodoro Christiano Vriezen dedicata* (1966) 81-93.

10. *The History of Edom*: F. Buhl, *Geschichte der Edomiter* (1893). T. Nöldeke, "Edom," *Encyclopaedia Biblica* 2 (1901) 1181-1188. R. H. Pfeiffer, "Edomitic Wisdom," *ZAW* 44 (1926) 13-25. H. Grimme, "Der Untergang Edoms," *Welt als Geschichte* 3 (1937) 452-463. K. Galling, "Das Gemeindegesetz in Dt 23," *Fests. A Bertholet* (1950) 176-191. V. Maag, "Jakob - Esau - Edom," *ThZ* 13 (1957) 418-429. M. Noth, "Edomiter," *RGG*³ 2 (1958) 308-309. J. R. Bartlett, "The Edomite King-list of Genesis XXXVI 31-39 and 1 Chron. I 43-50," *JTS* 16 (1965) 301-314. B. G. Boschi, "Sagezza di Edom: Mito e realtà," *Rivista biblica* 15 (1967) 357-368. J. R. Bartlett, "The Land of Seir and the Brotherhood of Edom," *JTS* 20 (1969) 1-20. R. de Vaux, "Téman, Ville ou Région d'Edom," *RB* 76 (1969) 379-385. J. M. Myers, "Edom and Judah in the Sixth-Fifth Centuries B.C.," *Near Eastern Studies in Honor of W. F. Albright*, ed. H. Goedicke (1971) 377-392. M. Weippert, "Edom: Studien und Materialien zur Geschichte der Edomiter aufgrund schriftlicher und archäologischer Quellen," diss. Tübingen (1971, typescript). J. R. Bartlett, "The Rise and Fall of the Kingdom of Edom," *PEQ* 104 (1972) 26-37; "The Moabites," in *Peoples of Old Testament Times*, ed. D. J. Wiseman (1973) 229-258.

11. *Individual Problems in Connection with Obadiah*: M. Haller, "Edom im Urteil der Propheten," BZAW 41 (*Fests. K. Marti*, 1925), 109-117. M. Bič, "Ein verkanntes Thronbesteigungsfestorakel im AT," *Archiv Orientální* 19 (1951) 568-578. J. Gray, "The Diaspora of Israel and Judah in Obadiah V. 20," *ZAW* 65 (1953) 53-59. B. C. Cresson, "The Condemnation of Edom in Postexilic Judaism," *Studies in Honor of W. F. Stinespring* (1972) 125-148. A. J. Braver, "The Name Obadiah — Its Punctuation and Explanation" (in Hebrew, Eng. summary), *Beth Mikra* 54 (1973) 418-419. E. Lipiński, "Obadiah 20," *VT* 23 (1973) 368-370. U. Kellermann, "Israel und Edom — Studien zum Edomhass Israels im 6.-4. Jh. v. Chr.," professorial thesis Münster i. W. (1975). P. K. McCarter, "Obadiah 7 and the Fall of Edom," *BASOR* 221 (1976) 87-91.

12. *Obadiah's Message*: J. van Gilse, "Tijdbepaling der profetie Obadjah," *NThT* (1913) 293-313. J. Theis, *Die Weissagung des Abdias* (1917). R. E. Gaebelein, *The Servant and*

the Dove: Obadiah and Jonah, Their Messages and Their Work (1946). A. H. Edelkoort, "De profetie van Obadja," *Nederlands Theologische Tijdschrift* 1 (1946/7) 276-293. G. Mennenga, "Obscure Obadiah and his Message," *Reformed Revue* 12/3 (1959) 24-32. R. A. Coughenouv, "A View of Value from a Servant of Yahweh," *Reformed Review* 24 (1971) 119-123.

13. *Miscellaneous Contributions on Obadiah*: A. Stifter, "*Abdias*," *A. Stifter Studien,* ed. M. Stefl (1956) 5-104. K. Weinberg, "Biblische Motive in Stifters Abdias," *Horizonte. Emuna* 7 (1972) 32-38.

The Crimes of Edom

Literature

H. Bekel, "Ein vorexilisches Orakel über Edom in der Klageliederstrophe — Die gemeinsame Quelle von Obadja 1-9 and Jeremiah 49, 7-22," *Theologische Studien und Kritiken* 80 (1907) 315-343. W. Rudolph, "Obadja," *ZAW* 49 (1931) 222-231. U. Masing, *Der Prophet Obadja*: vol 1, *Einleitung in das Buch des Propheten Obadja* (Tartu, 1937). R. Bach, *Die Aufforderungen zur Flucht und zum Kampf im alttestamentlichen Prophetenspruch*, WMANT 9 (1962). G. Fohrer, "Die Sprüche Obadjas," *Studia Biblica et Semitica (Fests. T. C. Vriezen*, 1966) 81-93. J. M. Myers, "Edom and Judah in the Sixth-Fifth Centuries B.C.," *Near Eastern Studies in Honor of W. F. Albright*, ed. H. Goedicke (1971) 377-392. J. R. Bartlett, "The Rise and Fall of the Kingdom of Edom," *PEQ* 104 (1972) 26-37; "The Moabites and Edomites," in *Peoples of Old Testament Times*, ed. D. J. Wiseman (1973) 229-258. A. Braver, "The Name Obadiah — Its Punctuation and Explanation" (in Hebrew, Eng. summary), *Beth Mikra* 54 (1973) 418-419. U. Kellermann, "Israel und Edom: Studien zum Edomhass Israels im 6.-4.- Jahrhundert v. Chr.," professorial thesis, Münster (1975). P. K. McCarter, "Obadiah 7 and the Fall of Edom," *BASOR 221 (1976) 87-91*.

Text

1   The prophecy[a] of Obadiah."[b]
    Concerning Edom.
    We[c] heard tidings from Yahweh,
        a messenger[d] is sent among the nations.[e]
    Rise up! Let us line up against her[f] for battle!
    [b]Thus has [the Lord][g]Yahweh spoken:[b]
2   Listen!
    I am making you small among the nations.
        You will be [a]utterly despised.[a]
3   Your presumptuous[a] spirit[b] deceives you,
        you (who) house[c] in clefts of rocks,
            who builds his[d] dwelling "in the heights,"[e]
    who speaks to himself:[f]
        "Who casts me down to the ground?"[g]

4   (Even though) you build[a] like an[b] eagle in the heights
        [c][or if] your nest [be set between stars][c]
            yet I am (nonetheless) bringing you down from there,
                                                            saying of Yahweh's.

5   If thieves fall upon you,
        [a][if plunderers by night, how will you be brought to silence],[a]
        is it not so?[b] They steal until they have enough.
      If grape gatherers fall upon you,
        is it not so?[b] they leave gleanings.

6   How Esau "will be"[a] searched through and through,
        his hiding places ransacked![b]

7   They drive you to the borders,
        All your allies deceive you.[a]
      Your friends[b] overpower [your bread].[c]
        They put[d] a trap for your feet[e] under you.
        [f][There is no discernment with him.][f]

8   Is it not so? On that day — saying of Yahweh's —
      I am stamping out the wise men from Edom
        and discernment from the mountains of Esau.

9   Then your[a] heroes will collapse, Teman,
        so that[b] everyone from the mountains of Esau will be wiped out.
      Because of the murder[c]

10   [because of an act of violence][a] against[b] your
                                            brother Jacob
        shame will wrap you round;
        you will be destroyed for ever.

11 . On the day when you stood by,[a]
          on the day when strangers carried off his army,
        when foreigners entered his gates[b]
          and cast lots[c] over Jerusalem,
        then you too were like one of them.

12   And you should not (gloatingly) look down[a] on the day[b] of your brother,
          on the day of his misfortune,[c]
        you should not rejoice over Judah's sons
          on the day of their downfall,
        you should not open your mouth wide[d]
          on the day of distress.

13   You should not enter the gate[a] of my people[b]
          on the day of his "misery,"[c]
        you of all people should not be amused[d] by his wretchedness[e]
          on the day of his collapse,
        you should not "grab"[f] at his possessions
          on the day of his "downfall."[g]

14   Nor should you stand in the escape route[a]
          to kill those of him who had escaped,
        and should not surrender those who had escaped
          on the day of distress.

15b[a]   As you have done will it be done to you;[b]
          Your deed returns on your own head.[c]

1a Gk, ὅρασις, "vision," is interpreted by σ᾽ ἔκστασις, "trance" or "ecstasy," as an event experienced by the prophet, and is thereby preserved from the narrower interpretation "vision" (Vg. has *visio*) in the light of the text that follows. The Targums' נבואת ע" "prophesying," brings out the sense of the text best here, as in Isa. 1:1 (cf. Ezra 6:14 MT).

1b The messenger formula is disconcerting at the point in the text at which it has been transmitted, for v. 1bα still first of all talks about Yahweh in the 3rd person; bβ cannot be separated from bα, since in both places the utterances are made in the 1st person plural. On the other hand, we miss the formula in v. 2, where the transition is made to Yahweh's 1st person utterance. This could be the omission of a copyist (it is also missing between Jer. 49:14 and 15), might then have been added in the margin, and from there have strayed into the text at its present point; cf. Jer. 49:7 and pp. 44f. below.

1c Gk, ἤκουσα, "I heard," can only be explained as a misinterpretation of MT, thinking the prophet is meant; or perhaps it is an assimilation to Jer. 49:14, שָׁמַעְתִּי. The correctness of the reading of MT is confirmed by the 1st person plural in bβ and by the history of this turn of phrase (cf. Jer. 6:24 and p. 46 below).

1d Gk, καὶ περιοχὴν εἰς τὰ ἔθνη ἐξαπέστειλεν, "sent a (Scripture-) message to the nations," reads שָׁלַח as verbal form and therefore sees צִיר, "envoy," as an object, meaning the ("comprehensive") content of the message: In Jer. 49:14 (Gk 29:15) translates the same Hebrew text similarly, καὶ ἀγγέλους εἰς ἔθνη ἀπέστειλε, "and has sent messengers to the nations," but sees "messengers" (plural, like σ᾽) as the object; α᾽ corrects this in Obadiah, and translates ἀγγελίαν, "message." Apart from Obad. 1 and Jer. 49:14 צִיר, "envoy," "messenger" is found as subject only in Prov. 13:17; 25:13; it occurs as object in Isa. 18:2; 57:9.

1e On the Gk reading cf. textual note to 1d above. Jer. 49:14 offers passive participle *qal* instead of 3rd masculine singular perfect of *puʻal*.

1f עָלֶיהָ, "against her," corresponds to Jer. 49:14, where the 3rd person singular feminine suffix is appropriate, being related to בָּצְרָה "Bozrah" in v. 13. Gk also translates throughout as ἐπ᾽ αὐτήν, "against her" (exception ἐπ᾽ αὐτόν, "against him," in G[86] for the first time — i.e., 9th to 10th century). The Vg reading however is *adversus eum*, "against him." MT is understandable if it is derived from a text which served as common source for both Obad. 1 and Jer. 49:14. Direct dependence on Jer. 49:14 is unlikely, because of the variants which are to be found here otherwise (see textual notes to 1c and 1e above). Moreover, in the Obadiah passage in its transmitted form the 3rd person feminine suffix is related to לאדום in 1bα; אדום, "Edom," in the sense of the country, is also feminine in Jer. 49:17; Ezek. 25:13; 32:29; 35:15; Mal. 1:4; cf. Ges-K §122h. In the case of the masculine forms used from v. 2 onwards, Edom is thought of as people or nation = Esau (vv. 8f.). As *lectio difficilior** עליה remains more probable than עָלָיו let alone נַעֲלֶה (beside קומו ונקומה; cf. Jer. 49:14; 6:4, 5; 31:6; 49:28, 31; for a different view cf. G. Fohrer "Sprüche," 85; W. Rudolph, KAT 13/2, 301f.

1g אדני "Adonai, Lord," may have been added later as substitute for the pronounciation of the divine Name (the Tetragrammaton); see C.A. Keller, 253; in the book of Amos, it is frequently found as a later addition, with this intention; see H. W. Wolff, *Joel/Amos*, BK 13/2 (Eng., *Joel and Amos*), textual note to Amos 1:8b; cf. also W. Zimmerli, *Ezechiel*, BK 13 [1969] 1250f. (Eng., *Ezekiel*, 1979-1983, excursus 1).

---

*The principle of textual criticism whereby "the more difficult reading is to be preferred," since a scribe will tend to assimilate the simpler or more familiar word or form, either inadvertently or in an attempt to correct a difficult or corrupt reading in his source (trans.).

2a-a Jer. 49:15 offers בָּאָדָם "among man," instead of אתה מאד, "you are very.. . ."
There is no reason to take over this reading, especially since MT is supported by Gk σὺ εἶ
σφόδρα, "you are very.. . ." In Jer. 49:15 בָּאָדָם in b can be explained by the parallelism
to בַּגּוֹיִם, "among the Gentiles," an obviously close variant in related traditional phraseology, which also conforms to the rhythm (mixed bicolon) of that context.

3a Here the *nomens regens* describes the characteristic of the *nomen rectum* and therefore takes the place of an adjective (cf. BrSynt §71a).

3b Here לב (generally translated as "heart") means the total personality, with its self-
awareness; cf. H. W. Wolff, *Anthropologie des Alten Testaments* (1973) 77, 89f. (Eng.,
Anthropology of the Old Testament [1974] 46, 54f.).

3c On י-*compaginis* as construct state, when a preposition is inserted between the construct state and its genitive (the absolute state) (see Ps. 123:1), cf. Ges-K §90, 1 and
Meyer³ 2 §45, 3e.

3d There is no reason to change the suffixes (to the 2nd instead of the 3rd person, as T. H.
Robinson proposes) in participial appositions (cf. Amos 5:12), especially since this seems
to be an independent interpretation of the text as it had been passed down (Jer. 49:16 has no
3rd person forms).

3e MT can easily be a misreading of מְרִים. This is W. Rudolph's view in *ZAW* 49 (1931),
223f.; he deviates from it later in KAT 13/2 (1971), where he reads, "in the height of his
sitting" = accusative of place. מְרִים is confirmed by Gk ὑψῶν and Vg. *exaltantem* (both,
"exalting") and is more probable between the participles שכני and אמר.

3f See textual note to v. 3b and H. W. Wolff, *Anthropologie*, 82, 85f., on לב as the place
of reflection (Eng., *Anthropology*, 49, 51f.).

3g V. 3b, with its reference to self-confidence, has no parallel in Jer. 49:16.

4a The link between v. 4 and v. 3 makes a more natural impression than the link between
Jer. 49:16b and 16a. Obadiah's conditional clause with אם in v. 4a picks up the accusation
of arrogance in v. 3, in order in 4b to announce the judgment (אורידך) which counters the
words cited from v. 3b (מי יורדני). In Jer. 49:16b an emphatic, or deictic, כִּי clinches the
indictment, which is also the condition for Yahweh's intervention, although here the catchword (מי יורדני, Obad. 3b) has not already been given; see textual note to 3g. The Maso-
retes read a suffix into תגביה (which can be absent in Jer. 46:16b). This was due to the separation of the object קנך through the addition of the second conditional clause with אם,
"even if." (Cf. textual note to 4c - c.)

4b In Hebrew the thing compared is as a rule determined, i.e., it is preceded by the (definite) article; cf. Hos. 8:1: Isa. 1:18 and BrSynt §21c; Meyer³ 3 §96, 4d, W. Schneider,
Grammatik des biblischen Hebräisch (1974) §52.5.

4c-c The clause is a later addition, for תגביה, transitive *hiphil*, requires קנך, "nest," as
its object (as also in Jer. 49:16); שׂים (past participle); "set," does not fit the direct form of
address of the context, to which Gk θῇς, Vg. *posueris* ("if you were to place"), Targ תשוי
all later adjust. The addition is also missing in Jer. 49:16b. It may perhaps be a reference to
Isa. 14:13.

5a-a The second conditional clause with אם in v. 5 breaks up the original cohesion of the
sentence, just as it does in v. 4; see textual note to v. 4c - c. The gloss "plunderers" interprets the images ("thief," "grape gatherer"); it draws on a different kind of language: אִיך
(cf. v. 6) instead of הלוא; consequently even a transposition of the second אם clause to a
position between v. 5a and b will hardly be sufficient to restore the original text, which
would then be a tricolon. Jer. 49:9 also has similar statements about "grape gatherers" and
"thieves," but makes no reference to "plunderers."

5b Here the negative statements in Jer 49:9aβbβ are changed into rhetorical questions.

6a Perhaps we should read נֶחְפַּשׂ, singular, "is searched out," like Gk ἐξηρευνήθη; but Esau can also be construed as a collective plural; cf. Meyer[3] 3 §94, 5a.

6b It is only thematically that this statement is reminiscent of Jer. 49:10a.

7a The transmitted text of v. 7aba has four finite verbs in the 3rd person plural, which can be assigned to four equal versicles; the first of these (aα[1]) and the fourth (bα) have no subject of their own. G. Fohrer, "Sprüche Obadjas" (1966), therefore puts the third versicle at the beginning; but this finds no support in the text transmission. W. Rudolph thinks that aβ is a marginal gloss, on the pattern of Jer. 38:22bα, "for strophic reasons," though these apply more to the present four-line strophe in its transmitted form (without לחמך and bβ, see textual notes to 7c and 7f - f below).

7b An אִישׁ שָׁלוֹם ("man of peace") is "a person with whom one shares fellowship or community," that is to say, a familiar friend or ally; cf. W. Eisenbeis, *Die Wurzel* שׁלם *im AT*, BZAW 113 (1969) 156f.; also Jer. 20:10; 38:22.

7c The surplus word seems to be added in order to interpret "men belonging to your company" as those who eat "your bread" (Ps. 41:9). Gk and Murabba'at have as yet no knowledge of this addition. J. Halévy, E. Sellin, C. A. Keller, and W. Rudolph read לַחֲמְיָך ("who ate your bread" = σ' and others, συνεσθίοντες σοι, Vg. *qui comedunt tecum* "who ate with you"; Targums, אכלי פתורך Gk (Codex Atheniensis) and others ἐπολέμησαν σε = "who fought against you"; cf. J. Ziegler and *Biblia Hebraica Stuttgartensia*, ed. K. Elliger and W. Rudolph.

7d Whereas Gk, Syriac (Peshitta), and Targums also presuppose the perfect (שׂמו), as in the preceding verb forms, Vg. changes the tense to the present (*ponent*, following *emiserunt, inluserunt, invaluerunt*), like MT. Here the imperfect in MT (progressive, according to J. D. Watts, 38f.) points to the fact that the "laying a trap" (as concrete form of the preceding statements) is dependent on the perfect forms; cf. vv. 5a and b, 9a and b.

7e This word is etymologically unexplained. It must designate some kind of trap which is to be set (שׂים) for the feet (תחתיך); cf. L. Koehler and W. Baumgartner, *Lexicon in Veteris Testamenti Libros* (1967ff.[3]) and Gk ἔνεδρα; Vg *insidias*, "ambush."

7f-f This sentence fits best thematically as a gloss to v. 8, since it departs from the direct form of address used in v. 7a.bα (cf. vv. 6, 8).

9a The 2nd person form of address must be retained because of the connection with vv. 10ff., although in the light of v. 8 we should rather expect גבורי here. See p. 40 below.

9b למען is normally used in the final, or purposeful, sense to mean the goal; but here, as in other passages too, it has the (consecutive) sense of the result (cf. Jer. 36:3; Ps. 51:4 and Joüon, *Gr* §169g).

9c Gk διὰ τὴν σφαγὴν καὶ τὴν ἀσέβειαν, "because of the slaughter and the godlessness," already links מקטל with the following verse and presupposes a copula before מחמס, "because of act of violence"; Syriac (Peshitta) and Vg do the same. Targums support MT. And yet it is hardly possible to go along with MT (T. H. Robinson, J. D. Watts) in assigning מקטל "because of murder") to the previous sentence; for in this case, v. 9b, as parallel to v. 9a, would be too long and the close of vv. 8bβ and 9b with their identical wording מהר עשׂו, "from the mountains of Esau") would be disturbed. Since this phrase is parallel to אדום ("Edom") in v. 8bα and to תימן ("Teman") in v. 9a, it is no more advisable to move מקטל ("because of murder") to the position now occupied by מהר עשׂו ("from the mountains of Esau"), and to view the latter phrase as a mistaken insertion of the two last words of v. 8bβ.

10a מחמס "because of the attack on life and limb" (see H. W. Wolff, *Joel/Amos*, BK 14/2, 232 [Eng. *Joel and Amos*]) is a gloss interpreting the preceding hapax legomenon קטל, "murder"; Gk and Vg (see textual note to v. 9c) fit this gloss smoothly into the original text by way of a copula. The gloss has its source in Joel 3:19. Perhaps it was originally a marginal note, prompted by the fact that ונכרת in v. 10b does not display any parallels that would bring it into correspondence with מקטל.

10b The context absolutely requires us to understand the *nomen rectum* in the construct state as an objective genitive; cf. BrSynt §77e; Joüon, Gr §129e; Meyer³ 3 §97, 4a.

11a The adverb signifies both distance and opposition; Gk ἐξ ἐναντίας, Vg *adversus*, both with the "hostile" sense of "contrary," "against," Targ, מקבל.

11b Targ עלו בקרווהי does not necessarily presuppose another text as source (בָּאוּ עָרָיו) as A. Sperber thinks (*The Bible in Aramaic* 4 B [1973] 68). It could correspond to the interpretation of שערים as "dwelling places" — an interpretation which was widespread from Deuteronomy onwards (Deut. 5:14; 12:17; 23:16; Jer. 14:2; 15:7). But this interpretation is probably less close to the meaning of the present text than the Gk εἰς πύλας αὐτοῦ, Vg *portas eius* (both, "his gates"). These at the same time confirm the plural in MT *Qere*, contrary to *Kethib*, which assimilates to v. 13a. Although the suffix is related to Jacob, and Jerusalem is only mentioned afterwards, the context does not suggest that the writer is thinking here of places in Judah other than, or outside, Jerusalem (W. Rudolph's view, KAT 13, 305).

11c On ידד I, perfect of *qal* (not נדה, as C. A. Keller thinks), cf. Joel 3:3; Nah. 3:10 and Koehler and Baumgartner, *Lexicon* (1967ff.³).

12a ראה ב = "to look on with interest," brings out the intense, emotional participation in the thing looked at; cf. Ps. 118:7.

12b Some scholars read an abbreviated בְּאָחִיךְ, "on your brother," instead of "on the day of your brother" (W. Nowack, T. H. Robinson, G. Fohrer, "Obadja"; cf. *Biblia Hebraica Stuttgartensia*), since this has an unpleasing effect beside the ביום, "on the day," which is regularly repeated at the end of the line. But the early versions confirm the MT; this first ביום in v. 12aα can be intended as an emphatic link with the double ביום in v. 11a, in this way depicting the whole of events connected with Edom's brother Jacob as the object of the sneers of the onlookers.

12c נֵכֶר, like נֶכֶר in Job 31:3, is a term used to describe an astonishing, disconcerting calamity. Gk ἐν ἡμέρᾳ ἀλλοτρίων, "in the day of strangers," Vg *in die peregrinationis eius*, "in the day of his wandering (to a foreign land)," probably already have the deportation in mind.

12d Literally: "Don't open your mouth wide!" Cf. Ezek. 35:13, where the similar phrase בְּפֶ" refers to behavior towards Yahweh.

13a Gk εἰς πύλας "into the gates," adapts to the plural in v. 11b; but the original text (MT is supported by Vg here) shows a fairly frequent switch from singular to plural, and vice versa, in this passage; cf. v. 12aα (נָכְרֹו) with v. 12aβ (אָבְדָם); on v. 13a see textual note to 13c.

13b Gk λαῶν, "peoples," genitive plural, may have read the plural form עַמִּים.

13c Gk πόνων αὐτῶν, "their distresses," very probably read אֹונָם (T. H. Robinson: אֹונֹו) since Gk never otherwise translates אֵיד by πόνος, but does frequently use this rendering for אָוֶן (1 Sam. 15:23; Jer. 4:14, 15; Ps. 9:28 Gk [= 10:7 MT]; 89 [90]:10). It must be said, however, that suffix forms of אָוֶן are not otherwise known. The plural suffix is from a scribal point of view more probable with the collective עַמִּי, and after v. 12aβ, than a singular (the view taken by T. H. Robinson and J. D. Watts); the copyist, picking up the אֵיד that follows in v. 13aβ, may have thought of "a wordplay on Edom" (W. Rudolph).

13d See textual note on v. 12a above.

13e Gk τὴν συναγωγὴν αὐτῶν erroneously read בַּעֲדָתָם; Vg, *in malis eius*, "in their distresses," = בְּרָעָתֹו and confirms the consonants in MT.

13f   The 2nd person feminine plural in MT is disconcerting; Gk, Vg and Targ. presuppose the 2nd person singular masculine form תִּשְׁלַח, as in the context. Targ. also takes יָדְךָ as object instead of the ending נה־; but this is probably intended to resolve the elliptical expression, which can also be found in 2 Sam. 6:6; Ps. 18:16; the afformative נה (תשלח) can be explained by the intensifying נָא־, which was misread (C. A. Keller et al.). An emphatic particle of this kind corresponds to the accentuating גם in the previous sentence.

13g   Gk ἀπωλείας αὐτῶν, "their destruction," presupposes אָבְדָם, "calamity," as in v. 12a; this is more probable than the immediate repetition of the אידו, "distress," "trouble," of the preceding sentence; צָרָה is also repeated only at greater intervals (vv. 12b-14b). The change to אֵידוֹ can here too be motivated by the echo of the word *Edom*; see textual note to v. 13c.

14a   In Gen. 27:40 פרק means "tear loose"; the noun here may mean the "way of escape" (Koehler and Baumgartner, "dividing way"; W. Rudolph, "crack," "chink"); cf. Gk διεκβολαί, "ways through," Vg. *exitus*, "ways out," σ᾽(φυγαδειαί) "(ways of) escape."

15b-a   On the problem of transposing 15b and 15a, see "Form," below.

15b   Cf. Lev. 24:19b.

15c   Bab. ms. Eb 25 (see *Biblia Hebraica*, ed. R. Kittel, 3rd ed.) offers יָשִׁיב "your deed can be put upon your head," and is just as improbable as יָשִׁיב, since both presuppose that Yahweh is the subject (cf. Hos. 4:9b; Joel 3:4, 7); MT fits better as parallel to the passive in the preceding sentence.

Form

What has led recent research generally to see vv. 1-14, 15b as *a single unit*, in spite of a number of difficulties? The cohesion of the individual sayings first of all becomes evident when the passage is set over against the continuation in vv. 15a, 16ff. In the first passage, the subject is simply and solely Edom's guilt and punishment; the nations are mobilized as Yahweh's instrument (v. 1; cf. v. 7). In the succeeding passage, on the other hand, the message of judgment applies to *all* the nations (vv. 15a, 16f.); now we are told for the first time that a remnant of Israel on Zion will be delivered (vv. 17a, 21a) — indeed, that Jacob and Joseph will themselves implement Edom's punishment (v. 18) to their own advantage (vv. 19-21). This thematic division is clearly borne out and underpinned by the style: in the first, major section, which we are considering here, and which constitutes the main part of the book, Edom is generally addressed in the 2nd person singular ("thou," or "you"); vv. 2-5, 7, 10-14, 15b). Later the addressee is no longer Edom, but Israel (vv. 16, 2nd person plural). These characteristics suggest that vv. 1-14, 15b should be considered as a single unit, both stylistically and thematically.

       What are the reasons that make a transposition of v. 15a and v. 15b plausible, so that 15b forms part of the passage vv. 1-14, while 15a is assigned to v. 16? The first point is the singular form of address in v. 15b. This is in line with the style prevailing in vv. 2-14. It should be noted, above all, that v. 16, with its plural form of address (though the addressees are not named), cannot possibly have originally followed directly on v. 15b, with its 2nd person singular; for v. 15b speaks to Edom, and v. 16 to Israel. On the other hand, v. 15a, which harmonizes ill with vv. 1-14, 15b (cf. 1b, 7), fits in well enough with v. 16, the catchword "all the nations" acting as a link. The transposition can be explained only in the framework of faulty scribal transmission.

The text's present order is explicable, because it puts the two כאשר ("just as") clauses in vv. 15b, 16a side by side (even though the sense is distorted in the process); in v. 15a, Edom's destiny is placed in the context of the eschatological judgment on the nations (like Isa. 34:2, 5f., 8; Joel 3:2, 12, 19; in spite of the disharmony with vv. 1, 7) and the "surrendering" theme in 14b finds some kind of commentary in 15a. But it is only possible to see the passage in this light through a forced process of hindsight. The reasons I have adduced for believing that, in the original text, v. 15b belonged to vv. 1-14 are cogent ones, and have come to be increasingly accepted, ever since Wellhausen.

Yet, what has been said about the general coherence of vv. 1-14, 15b must not blind us to the internal stresses and strains in the text. In v. 4 a speech unit is concluded with the oracle formula נאם יהוה, "utterance of Yahweh," although it opened with the messenger formula, כה אמר יהוה, "thus says Yahweh"; in v. 8 a new saying is introduced with the same oracle formula, but this time it is interpolated parenthetically. In the intervening passage, vv. 5-7, the direct address *to* Edom, which otherwise runs through the whole passage, is interrupted by statements *about* Edom, in the 3rd person, of the kind we also find in v. 8. These sayings in vv. 1-9 (which also vary greatly in their content) deal almost exclusively with Edom's future downfall (on v. 3 see p. 47 below; on the perfect forms, p. 48). The sequel, on the other hand, from the last word of v. 9 onwards, gives the reasons for the catastrophe — and again the reasons are not unified in form. First, we have a brief adverb (vv. 9bβ-10a מקטל see textual note on 10a); then a short nominal clause (v. 11bβ) following a detailed description of the situation (v. 11a, bα); and finally comes a sequence of eight warnings. These are quite unusual in their function as justification for punishment, but the close in v. 15b makes it clear that this is what they are. These incisions and divergences in the text raise the question: how far can it be understood as a single unit at all? In order to decide this, we must first of all look at the form of the individual, self-contained passages.

The text begins with the audition account, telling of Yahweh's command to the Gentile nations to line up for war against Edom (v. 1). The reason is explained in an extensive divine utterance (vv. 2-4). Calls to battle of this kind, justified by threats of disaster, had been familiar forms of speech in prophecy ever since Hosea (5:8f.), Micah (4:13), and Jeremiah (5:10f.; 6:4-6); cf. R. Bach, *Aufforderungen* (1962) 51ff. What is now of immediate importance is that this opening saying has not only form-critical precursors but also an almost word-for-word parallel in Jer. 49:14-16. In Obad. 5 a further parallel to Jer. 49:9 follows. In vv. 1-5 three-quarters of the words used are exactly those found in Jer. 49:14-16. This finding compels us to assume dependency at this point. But is the original passage Obad. 1-4 (as M. Haller and W. Rudolph think) or Jer. 49:14-16 (J. A. Bewer's view)? Or do both texts derive from a third, earlier text (an opinion supported by J. Bekel, J. A. Thompson, and J. D. Watts)? A decision can be arrived at only through a consideration of the differences between the two texts. The relevant passages are set side by side below, the differences being underlined:

Jeremiah 49:14-16, 9	Obadiah 1-5
¹⁴שְׁמוּעָה שָׁמַעְתִּי מֵאֵת יהוה	¹ שְׁמוּעָה שָׁמַעְנוּ מֵאֵת יהוה
וְצִיר בַּגּוֹיִם שָׁלוּחַ	וְצִיר בַּגּוֹיִם שֻׁלָּח
הִתְקַבְּצוּ וּבֹאוּ עָלֶיהָ	קוּמוּ וְנָקוּמָה עָלֶיהָ
וְקוּמוּ לַמִּלְחָמָה	לַמִּלְחָמָה
¹⁵כִּי־הִנֵּה	² (כֹּה־אָמַר אדני יהוה) הִנֵּה
קָטֹן נְתַתִּיךָ בַּגּוֹיִם	קָטֹן נְתַתִּיךָ בַּגּוֹיִם
בָּזוּי בָּאָדָם	בָּזוּי אַתָּה מְאֹד
¹⁶תִּפְלַצְתְּךָ הִשִּׁיא אֹתָךְ	³ זְדוֹן לִבְּךָ הִשִּׁיאֶךָ
זְדוֹן לִבֶּךָ	
שֹׁכְנִי בְּחַגְוֵי הַסֶּלַע	שֹׁכְנִי בְחַגְוֵי־סֶּלַע
תֹּפְשִׂי מְרוֹם גִּבְעָה	(מֵרִים?) מְרוֹם שִׁבְתּוֹ
	אֹמֵר בְּלִבּוֹ
	מִי יוֹרִדֵנִי אָרֶץ
כִּי־תַגְבִּיהַ כַּנֶּשֶׁר	⁴ אִם־תַּגְבִּיהַּ כַּנֶּשֶׁר
	[וְאִם־בֵּין כּוֹכָבִים שִׂים]
קַנֶּךָ מִשָּׁם אוֹרִידְךָ	קִנֶּךָ מִשָּׁם אוֹרִידְךָ
נְאֻם יהוה	נְאֻם יהוה
⁹ אִם־בֹּצְרִים בָּאוּ לָךְ	⁵ אִם־גַּנָּבִים בָּאוּ־לְךָ
	[אִם־שׁוֹדְדֵי לַיְלָה]
	אֵיךְ נִדְמֵיתָה
לֹא יַשְׁאִרוּ עוֹלֵלוֹת	הֲלוֹא יִגְנְבוּ דַיָּם
אִם־גַּנָּבִים בַּלַּיְלָה	אִם־בֹּצְרִים בָּאוּ לָךְ
הִשְׁחִיתוּ דַיָּם	הֲלוֹא יַשְׁאִירוּ עֹלֵלוֹת

Apart from later additions apparently made for literary reasons (see textual notes to vv. 4c-c and 5a-a), the Obadiah text shows only one considerable expansion (in v. 3b) compared with Jeremiah 49. Jeremiah 49 has some small additional words and phrases in vv. 14bα, 16aα.γ that go beyond the text of Obad. 1 and 3: in Obad. 1, the war that is proclaimed seems to be rather more imminent, since the text contains only the message about the call to battle, and not also the call to gather together and to move up to the battlefield. In v. 3 Obadiah makes Edom's arrogance particularly explicit by additionally referring to its self-confidence. Neither the omission of particular passages nor the additional words and phrases point to any direct literary dependence. In fact, a whole series of slight variants actually serves to exclude direct dependence, since they are only fully explicable in the framework of oral transmission. No misreading or scribal error can explain why Obad. 2b should run: ''you will be utterly despised,'' whereas Jer. 49:15b reads: ''despised among men''; or why the wording of Obad. 3aα is shorter and transposed compared with Jer. 49:16aα; or why the conditional clause in Obad. 4a is introduced by אִם, whereas in Jer. 49:16b it begins with כִּי. The variants between Obad. 5 and Jer. 49:9 are particularly significant: the two sentences about the ''thieves'' and the ''grape gatherers'' appear in a different order; in Obadiah the verb in the conditional clauses is the same, but not in Jeremiah; the consecutive, or result, clauses are rhetorical questions in Obadiah, indicative statements in Jeremiah; and moreover the verb in the sentence about the thieves is different in the two passages.

If we take into account these differences, together with the very large measure of agreement, only one conclusion is possible: the two passages derive from one and the same orally proclaimed text. We should note here that in the case of Obad. 1-4 the text is framed and formulated as a self-contained messenger speech; the same may be said of Jer. 49:14-16, with its concluding ''saying of Yahweh.'' Obadiah therefore evidently goes back to a text passed down by word of mouth. (On the process of oral transmission, cf. C. Hardmeier, ''Kritik der Formgeschichte auf texttheoretischer Basis,'' diss. Heidelberg [1975] 105f.) Verse 5 picks up another text about Edom, which appears in v. 9 in the collection of sayings about Edom in Jer. 49:7-22, and is consequently not connected there with Obadiah's opening saying. The fact that here rhetorical questions take the place of statements in the indicative shows the character of living speech; it is as if Obadiah wanted to gain the assent of his listeners with a saying against Edom which was already familiar to them. In the same way, v. 8 with its ''is it not so?'' introduces a new ''saying of Yahweh'' which, like vv. 2-4, 5 addresses Edom (in the 2nd person singular) and, like vv. 2-4, employs the ''I'' of the Yahweh utterances. This saying in v. 8 touches on themes which we find again, stylized in a different way, in Jer. 49:7; there the Edomites' wisdom is called in question; here Edom's annihilation is proclaimed, with all the consequences issuing from a downfall that is to be political as well (vv. 9f.). The threat in vv. 9f. is not determined by any traditional material known to us, and it again uses the direct form of address (2nd person singular), whereas v. 8 talked about Edom in the 3rd person, which makes the link with traditional material of the sentence introduced by הֲלוֹא even more comprehensible.

Between the ''is it not so?'' sentences in vv. 5 and 8, which seek contact with the listener through the pointer to what is already familiar, we have first of all in v. 6 a clause introduced by an exclamatory אֵיךְ ''how!'' (cf. Jer. 3:19; 49:25; also p. 50 below); this corresponds in thought to the Edom saying in Jer. 49:10, seeking in a similarly exclamatory way for new assent to what is already known. This sentence too interrupts the ''direct address'' style, and this can again be explained by the absorption of traditional material. Verse 7, on the other hand, again reverts to the 2nd person singular form of address, although there is no detectable relation in either form or content to any sayings about Edom known to us.

From v. 11, the address style is preserved unbroken until the end in vv. 14, 15b and — apart from the final, apodictic utterance in v. 15b (see p. 56 below) — offers only highly topical comments, which are in no way modeled on the pattern of earlier statements. The phrase ''on the day'' introduces the sayings twice (v. 11aα.β) and closes them eight times (vv. 12-14), gathering the sayings into an impressive whole. The sequence of eight prohibitions in vv.12-14, in which warnings act as justification for punishment, is original (cf. Prov. 24:17; 27:10; Amos 5:5f.; Hos. 9:1). These indirect accusations in the form of prohibitions ("you really should not. . .") give the impression that the events referred to are very recent.

The final sentence in v. 15b formally announces to Edom that its punishment will correspond precisely to the acts it has committed. If, from this point, we survey the trend of the sayings hitherto, we see that the last original sentences in vv. 11-24 speak solely about Edom's deeds, whereas vv. 1-10 deal, essentially speaking, with the punishment which is to be expected; only v. 3 (and vv. 9bβ-10aα very faintly) touch on the guilt, but much less distinctly than vv. 11-14. What we therefore have here is a large-scale example of an announcement of punishment with a number of different parts, and the justification for that punishment.

We can make the singular development of this passage clear to ourselves in the light of our observations about the units of speech which had already received their fixed form, and if we also bear in mind the incongruities of style. The prophet starts with the wording of a saying that had been passed down orally (vv. 1-4), which was essentially a proclamation of judgment; the interpolated reason for this condemnation (v. 3) talks only about the Edomites' self-confidence. What follows is clearly an application of what has been said. Rhetorical questions (vv. 5ab, 8 הלוא ["is it not so"] and v. 6 איך ["how"] play on more or less familiar sayings directed against Edom. Insofar as we can compare this passage with the numerous sayings against Edom that have been passed down to us, however (see p. 50 below), it can be said that the prophet frees himself increasingly from familiar material as he goes on and — using his own language — turns to live issues (vv. 7, 9f.). All in all, therefore, in vv. 5-10 he expounds and applies the announcement of punishment uttered in vv. 1-4, using material that is both traditional and new. In vv. 11-14 the guilt of the Edomites is then given a topical reference (after the brief hint in vv. 9f.). Whereas the old "foundation" text in v. 3 talked only about self-confidence, now the prophet goes on to the Edomites' base behavior toward the people of Jerusalem after the conquest of the city by Nebuchadnezzar II in 587. Thus an earlier saying of Yahweh is proclaimed anew, in accusation of the Edomites and as a proclamation of the divine judgment.

The transition is reflected in *the rhythms* and the style as well (insofar as the uncertainties about Hebrew prosody permit comment here). It is only where the number of stresses corresponds to the thought rhyme that the rhythm is not very uncertain. Uniformly parallel cola (rhythmical periods) can be found from v. 9 onwards, roughly speaking (clearly so from v. 12), at the point where Obadiah breaks completely free from already existing sayings. Before that we may, with considerable caution, divide the lines as follows, the symbol "//" pointing to what are clearly synonymous parallels:

Verse 1bα[2]: 3 + 3; v. 1bβ: 2 + 2 (?); v. 2: 3 + 3 (without הנה); v. 3aα: 3; v. 3aβ-b: 3//2// 2 + 3; v. 4: 3 + 2 (without נאם יהוה, see textual note to v. 4c-c);

v. 5: 3 + 3//3 + 3 (see textual note to v. 5a-a); v. 6: 3//2; v. 7: 3//3//3//3// (see textual note to v. 7a,c and f-f); v. 8b: 3//3. From vv. 9-11bα we can read twice two parallel seven-stress cola (3 + 2 + 2?), which first of all close with a single emphatic colon of three stresses in v. 11β. (The repetition of the phrase מהר עשׂו ["from the mountains of Esau"] from v. 8b at the end of v. 9 [see textual note to v. 9c] is just as significant stylistically as the repetition of ביום ["on the day"] in v. 11a; cf. v. 5 and vv. 12-14.) Eight clearly synonymously parallel cola of five stresses follow, most of which should be read as mixed bicola with 3 + 2 stresses. The style clearly marks these as constituting the compelling climax of Obadiah's own utterance, especially through the eight uniform opening prohibitions (אל־ת[ו]") and the seven uniform conclusions with. . .ביום (v. 14a is the exception). The final all-concentrating utterance in v. 15b (2//2//3) is no less striking; here the inwardly antithetical two-stress bicolon is synonymous outwardly to the three-stress colon.

Setting

Only verses 11-14 make it possible *to date* the text. They presuppose more clearly than almost any other Edom texts the conquest of Jerusalem by the Babylonians in 587 (cf. Ezek. 35:5; Ps. 137:7; also pp. 53-54 below). Unlike all the other texts, Obadiah cites details which can neither be ascribed to tradition nor be the work of the imagination; they can best be understood in the light of the specific experience of eyewitnesses. But this means that this proclamation must be dated not much later than 587. Where the actual date of Jerusalem's catastrophe is concerned, E. Kutsch would seem to me to have the strongest arguments on his side (see "Das Jahr der Katastrophe: 587 v. Chr.," *Biblica* 55 [1974] 520-545). E. Vogt, on the other hand, considers that "the reasons in favor of 586 seem to have more weight" ("Bemerkungen über das Jahr der Eroberung Jerusalems," *Biblica* 56 [1975] 223-230; quotation from 230).

In what *framework* can this proclamation have been made? Our analysis has shown that — in terms of form criticism — our text must be understood as both a new proclamation and the exposition of an already existing Yahweh saying. We know from Zech. 7:3, 5; 8:19 that national ceremonies of lament were held every year in Jerusalem on the 9th day of the 4th month (the date when the city fell in 587; 2 Kings 25:3f.), on the 7th day of the 5th month (when the temple was burnt to the ground; 2 Kings 25:8f.), in the 7th month (when Gedaliah was murdered; Jer. 41:1ff.), and on the 10th day of the 10th month (when the siege of Jerusalem began in 589; 2 Kings 25:1). The book of Lamentations makes it seem very probable that some, at least, of these lament ceremonies were already held quite soon after 587 (cf. H. J. Kraus, *Klagelieder*, BK 20 [1968³] 12ff.). Here the remembrance of Edom's behavior on the fall of Jerusalem would certainly have played a part; cf. Lam. 4:21f.; also U. Kellermann, *Edom* (1975) 226ff.

At the same time, it will hardly be permissible to attribute all prophetic sayings against Edom to the period following 587 (J. A. Thompson too believes that Obadiah took over preexilic oracles in vv. 1-9). Ezekiel 35:5 sees Edom's hostile attitude in 587 in the context of "age-old enmity" (אֵיבַת עוֹלָם); the same expression is applied to the traditional enmity of the Philistines (Ezek. 25:15). This enmity will no doubt often have received nourishment from the days of David (2 Sam. 8:13f.) and Solomon (1 Kings 11:14ff., 25) onwards (cf. also 2 Kings 8:20-22). Amos 1:6 tells us that the Edomites bought Israelite slaves from the Philistines. This being so, it is surprising that among all the prophetic sayings against foreign nations passed down from the 8th and 7th centuries, no clearly datable, earlier threat directed against the Edomites is to be found. On the other hand, it would be strange if the collection of highly various sayings against Edom in Jer. 49:7-22 were not to include a single saying dating from the years before 587; for — unlike Ezekiel's sayings about Edom (25:12ff.; 35:1ff.) — these hardly refer at all to the fall of Jerusalem (49:12 is the exception). Now, according to Jer. 27:3, in 594 negotiations about a coalition against Babylon were being carried on in Jerusalem, with Edom as well. Is it likely that no prophetic voices were raised in protest when a pact of this kind, entered into before 587, was revoked by Edom, at least for all practical purposes? At all events, the accusation of self-confidence which finds a place in both Jer. 49:16 and in Obad. 3, and in very similar terms, would be much more comprehensible if it belonged to the period before 587, rather than to the succeeding years. Earlier, it was a serious blow to Jerusalem when, as the Babylonian peril came closer, Edom preferred to withdraw to its rocky terrain south of the Dead Sea and east of the Arabah (see p. 48 below), rather than to hasten to Jerusalem's help (see pp. 35-36 below). Later on, the Judaeans would rather have seen Edom further off still (cf. vv. 11-14).

We may therefore assume that between 594 and 587 cultic prophets in Jerusalem had a critical word to say about Edom's withdrawal into self-security. We see Obadiah taking as his starting point just such a "saying of Yahweh," as a message that he had received (v. 1: שְׁמוּעָה שָׁמַעְנוּ). We hear him expound and apply this saying to the situation after 587, adding to it other sayings that had been passed down, as well as words of his own.

Lamentations 4:21 indicates that the ceremonies of lament that were held in commemoration of the catastrophe did not merely offer scope for prayer, but that this was followed (cf. Lam 4:17-20), not by an assurance of salvation for Israel, but by a threat directed against Edom, in this case in ironic guise (cf. H. J. Kraus, BK 20, 82f.). Since this is the background — the *Sitz im Leben* — we find it strange that, with a few exceptions, Obadiah should adhere throughout to the direct form of *address to* Edom. (In Mari a cultic prophet already addressed Babylon threateningly in an oracle to foreign nations, on behalf of his own king, Zimri Lim: See *Archives royales de Mari: Textes cunéiformes*, 13, 23; also H. Schult, *ZDPV* 82 [1966] 228-231; H. B. Huffmon, *BA* 31 [1968] 109: F. Ellermeier, *Prophetie in Mari und Israel* [1968] 40-42.) As in the case of Ezekiel (cf. 35:2 as well as 6:2 and frequently) we shall have to think of this verbal proclamation in conjunction with an "expressive action" (W. Zimmerli, *Ezechiel* BK 13 [1969] 142-144; Eng., *Ezekiel* [1979]), in which, as in a symbolic act, the prophet turned his face towards the dwelling place of the people threatened. (We meet this elsewhere, in 1 Kings 8:44, 48; Dan. 6:11, when exiles turn in a certain direction for prayer.)

So in the ruins of the Jerusalem sanctuary a service of prayer and worship had begun to be held in which it was not only the prayer of lament that found a place, but proclamation as well. Moreover this proclamation took the form, not only of a prophetic-priestly assurance of salvation, or a threat to the enemy spoken by a cultic prophet; it could also pick up earlier sayings of Yahweh, which were now proclaimed again for a new situation. This is the only way in which we can understand the tension-laden complex of vv. 1-14, 15b, in its themes, and with its abruptly changing and characteristic forms of speech.

Commentary

[v. 1]   No prophetic writing has a shorter heading than this. The fact that we are given no information about place and time, the name of the prophet's father, or his own profession may indicate that the main text was written down soon after it had been proclaimed. As is shown by what follows, חֲזוֹן no longer means the process through which the prophet arrives at his perception or knowledge; it is simply the content of that knowledge itself: the revealed Word. Luther already often translated the expression as *Weissagung*, "prophecy" (e.g., Hos. 12:11; Nah. 1:1; Hab. 2:3; cf. G. Krause, *Studien zu Luthers Auslegung der Kleinen Propheten* [1962] 99), not as *Gesicht*, "vision," as he does here and in Mic. 3:6; Hab. 2:2. It is in the sense of "prophecy" that the word is also to be understood in the headings to the books of Isaiah (1:1) and Nahum (1:1); cf. Köhler and Baumgartner, *Lexicon*. With its recollection of visionary experiences, the expression clearly brings out the fact that what is being uttered here does not derive from the prophet himself, but is a word he has received (cf. 1. Sam. 3:1).

Obadiah was too common a name in Israel for it to be a recognizably symbolic name, meaning "worshiper of Yahweh." The Old Testament alone mentions eight different people with this name; cf. Köhler and Bamgartner. If a symbolic intent were present, we should at least expect the longer form עֹבַדְיָהוּ, which stresses the name of Yahweh more emphatically; though this form, too, occurs three times as the name of a person. When parents called their son Obadiah, they were more or less consciously expressing the hope that he would be someone "who serves Yahweh." The suggestion has been made (by A. J. Braver, "The Name Obadiah") that the name should be vocalized as Abadiah. The parallel עֲשָׂהאֵל (2 Sam. 2:18ff.) and the vocalization in the Septuagint ('Aβδιας) and the Vulgate (*Abdias*) could serve as evidence for this. In this case the theophorous element would be the subject of the perfect עבד, not its object, the meaning then being "Yahweh has worked (served)." What speaks decisively against this proposal is that it would be quite unusual to find Yahweh as the subject of עבד, "work" (in contrast to עשׂה, "make or do"), and that Gk and Vg in their vocalization were not thinking of a perfect (in which case the second vowel of the verb would have to have been preserved, as in the case of 'Aσαηλ and Asahel in 2 Sam. 2:18ff. They were thinking of the abbreviated form of the noun עֶבֶד ("servant" of Yahweh), which coincides with the meaning of the Masoretic vocalization (cf. M. Noth, *Die israelitischen Personennamen im Rahmen der gemeinsemitischen Namengebung*, BWANT 46 [1928] 137).

The heading probably originally found its continuation in לאדום "concerning Edom" (see textual note to v. 1b). As prolongation of the messenger formula כה אמר יהוה, "thus says Yahweh," the addressee is very occasionally introduced with ל "concerning" or "to" (see Amos 5:4; Jer. 14:10; Ezek. 36:4), but it is never Edom nor other comparable foreign nations. In Obadiah's time especially, however, ל with the addressee is repeatedly found as a heading to collections of prophetic sayings, for example, even in Jer. 21:11 ("to the house of the king of Judah") and 23:9 ("concerning the prophets"), and especially in the case of sayings about foreign nations (Jer. 46:2; 48:1; 49:1, 7, 23, 28); Jer. 49:7 is deserving of special note, since here כה אמר יהוה (the messenger formula) follows the heading of the collection, לאדום "concerning Edom." This suggests that the book of Obadiah is also intended to be understood as a *collection* of sayings relating to Edom.

The name *Edom* can have grown up as description of a landscape, especially in view of the red (אָדֹם) rock of the rugged country east of the Arabah, particularly the region round Petra. Genesis 25:30 (cf. v. 25) already connected the name *Edom* with the color red. But although the area in which the Edomites lived was called the red country, we should remember that for the ancients "red" was a color that included a wide spectrum, from pale yellow to dark brown; cf. W. F. Albright, *BASOR* 89 (1943) 14, n. 36, and his contribution to *JBL* 63 (1944) 229, n. 128; R. Gradwohl, *Die Farben im Alten Testament*, BZAW 83 (1963) 4-16, 26f.; F. Bender, *Geologie von Jordanien* (1968) 40f.; M. Weippert, "Edom," diss. Tübingen (1971) 393. In v. 8 "Edom" is clearly used for the area in which the people lived, parallel to "the mountains of Esau"; but our heading is thinking of people and land as a whole; see textual note to vv. 1f.

The collection begins with the saying (vv. 1b-4) which has been passed down in very similar form in Jer. 49:14-16 (see pp. 38-39 above). The two alliterative words from the same root שמע indicate that this is the tensely exciting opening of living speech. It unites what is traditional with what is original, by linking a call to battle with the account of "tidings that have been heard."

The exegetical problems raised by the opening of this saying are concentrated round the question of how to interpret the 1st person plural in שמענו, "we heard," and then also in נקומה. The first sentence, "we heard," is generally explained on the model of those accounts in which a prophet, in the hour of receiving a revelation, sees himself drawn into the heavenly council gathered round Yahweh; cf. 1 Kings 22:19-22; Isa. 6:8; Jer. 23:18, 22; Isa. 40: 3, 6; also K. Ellinger, *Deuterojesaja*, BK 11 (1978) 6ff. But the fact that we have a parallel tradition in Jer. 49:14 where the 1st person singular is used ("I heard tidings") could rather suggest that here Obadiah is associating himself with other cultic prophets who received the same message earlier. The text goes on to mention "the messenger sent among the nations." He too apparently had to communicate this Word. But since he is mentioned separately, it seems improbable that it was with this messenger, let alone with the nations, that Obadiah was associating himself in the preceding "we" (cf. R. Bach, *Aufforderungen* [1962] 53; W. Rudolph, KAT 13/2 [1971] 302). This is the more improbable, since the prophetic voice in Jer. 49:14 does not do so either. "We heard" should accordingly be explained in the light of Obadiah's special situation, in the context of cultic history (see pp. 42-43 above). Obadiah reminds his listeners of the prophetic Word that has been passed down, thereby identifying himself with the congregation in the circumstances of the present (cf. U. Masing, *Obadja* [1937] 75). The reminder is part of one of the lament ceremonies held after the destruction of Jerusalem, and is an answer to the imploring complaint of the congregation; cf. Lam. 4:21f., following 4:17ff. The fact that the prayers particularly mentioned Edom and its gloatingly hostile behavior (cf. Lam. 1:2, 7, 17) also explains why the prophetic saying promising that the prayer had been heard does not mention Edom by name, but only refers to it in the 3rd person feminine singular (עליה, "against her"). The emphatic opening position given to the phrase שמועה שמענו מאת יהוה ("we heard tidings from Yahweh") is also comprehensible in the context of that particular ceremony, in which, after the lament of the people, the cultic prophets had first to listen for Yahweh's Word and then had to proclaim "what he says" (Ps. 85:8; cf. Hab. 2:1; also J. Jeremias, *Kultprophetie* [1970] 104ff.). שמועה is therefore the "tidings" which are passed on to the congregation (cf. Isa. 53:1; Jer. 51:46) as the prophetic Word of revelation (cf. also Isa. 28:9, 19). A communication of this kind is a message "from Yahweh" and as such is initially something to be heard, not yet seen (cf. 1 Kings 10:7); but it already crosses the borderline between the two (cf. Jer. 10:22).

Thus, the suffering community is supposed to know that God is at work (cf. vv. 2, 4). A messenger is simultaneously on the way in their service. ציר is a word used for the ambassador engaged in international affairs (Isa. 18:2; 57:9), his preeminent characteristic being reliability (Prov. 13:17; 25:13). He is essentially speaking as "envoy"; the word שלח ("send") is also used in the same context as ציר in Isa. 18:2; 57:9; Prov. 25:13. It is not clear whether this is a reference to some diplomatic activity which has actually been observed (cf. Jer. 51:31) or whether what is being thought of is a message directly sent by Yahweh through the agency of a "heavenly" messenger. What is clear is that God's Word to the congregation and Yahweh's authority in the world of the Gentile nations are coordinated.

The command to mobilize for the fight against Edom therefore probably applies to both. It is not easy to arrive at a decision, for at this point highly formalized material appears in tersest form; cf. Jer. 6:4f. (עָלֶיהָ מִלְחָמָה קוּמוּ); 49:28, 31 and R. Bach, *Aufforderungen* 61ff. But the syntax should be noted. If we consider that the call to battle is limited to the Gentile nations, this means presupposing that the little sentence about the sending of the ambassador is part of the content of the tidings that have been heard from Yahweh. But what speaks against this is the simple way it is connected with the previous clause through ו (circumstantial clause with inversion of the subject; see Ges-K §142d), which means that the content of the two clauses is parallel ("We heard tidings from Yahweh while a messenger was sent among the nations"). It is only then that the message received from Yahweh begins: "Rise up! Let us line up against it for battle." It is improbable that now it is the envoy who joins together with the nations (in the 1st person plural cohortative) and that the majority of the Jerusalem prophets and their congregation (who speak in the 1st person plural in the previous sentence) should be excluded here. It would seem to be more natural to assume that here Jerusalem is being summoned to fight against Edom, together with the other nations (W. Rudolph takes a different view). In Jer. 49:14 the 1st person plural is missing in the call to battle. This corresponds to the fact that it is the 1st person singular that appears at the opening of the saying, instead of the 1st person plural. Ezekiel 25:14 also states that Yahweh is putting the punishment he has designed for Edom into the hands of his people Israel; and our present book presupposes the same thing in a later saying (v. 18). Above all, however, v. 21 talks about the people on Mount Zion who have been delivered as trooping up to Edom (see p. 22 above). Our saying here leaves this point unemphasized; nor does it develop the idea any further later on, any more than it elaborates the action of the nations — unless, indeed, v. 21 constitutes the conclusion of the discourse in 1b-14, 15b (see pp. 68f. below). Stress here is rather on Yahweh's own action (vv. 2, 4). Accordingly, in considering the form given to the command to mobilize ("Let us rise up. . .") we should notice particularly that Yahweh himself, the commander-in-chief, as their leader thereby joins his troops from Israel and the Gentile nations (cf. J. A. Thompson, *Obadiah*, IB 6 [1956]). The war of the nations against Edom, which is announced in this way in traditional phraseology, is Yahweh's will: this is made clear through the Word of judgment in vv. 2-4, which the messenger formula introduces as a saying of Yahweh (on the transposition, cf. textual note to v. 1b); Jer. 49:15 links up the judgment speech with the call to battle by means of a justifying כִּי ("because," "for").

[vv. 2-3] For the sake of contrast, the dominant announcement of punishment (vv. 2, 4) includes a saying (v. 3) which is indirectly a reason for the punishment. (W. Rudolph, *ZAW* 49 [1931] 227, underlines the literary function of the contrast, while G. Fohrer, "Sprüche Obadjas" [1966] 85, and J. M. Myers, "Edom" [1971] 383 stress its substantial function, as justification.) Here the emphatic interjection הנה ("Listen!") stresses above all the following word "small" (cf. Gen. 34:21; 42:22). A similar use can already be found in Ugarit, where the particle can also be used to emphasize whole clauses or sentences; cf. K. Aartun, *Die Partikeln des Ugaritischen*, AOAT 21/1 (1974) 63f., 68f. Israel and the Gentile nations are to know what kind of people it is, against whom they have to line up for battle on Yahweh's instructions; it is small and despised. In the declarative perfect, Edom itself (on the "address" style, see p. 43 above) is shown what has already actually come about, in Yahweh's eyes, since it is his act that causes it to happen: "I am making you small among the nations." The noun clause describing a circumstance adds the subjective effect to the objective one. We are supposed to think of the decimation of the population and the reduction of living space: a "small" Edom like this cannot evoke either fear or respect from others. We

should note that v. 2 describes the effect (in the perfect) before the act of Yahweh's which is the cause (v. 4, in the imperfect). Although here Yahweh threatens
that Edom will be reduced in size and will be despised, this expectation is
nonetheless clearly distinguishable from the latter presumption that it will be totally destroyed (cf. v. 18, earlier, v. 9). This difference is explicable, if here, at the
beginning of his speech, Obadiah is picking up a Yahweh saying from the period
before 587 (see p. 43 above); for it is also noticeable that what is said about Edom
in v. 3 includes none of the features that characterized its behavior after the conquest of Jerusalem. The fact that it is going to be ''small'' and ''despised'' is in no
way here related to its own contempt of Jerusalem (vv. 11-14), as a kind of retaliation. It is contrasted solely with Edom's own conceit and its self-assurance.

Edom's ''heart'' — that is to say here, its self-awareness and the bearings
from which it lives — is characterized by זדון. The root זוד means immoderate,
exaggerated, hybristic behavior. The noun זדון accordingly means a presumptuous, overweening opinion of oneself (Deut. 18:22; 1 Sam. 17:28; Prov. 11:2) and
the impudent disregard of other people (Deut. 17:12; Ezek. 7:10; Prov. 13:10).
Arrogance of this kind is attributed especially to the great power Babylon (Jer.
50:29, 31). By adopting the same arrogance, Edom is deceiving itself. Overweening pride is deceiving Edom, just as Eve was tricked by the serpent (Gen. 3:13).
The perfect השיאך is declarative here, as it was in v. 2. The imposture will come
to light, but the threat of Yahweh's intervention in itself already shows that life
lived in presumptuous arrogance is life lived in illusion or fraud.

Edom's arrogance is based on its geographical situation. The prophet is
thinking especially of the rocky fastnesses east of the Arabah. They are easy to de-
fend against intruders from the north, where the deeply scored valley of the Zered
(Wādi Ḥasā), east of the southern tip of the Dead Sea, already forms a natural bar-
rier against Moab, but above all against danger from the west; since from the
Arabah (the rift between the Dead Sea and the Gulf of Aqabah) an average difference in height of more than 5000 feet has to be surmounted in a distance of 15 to
25 miles. The rugged cliffs with their many caves offered natural protection to the
Edomites living there. Fortifications also secured the land towards all sides; cf. N.
Glueck, *The Other Side of the Jordan* (1940) 128, 133ff. Except for the parallel
passage, Jer. 49:16, we meet the phrase חגוי סלע (''clefts of rock'') in the Old
Testament only in Song of Sol. 2:14, parallel to ''hiding place'' (סֵתֶר), where the
nests of doves are mentioned. So Edom knows that it is secure in its nests in the
caves and the clefts of the rocks. The word סלע (''rock'') is used here without the
article, unlike Jer. 49:16; Song Sol. 2:14. This could be a reminiscence of the
word's use as the name of a person, and we should perhaps see it as a reference to
the rocky city of Petra (which dates from the late Nabataean period; cf. 2 Kings
14:7; also Judg. 1:36; Isa. 16:1, although the identification of the locality remains
uncertain; see H. Wildberger, *Jesaja 13ff.*, BK 10/2 [1978] 619f.). Edom's pride
is its general ability to settle in the regions of the high mountains (see textual note
to v. 3e). The people who had moved into the country west of the Arabah and into
southern Palestine found a secure place of retreat in the ancestral mountain
country.

The quotation that follows is missing in Jer. 49:16. It shows that the prophet does not merely wish to point to Edom's natural conditions and its attitudes of mind, in contrast to what Yahweh brings about; he also wants to bring out the culpable nature of its arrogance, as reason for Yahweh's intervention. In the prophetic saying, the quotation frequently serves precisely this purpose (H. W. Wolff, *Gesammelte Studien* 94ff.). The reflective soliloquy (''he says in his heart. . .'') provides evidence of presumptuous self-confidence (''Who casts me down to the ground?''). It is not its satisfaction over its objectively favorable geographical locality which constitutes Edom's guilt. It is merely its exaggerated opinion of itself, compared with other nations. This becomes historically comprehensible in the context of Edom's withdrawal from the anti-Babylonian coalition of 594 (Jer. 27:3; see p. 43 above; cf. also J. R. Bartlett, ''Edomites,'' [1973] 241: ''Edom's behavior from 594 to 587 B.C. suggests that her chief motive was not enmity with Judah but a desire for self-preservation''). Edom knows that it is much more secure than the northerly partners in the coalition, Israel, Moab, Ammon, Tyre, and Sidon. In the case of a Babylonian advance, these people will be much more likely to need Edom's help than Edom theirs. For the cultic prophet in Jerusalem, this hybris documents God's judgment.

[v. 4]   Yahweh presupposes that the opportunities for defense are exceedingly favorable. Edom's fortifications may be as inaccessible as an eagle's nest (cf. Job 39:27) — the interpolator (see textual note to 4c - c) even makes Edom emulate the plan of the Babylonian king who, according to Isa. 14:12-14, desires to place his throne above the stars. But in spite of that Yahweh will fetch Edom down (cf. Isa. 14:15). The nest in the rocks, as an image for safe human dwelling, is also applied to the Kenites in Num. 24:21. The phrase used for something that is inescapable (''even though you remove yourself. . .I will still fetch you from there. . .,'' מִשָּׁם. . .אִם) is modeled on Amos 9:2-4a, in the series of five similar formulations. There too it is the divine ''I'' whom not even a remnant will escape. The final formula in the Yahweh saying underlines that it is Yahweh himself from whom the highest fortifications provide no security. The self-confident man's rhetorical question in v. 3b finds its clear answer: ''I, Yahweh, will fetch you down from the heights which seem to be impregnable.'' Verse 4 completes the quotation of the saying also passed down to us in Jer. 49:14-16. The saying about Yahweh's judgment on the self-confident is expounded further in what follows.

[v. 5]   For this exposition Obadiah first of all draws on other traditional sayings about Edom. Thus, Jer. 49:9 attests that v. 5 is a saying independent of Obad. 1-14 = Jer. 49:14-16. Obadiah may have linked it on to v. 4 because of the similar conditional structure (double אִם clause). But the saying is not simply quoted; through the rhetorical הלוא (''is it not so?'') the congregation is reminded of the saying as something with which they are familiar. Prophets not infrequently jog the memories of their listeners with phrases of this kind (Amos 9:7b; Mic. 3:1b, 11bβ; Hab. 1:12; Zech. 7:7; Mal. 1:2b; 2:10; cf. also Josh. 1:9; 2 Kings 15:21; Prov. 8:1; Job 22:12). The rhetorical particle simultaneously emphasizes the statement that follows, by rousing attention; cf. K. Aartun, *Die Partikeln des Ugaritischen*, 72f. In this way Obadiah comments on the introductory saying. But when he remodels the sentence which Jer. 49:9 passes down to us in the indicative, it is a question whether his intention is merely to give it rhetorical form. In Jeremiah the saying seems to threaten a complete and utter plundering. There the possibility of any gleanings after the grape harvest is categorically denied. The prophet announces ruin or destruction (שחת *hiph'il*) through the thieves. But in Obadiah a question is put — the question whether thieves do not merely ''steal'' until their ''requirement'' (די) has been met, and whether grape gatherers do not leave gleanings for the poor and for strangers, as the ordinances of the law require (cf. Lev. 19:9f.; Deut. 24:21). Here the comparison between Edom and the house that has been robbed and the vineyard that has been harvested serves to intensify what is said, like the comparison with the eagle's nest in v. 4.

[v. 6]   Verse 6 makes it clear that worse is going to befall Edom. As rhetorical interrogative, איך is here (as in the addition in v. 5; see textual note to v. 5a - a) an expression of astonishment. *Esau* as a name for Edom probably goes back to a relatively late combination; cf. Gen. 25:30; 36:9; also M. Noth, *Überlieferungsgeschichte des Pentateuch* (1966³) 104 [Eng., *A History of Pentateuchal Traditions*, 1972]. The country is going to be searched through and through and its most secret hiding places will be ransacked. Only the theme of the saying in Jer. 49:10 has been taken over, not its wording, and this indicates the heightening, compared with the images in v. 5: the plundering of thieves is limited by their own wishes, and the harvesting of grape gatherers is restricted by the rule that gleanings have to be left for the poor; and in the same way, the ransacking of Edom is dependent on Yahweh's will towards judgment (vv. 2, 4). With the exclamatory interrogative particle איך, Obadiah again strives to win assent to the proclamation of judgment on Edom that had been passed down. The change from the 2nd person of the address in v. 5 to the 3rd person, like the איך, points to a different stylization of the announcement of disaster. The rhythm of the song of lament mingles with the description of the catastrophe and the complaints of those who are involved in Edom's downfall. We find something similar in Zeph. 2:15 (cf. Jer. 9:19); see also C. Hardmeier, ''Kritik der Formgeschichte,'' diss. Heidelberg [1975] 337f., 355).

[v. 7]   In v. 7 Obadiah for the first time gives more specific political form to what he says. We can show no parallels for the threats that follow, so that we lack a secure basis for assuming that this is traditional material belonging to the context of cultic prophecy. At the same time, the renewed transition to the direct form of address, as well as the parallelism of four three-stress cola (see pp. 41f. above) could be an indication of this. We find here a triple use of the *perfectum propheticum*, used also in vv. 2f. and 6. Yahweh's threat to the self-confident (vv. 2, 4) is now no longer interpreted as plundering (vv. 5f.), but as a disappointing harassment by old allies. They are described twice, both as partners to a covenant (אנשי בריתך) and as members of an alliance (אנשי שלמך ''men of your peace''; see textual note to v. 7b). Here an explanation is bound up with two, linked questions. Who are these people? and What do they do? Apparently they do not perform any destructive and annihilating acts of war. They do just what Edom's own arrogance and conceit do: "they deceive" (cf. הִשִּׁיאוּךָ with v. 3a); "they show that they are above everyone else" (on יָכְל ל cf. Gen. 32:26; Num. 13:29; Judg. 16:5; Jer. 1:19; 20:10; 38:22; Ps. 129:2). The last statement is the clearest, although it is etymologically the most difficult to explain (imperfect after the preceding three perfect forms; see textual note to v. 7d). In the context and according to the old translations, it is best rendered as: "they lay traps (snares, pitfalls) for your feet under you." In some form, that is to say, they are barring the way for their former allies.

What is really meant ought to emerge from the first sentence; but שִׁלְּחוּךָ presents scholars with the greatest puzzle. The idea of deportation (G. Fohrer, "Sprüche Obadjas" [1966] 87) is the most improbable solution, for there is no suggestion that the people addressed are going to be driven beyond their own Edomite frontiers, or that they will be delivered up to the enemy. The word שׁלח *pi'el* ("send away") is relatively unbelligerent, and could be a reference to the expulsion of Edomite negotiators who were seeking help from friendly tribes. But then what are the traps for their feet supposed to be (bα)? We should most probably think of refugees who hoped to find protection among friendly neighbors. If we assume this, the various statements all fit: the refugees are certainly not physically attacked, but they are definitely sent back to the frontier. In this way the friendship proves deceptive; the ancient allies show their superiority by securing their frontier through mantraps (?). The text does not show at all who the former allies, or partners to an agreement, are. Ezekiel 25:3-10 (cf. esp. v. 8) suggests that they may have been Arab tribes in the eastern and southern desert, who also caused the Ammonites and the Moabites trouble; cf. J. R. Bartlett, "Rise," *PEQ* 104 (1972) 36f. The gloss in v. 7bβ (see textual note to v. 7f-f) already interprets the previous four short sentences in the light of v. 8: the wisdom which would know how to avert the life-threatening danger can no longer be found in Edom. The new saying tells us why this wisdom is lacking.

[v. 8] This saying is again introduced by "Is it not so?" as a saying of Yahweh's of which listeners only need to be reminded (see above, on v. 5). Obadiah's speech goes on to explain the earlier divine Word through another saying. "On that day" often acts as a temporal link in expansions and explanations (Hos. 1:5; 2:18; Joel 3:18; Amos 9:11; Isa. 7:18, 20; 21:23) and is not infrequently associated with a "saying of Yahweh" (נְאֻם יהוה; Hos. 2:16, 23; Amos 8:9).

The saying itself goes back to Yahweh's own acts (cf. vv. 2, 4). In this "I" utterance, he threatens more drastically than before to implement his work of destruction. He is annihilating "the wise" and their "wisdom." The result is that Edom will lose the basic values which had especially characterized it, according to Jer. 49:7; cf. Job 1:1 (Lam. 4:21); 2:11; 1 Kings 4:30f. The wisdom of the wise does not mean merely reflection about questions of teaching, law, natural phenomena, and theology. It also covers the examination, discernment, and guidance of right and successful action in public life. Here Edom is notified of nothing less than the end of a serviceable political policy, a reasonable diplomacy, and successful military tactics in its own country; cf. Isa. 19:11f.; 29:14. Just as in v. 6 the Edomites are called after their progenitor Esau (see p. 50 above), so here (as in vv. 9, 19, and 21) the country itself is called "the mountains of Esau."

[v. 9] In v. 9 *Teman* is mentioned, parallel to "the mountains of Esau." In the Old Testament, the name *Teman* is not usually applied to a city or town (a town which N. Glueck believed could be identified with Tuwilan, northeast of the village of El-dji, in the region just east of Petra; see *The Other Side of the Jordan* [1940] 24ff.). Genesis 36:34 talks about "the land of the Temanites." In Ezek. 25:13 and Hab. 3:3, Teman also represents a considerable region, and in Jer. 49:20 (cf. v. 7) is parallel to Edom; cf. R. de Vaux, "Téman, ville ou région d'Édom?" *RB* 76 (1969) 379-385. It is only in Amos 1:12 that Teman is parallel to the town of Bozrah; cf. H. W. Wolff, *Joel/Amos*, BK 14/2, 195 (Eng., *Joel and Amos*, on Amos 1:12). Perhaps Teman sometimes meant the southern part of the Edomites' ancestral mountain country, east of the Arabah, while Bozrah was the name given to the northern part of the country (cf. N. Glueck, 26); but here Teman means the country as a whole. The verse describes the consequences, when God robs Edom of its wisdom. Then its warriors collapse. In Jer. 51:56 חתת stands for the breaking of the bows used in war; in 50:2 for the destruction of idols; in Jer. 48:1 for the breaking down of a fortress; in 40:20, 39 for the collapse of a whole country and for the terrible breakdown of human beings, especially soldiers, as here, Isa. 8:9; 37:27; Jer. 8:9. The result (on למען, "so that," see textual note to v. 9b) is that in the mountains of Esau the inhabitants will be exterminated. That means that this threat is much more terrible than what was threatened in vv. 2-4, 5f., and 7: Edom will be so small and despised (v. 2), so reduced (v. 4), so plundered (v. 5f.), so betrayed (v. 7) that the outcome will be the annihilation of its wisdom (v. 8), the collapse of its army (v. 9a), and the extermination of its population (v. 9b).

[v. 10] It is only after the climax of the downfall has been reached that the final ground for God's judgment is named: Edom has committed "murder" against its brother Jacob. This nonce word for the deadly use of force is explained in the transmitted text itself (see textual notes to v. 9c and 10a). Amos 1:11 also mentions the sword with which Edom pursues its brother. Why does Obadiah call Edom Israel's *brother* here? Scholars have thought of the contractual relationship between partners to a treaty, which in the ancient east could be expressed in language of this kind; cf. Amos 1:9, 11; 1 Kings 9:13; 20:32-34; Num. 20:14; H. W. Wolff, *Joel/Amos*, BK 14/2, 193f. (Eng., *Joel and Amos*); M. Fishbane, "The Treaty Background of Amos 1:11 and Related Matters," *JBL* 89 (1970) 313-318. But Obadiah is evidently aware of the patriarchal tradition which formed a part of salvation history and which saw the blood relationship as ground for a common history of promise (Gen. 25:21ff.; 27:27ff., 39f.; Deut. 2:8; 23:8). This is the only way we can explain why it is here alone, in the context of Obadiah's speech, that the "brother" is called "Jacob" (which is in line with the confrontation between Jacob and Esau in Gen. 25:27); for otherwise Obadiah talks about Jerusalem (v. 11), "Judah's sons" (v. 12), or "my [Yahweh's] people" (v. 13). (On "the house of Jacob" in vv. 17f., see p. 65 below.) Verses 13f. bring out more clearly the specific acts which Obadiah is thinking of when he talks about fratricide, and we shall discuss that further in connection with those verses. Following vv. 8f. Edom's extreme bloodguiltiness is only briefly touched on; it explains why (מֵן) the "shame" of the downfall (vv. 8b, 9a) "shrouds" Edom, so that nothing but shame is to be seen, and tells why Edom is going to be finally "annihilated": the carrying over into v. 10b of כרת *niph'al* from v. 9b rounds off the saying in vv.8-10 (on לְעוֹלָם "finally," "for ever," see Isa. 14:20; 25:2; cf. Mal. 1:4 and H. W. Wolff, *Hosea*, BK 14/1, 64 [Eng. *Hosea*, on 2:21]). This is the last saying about Edom which Obadiah has taken over. With its brief accusation of fratricide, it has given the keyword which will now be explained more precisely in extempore, living speech, in vv. 11-14.

[v. 11] The accusation that runs throughout revolves round the events that followed immediately on the conquest of Jerusalem in 587. This "day" is mentioned no less than ten times in vv. 11-14, יוֹם ("day") always meaning both the period of time and the event occupying that time; cf. H. W. Wolff, *Anthropologie* (1973) 127 (Eng., *Anthropology* [1974] 83ff.). "The day" is defined more precisely as the occasion when foreigners led off the Judean troops into captivity and when "lots were cast over Jerusalem" as well. In this last description we should probably think, not of the actual tillable soil of Jerusalem, but of the people. Also in Joel 3:3 lots are cast for the people, apart from the division of the land in v. 2; while in Nah. 3:10 it is the ruling class for whom lots are cast. Consequently, "Jerusalem" in v. 11b, parallel to חיל ("army") in v. 11a, probably means the civilian population of the conquered capital city, and especially its leaders (cf. 2 Kings 25:11f., 18ff.). Among the foreigners who streamed through Jerusalem's gates (bα) Edom also "stood by" (aα), indeed it was Edom who "like one of them" (bβ) put together the convoys of prisoners.

How is the historian supposed to imagine this "standing by" on Edom's part (on the adverb itself, מִנֶּגֶד, see textual note to v. 11a)? It is difficult to answer this, because here Edom is indicted as a whole, as it is in vv. 2-5, 7, 9f. Jeremiah 13:18f. attests that during the immediately preceding years (at latest from the time of Nebuchadnezzar's second siege of Jerusalem) the Edomites had thrust forward from the south, deep into Judean territory, as far as the region round Hebron; cf. A. Alt, "Judas Gaue unter Josia," *Palästinajahrbuch* 21 (1925) 100-116 = *Kleine Schriften* 2, 276-288; M. Noth, *Geschichte Israels* (1966⁶), 265 [Eng., *History of Israel*, 1960²]; also ZDPV 74 (1958) 155f. = *Aufsätze zur biblischen Landes- und Altertumskunde* 1,131f.; U. Kellermann, *Nehemia*, BZAW 102 (1967) 164-166; and S. Herrmann, *Geschichte Israels* (1973) 344f. [Eng., *History of Israel*, 1975, 1980², 315). According to Ezra 2:21, Bethlehem was one of the southernmost places in Judah, and according to Neh. 3:5 Tekoa seems to have lived under the rule of an Edomite aristocracy; cf. 1 Macc. 5:65. Ezek. 36:5 (cf. 35:10, 12) shows that even the exiled community in Babylon knew about the

Edomite advance into the southern parts of Judah (cf. W. Zimmerli, *Ezechiel*, BK 13, (1969) 862 [Eng., *Ezekiel*, 1979]; E. Höhne, "Idumäa," *Biblisch-Historisches Handwörterbuch* 2, 759; the frontier of Idumea on the map of the Hasmonean empire: *Biblisch-Historisches Handwörterbuch* 2, 654; and in Nehemiah's time: G. E. Wright and F. V. Filson, *Historical Atlas to the Bible* [1946], pl. VII D). But all the same, Judean refugees had certainly found refuge in Edomite territory, as well as in Moab and Ammon (Jer. 40:11), so we cannot talk unreservedly about a completely hostile attitude. Above all, however, the statements in v. 11 give the impression that it is particular Edomite groups that are under discussion here, groups that lingered in Jerusalem's gates and in the city's immediate environs. If they were "like one of those" who put together the treks of prisoners, did they then belong officially to the foreign contingents among the conquering Babylonian troops? According to 2 Kings 25:1 (compared with 24:2, where ms. S [cf. *Biblia Hebraica*, ed. R. Kittel, 3rd ed.] reads "Edom" instead of "Aram," though probably mistakenly) this possibility cannot be entirely excluded. According to 1 Esdr. 4:45 it was Edomites who burnt down the temple (but see 2 Kings 25:8f.). The nature of the other things Obadiah has to say about Edomite behavior does not make it very probable that the Edomites belonged to the Babylonian army. All the same, the Edomites do seem to have succeeded in acquiring a better relationship to the Babylonian occupying power than Moab, for example (cf. Jer. 40:11ff.; 48:14ff.); for according to Josephus (*Ant.* 10.9.7 [§181]) five years after the conquest of Jerusalem, in the 23rd year of Nebuchadnezzar (582), Moab too, like Ammon, was subjected by Babylon; whereas we are subsequently told nothing about Edom's fate; cf. Noth, *Geschichte Israels* 265 (Eng., *History of Israel*) and U. Kellermann, *Edom* (1975) 51f. What Obadiah probably had in mind, therefore, were freebooter Edomite reconnaissance patrols, who were friendly towards the Babylonians and hostile towards the people of Jerusalem. The fact that they made themselves conspicuous when the processions of military and civilian prisoners were being put together is important for an understanding of what Obadiah goes on to say in vv. 12-14.

[v. 12]   Verse 12 describes these happenings as "the day of misfortune" (see textual note to v. 12c), as the day of "downfall" and of "distress." As those who stood by (v. 11aα), the Edomites should have veiled their faces at the sight of the terrible situation of their "brother." Instead, they enjoyed the spectacle (see textual note to v. 12a). The accusations that follow (in the form of warnings; see p. 41 above) show, step by step, what happens to these "onlookers" as a consequence of their wrong attitude. Malicious observation is followed first of all by a gloating pleasure in the misfortune of others. Lamentations 1:7 also complains that "seeing" makes the malevolent laugh at Jerusalem's ruin. Obadiah says that Edom "rejoices over the Judeans." Ezekiel 35:14f. also talks about Edom's pleasure at the desolation of Israel. It is surely not by chance that Obadiah, thinking of the exile, talks about יום אבדם ("day of distress"), for אבד often means "being dispersed" or "cut off" (it is applied to the "going astray" of sheep in Ps. 119:176 and to the "being dispersed" of exiles in Isa. 27:13). Israel has been thrown back to the time before its history of election began, as it were: "A dispersed (אֹבֵד) Aramaean was my forefather" (Deut. 26:5, in Martin Buber's version). Watching and rejoicing are followed by words. The way Edom "makes its mouth big" during Jerusalem's tribulation is brought out elsewhere through direct quotation. Psalm 137:7 reminds its hearers that the Edomites egged on Jerusalem's destroyers, crying, "Rase it, rase it! Down to its foundations!" According to Ezek. 35:12, they scoffed over Israel's mountains: "They are laid desolate, they are given us to devour." Cf. textual note to v. 12d.

[v. 13]   The Edomites did not content themselves with gloating looks and encouraging cries from the sidelines. Like the Babylonians and other foreigners (v. 11ba), they too pushed their way into the city gate, "into the gate of my people." It becomes evident here that these accusations, formulated as warnings, as divine words in the form of the messenger's speech, are — like vv. 2, 4 and 8 — an expression of Yahweh's own self. The prophet, on the other hand, introduced himself with the 1st person plural (v. 1b). Once the enemy is in the gate, the city has finally been conquered (Ezek. 26:10). Lamentations 4:12 cries out complainingly that it is unheard-of that "a foe and an oppressor could enter the gates of Jerusalem." Now Edom also looks on at the great disaster at close quarters; the new position in the gateway brings the intensification here, compared with v. 12a. The indignant "you of all people" in aβ is in line with the reminder of brotherhood in the previous verse. Here at least, if not at the end of all three lines in v. 13 (see textual note to v. 13c, g), the day of utter collapse is called (יום אידו (אידם ("day of his calamity"), the sound perhaps being intended as a play on "Edom"; cf. Ezek. 35:5 and W. Zimmerli, BK 13, 861 (Eng., *Ezekiel*). In the jostling throng in the gateway, the glance does not lead to the word (as it did in v. 12, where the onlookers were standing at a distance). Now it leads to actual "grasping" (see textual note to vv. 13f.). What is the hand stretched out for? The word חיל, though it can have other meanings as well as "army," can hardly have a different meaning here from the one it bears in v. 11; so we have to think of the army that was gathered at the gate before being marched off into exile. Now שלח (יד) ב can certainly also mean "kill" (Gen. 37:22; 1 Sam. 24:7, 11; 26:9; cf. Gen. 22:12); but in that case it would hardly have as object "his (whole) army." We should here more probably think of possessions in general, or even valuables that had been rescued (cf. Lam. 1:10) and which a defeated army still had with it.

[v. 14]   The killing takes place elsewhere. Edomites had taken up their position at points where escape was possible (on פרק see textual note to v. 14a) — breaches in the walls which were not kept under observation by official Babylonian troops (cf. 2 Kings 25:4f.; Jer. 39:4f.), or forks in the road, which offered a favorable chance for escape from the line of deportation (cf. Ps. 60:4b, 9 and H. J. Kraus, *Psalmen*, BK 15 [1978] 589; Eng. forthcoming). If someone tried to flee at one of these points, he could fall into the hands of an Edomite there. Obadiah knows Edomite commandos of this kind, which either killed the refugees they captured, or delivered them over to the Babylonians. This is the justification for the accusation of fratricide (vv. 9f.). The word used here is כרת *hiph'il*, "annihilate"; and this is the precise reason why Edom's punishment should also be annihilation (cf. כרת *niph'al*, vv. 9b, 10b). This indirect pointer to the law of retaliation brings us to the final pair of sentences in the speech.

[v. 15b]   These sentences sum up the proclamation of Edom's punishment and guilt. Impressively, the verse puts a two-stress bicolon parallel to a tricolon. These give a different form to the generally accepted answers to the question of what was to be expected as a consequence of the crimes that were forbidden and had nonetheless been committed. In the process of this modification, the two sentences take the legal principles which are otherwise formulated in the 3rd person, as precepts, and transpose them into the form of a threatening address. In this way they adapt them to the style that dominates vv. 2-14, with its 2nd person masc. singular form. The first sentence transforms the rule passed down in Lev. 24:19b: "As a man has done, it shall be done to him." Leviticus 24:17-21 explains this law of retaliation which, according to v. 22, applies explicitly to "the sojourner" (or stranger) and to "the native" alike. So its application to Edom is not surprising, especially since it counts as a rule of international wisdom, of which there were excellent exponents in Edom (cf. v. 8b and p. 51 above). The rule which Obadiah takes over merely establishes the nature of the punishment. It does not say who will carry that punishment out. Ezekiel 35:11a proclaims to Edom that it is Yahweh (cf. Obad. 2, 4, 8). In a corresponding saying directed against Babylon, Jer. 50:29 calls upon the nations: "Requite her according to her deeds!" (cf. Obad. v. 1b and p. 47 above). Obadiah leaves the question open. By doing so he stays close to his parallel sentence (bβ), which is to be found similarly formulated, though in generalized form, in Prov. 12:14: "The work of a man's hand comes back to him." Even proverbs and sayings (e.g., Prov. 19:17b) can testify that it is Yahweh's act when what a person does "comes home to roost" in this way; and this is especially emphasized in prophecy (e.g., Hos. 4:9b, cf. H. W. Wolff, BK 14/1, 103 [Eng., *Hosea*, on Hos. 4:9]; on the absorption of Obadiah's language in v. 15bβ in Joel 3:4bβ, 7b cf. H. W. Wolff, BK 14/2, 94, *Joel/Amos* [Eng. *Joel and Amos*]). Obadiah restricts himself to the threat that the act carried out and completed (גמול) against other people will itself have its effect on the agent; like a boomerang, it will return to the head of the perpetrator — which means his life.

Purpose

With these final threats, the cult prophet Obadiah achieves two things. First, he again powerfully emphasizes the crimes committed by the Edomites in the recent past, when the people of Jerusalem were carried off into exile. In this way he brings out the full force of the last part of the speech (vv. 11-14), which he himself formulated in his own words: "*As you have done* will be done to you; *the deed you have committed* returns onto your own head." If you wish to know what you have to expect, remember exactly what you did to the Judeans! Second, with his terse final sentences, without any topical addition (unless indeed v. 21 should belong to

v. 15b; see p. 22 above), Obadiah points back to the divine words of judgment uttered against Edom (vv. 1b-10), which he took over in the first part of his speech. The people who have made common cause with the conquerors of Jerusalem (v. 11) will themselves experience the onslaught of the nations (v. 1b); those who look down gloatingly and arrogantly on the defeated inhabitants of Jerusalem (v. 12) will have to become quite small themselves (vv. 2-4); those who have laid hands on the poor army of prisoners (v. 13) will themselves learn what it is to be plundered (vv. 5f.); the people who delivered up the refugees belonging to the people of the covenant (v. 14b) will themselves find no refuge among their friends any more (v. 7); the men who killed those who had escaped (v. 14a) will as fratricides themselves fall victim to annihilation (vv. 8-10). ''As you have done *will be done to you*; the deed you have committed *returns onto your own head.*'' If you look at what you have done you will see exactly how just Yahweh is, in the judgment he has announced.

This word is addressed to the still presumptuous Edom; but it is desolate, lamenting Jerusalem who is supposed to hear it (see p. 42). On the possible close of the speech in v. 21, see p. 47 above.

When we turn up our noses at pre-Christian notions of retaliation, have we really grasped the validity of that prophetic speech, spoken in the 6th century B.C., in the framework of the cult? Should we not first of all ask where nowadays Edom is taking up its position (vv. 11 and 14; cf. עמד, ''stand'') towards an Israel which has suffered over and over again? And should we not inquire on which side the Christian churches stand? Perhaps here and there the Christian church itself finds itself in the position of derided and threatened Israel. Perhaps — under the superior power of its opponents — it is exposed to the contempt and the greedy grasp of false ''brothers'' (vv. 10 and 12; cf. אחיך). From time to time we ought to make sure to whom vv.11-14 applies today — for whom it is intended as a mirror, and a guide to conscience. And who should be looking at vv. 1-10, so that they may discern their future more clearly?

Then and only then will the truth of the precepts in v. 15b (see pp. 56f. above) show us how necessary it is for Edom and for Israel, for Christians and for their opponents, that Jesus Christ, as the one crucified, has taken upon himself everything in this saying that applies to us and everything that is true of us. He is the living witness of God's unconditional mercy on all human beings. Obadiah is Jesus' precursor inasmuch as, with his threats and his accusation of Edom, he indirectly declares God's compassion with Jerusalem who, after all, had well deserved its downfall, according to the testimony of the earlier prophets.

After Jesus Christ entered human history, Obadiah took on a double function. His message of judgment (vv.1-10, 15b) shows everyone that it is completely hopeless to go on practicing enmity, leaving God's compassion on one side. This is the message to all of us, that we should treat the people of God (v. 13aα: ''my people'') with brotherly affection (vv. 10a, 12a); and it is the message to God's people themselves as well. Obadiah's accusations (vv.11-14) turn into new warnings, sentence by sentence, warnings against departing from the path of Christian discipleship, in our specific relationship to Israel and in our relationship to the suffering Christian church today.

Deliverance on Mount Zion

Literature

J. Gray, ''The Diaspora of Israel and Judah in Obadiah v. 20,'' *ZAW* 65 (1953) 53-59. E. Lipiński, ''Obadiah 20,'' *VT* 23 (1973) 368-370. J. R. Bartlett, ''The Moabites and Edomites,'' *Peoples of Old Testament Times*, ed. D. J. Wiseman (1973) 229-258. D. R. Ap-Thomas, ''The Phoenicians,'' ibid., 259-286. U. Kellermann, ''Israel and Edom,'' professorial thesis, Münster (1975) 17-28. B. Diebner and H. Schult, ''Edom in alttestamentlichen Texten der Makkabäerzeit,'' *Dielheimer Blätter zum Alten Testament* 8 (1975) 11-17.

Text

15a Yes, Yahweh's day is near for all nations.[a]
16 For,
> as you[a] had to drink upon my holy mountain,
>> so all nations will have to drink without ceasing.[b]
> They shall drink and gulp it down to the dregs.[c]
>> They shall be as[d] those who had never been.
17 But on Mount Zion there shall be exemption
> [a][and it shall be a sanctuary].[a]
> And the house of Jacob shall[b] take possession of those
> [c]'who had possessed it.'[c]
18 Then the house of Jacob shall become[a]a fire
> And the house of Joseph a flame,
>> but the house of Esau straw.
> They set light to them[b] and consume them,[ba]
>> so that no survivor remains
>>> from the house of Esau.
> For Yahweh has spoken.
19 And they[a] shall take the southland [b][the mountains of Esau][b]
> and the lowland [b][the Philistines][b] in possession,
> they[a] shall take Ephraim's fields[c] [d][and the fields of Samaria][d]
>> and [e][Benjamin][e] shall take Gilead in possession.

20   And the exiles ᵃ[that was the beginning]ᵃ from Israel's sons
     'shall' 'possess'ᵇ 'the land of the'ᶜ Canaanites as far as Zarephath,
     and the exiles of Jerusalem who are in Sepharad
     shall possess the cities of the southland.
21   The 'delivered'ᵃ onᵇ Mount Zion shall go up
     to rule Mount Esau.
     But the sovereignty shall belong to Yahweh.

15a   See textual note to 15bᵃ, p. 37 above.

16a   Gk ἔπιες and Vg *bibisti*, "you [sing.] have drunk," assimilate to the sing. in v. 15b.

16b   Many MT manuscripts write סָבִיב, "round about," probably picking the substance of Jer. 25:15ff.; cf. 25:9; Joel 3:11; Zech. 14:14. But the continuation in bα speaks in favor of MTᴸ. Gk οἶνον, "wine," probably instead read a (perhaps damaged?) תמיד, "incessantly," as the frequently occurring תִּירוֹשׁ, "unfermented wine"; cf. Hos. 2:8f., 22; 7:14; 9:2; Mic. 6:15; Joel 1:10; 2:19, 24; Hag. 1:11; Zech. 9:17. Targ puts כס פורענותהון, "cup of punishment," in front of תמיד as object; cf. כּוֹס, "cup," in Jer. 49:12; 25:15, 17, 28; Lam. 4:21 and Isa. 51:17, 22 ("cup of wrath").

16c   The nonce form of לֹעַ (cf. Koehler and Baumgartner, *Lexicon*) is probably the original reading (Vg *absorbent*, "they shall suck in"). Gkⱽᴸ ἀναβήσονται, "they shall go up," mistakenly read the common וְעָלוּ (as they do correctly in v. 21); but earlier Gk texts (notably W; cf. Ziegler) have καταβήσονται, thereby surely confirming MT.

16d   כלוא corresponds to כַּאֲשֶׁר לֹא (Joüon, *Gr* §174d; W. Rudolph) but it probably wishes to compare the nations in their existence rather in what they do.

17a-a   Two Gk 10th-century miniscule manuscripts leave out καὶ ἔσται ἅγιον, "and it will be holy." Is this an internal corruption in the Greek, caused by the homoeoarchy καὶ. . .καὶ (i.e., the eye jumping straight from the καὶ, "and," introducing 17a to the "and" at the beginning of the following line)? Or is the omission a confirmation that the mention of the sanctuary (וְהָיָה קֹדֶשׁ) is a later interpolation? As the sentence runs at present, the words give the impression of being an addition; in the light of Joel 3:17bα; 2:32bα (cf. Isa. 4:3), the interpolator is put out because here Mount Zion, as the place of refuge for those who have been spared, is not called קֹדֶשׁ, "holiness," (as in v. 16). C. A. Keller expresses the character of the clause as explanatory addition by translating it as a relative clause, *qui redevient sainte*, "which will again be sanctified."

17b   As a collective, בית, "house," takes a plural verb.

17c-c   MT mistakenly reads "their possessions," leaving it unclear to what the suffix is related; מוֹרָשׁ, "possession," is otherwise found only in Isa. 14:23. Gk τοὺς κατακληρονομήσαντας αὐτούς and Vg. *eos qui se possederant*, "those who had possessed them," as well as Targ עממיא דהוו מחסנין להון all suggest that מוֹרִישֵׁיהֶם was the original reading. This is confirmed by Murabbaʿat (*Discoveries in the Judaean Desert* 2, 88); cf. *Biblia Hebraica Stutt.* and Jer. 49:2.

18a-a   On the image in v. 18a cf. Isa. 5:24; 47:14; also Isa. 10:17 and p. 66 below.

18b   The plural forms בהם and ואכלום show that in the case of בית, "house," it is again the many individual members who are being thought of; cf. textual note to v. 17b and the continuation in v. 18b.

19a   The phrases are a subsequent interpretation of v. 17b; the logical subject of v. 19aα is accordingly "the house of Jacob," for v. 19aββ "the house of Jacob" and "the house of Joseph" (cf. v. 18a). Gk οἱ ἐν Ναγεβ, "those in the Negev," takes הנגב, the Negev ("the southland") as well as the following השפלה "the lowland" (οἱ ἐν τῇ Σεφηλα, "those in the Shephelah'') as subject, but then finds no corresponding subject for b. Vg, more consistently, treats as object only the regions prefixed with the sign of the definite object אֵת, and accordingly translates the last three words: *et Beniamin possidebit Galaad*, "and Benjamin shall possess Gilead'' (similarly Targ), thereby presupposing a further (וירשׁו) ("and shall possess'') for which we have no record in the transmitted text. Both grammatically and in substance, it is difficult to see the southland, the lowland (and Benjamin), as the (collective) subject of the act of taking possession; cf. also v. 20b.

19b-b If southland and lowland are objects, the statements about them added asyndetically in the accusative case (i.e., without the conjunction or copula "and'') must be viewed as explanatory glosses.

19c It remains uncertain whether אֶת־שְׂדֵה ("field'') is a later addition or not. Gk τὸ ὄρος, "the mountain,'' presupposes אֶת־הַר. In this case the parallel to v. 19aα would be pared down even more; otherwise the accusative case belongs only to the glosses.

19d-d The gloss is extended further.

19e-e The second object of the second וירשׁו ("and they shall possess'') clause will have been והגלעד, "and Gilead,'' since previously, too, the names of geographical regions appeared thrice as objects in the original text; in Jer. 50:19 Ephraim and Gilead are also mentioned side by side. The fact that אֵת בנימן, "Benjamin,'' which was originally a marginal gloss, has been absorbed into the text in the wrong order (בנימן אֵת), with the sign of the definite object, אֵת, succeeding the noun instead of preceding it, shows particularly clearly that this is an interpolation.

20a-a Gk ἡ ἀρχὴ αὕτη, probably read (הֶ)הָחֵל הַזֶּה or תְּחִלָּה זֶה; a (mutilated) gloss may therefore perhaps have been a reference to a first experience of deportation — the experience of the Northern Kingdom of Israel. σ' and θ'(τῆς δυναμεως ταυτης) Targ עמא הדין and Vg *exercitus huius*, "of this army,'' understand חֵל = חַיִל (cf. 2 Kings 18:17; Isa. 36:2): "the state of exile of this army [Targ people] of Israelites,'' α'(τῆς ευποριας αυτων), but in the sense of "property.'' B. Duhm proposed an emendation which has been widely accepted (by J. A. Bewer, E. Sellin, W. Rudolph, and others); he suggested reading חֲלַח זֶה as a marginal gloss which was intended to point to the place of exile (*Kalah*); cf. *Biblia Hebraica Stutt.* and 2 Kings 17:6; 18:11).

20b The text is obviously corrupt at this point. אֲשֶׁר ("which'') can have been followed by the name of a place, as in aβ; a verb is missing as well, probably יִרְשׁוּ, "they shall take possession,'' as in b (cf. Neh. 9:24).

20c Before כנענים, "Canaanites,'' too the definite article at least must have been omitted. Gk γῆ τῶν Χαναναίων, "the land of the Canaanites, Targ דבארע כנענאה even presuppose אֶרֶץ־הַכְּ, Vg *omnia Chananeorum*, "all the things of the Canaanites,'' presupposes כָּל־הַכְּ.

21a MT ("saviors'') is supported by σ' σωζοντες and Vg *salvatores*. But in the framework of the interpretation of v. 17 (see p. 65 below), נוֹשָׁעִים is probable, and this is presupposed by Gk (ἄνδρες σεσφσμένοι), α', θ', Syr, and Targ^M - if indeed the original reading was not the *hoph'al* participle מֻשָׁעִים. It is true that ישׁע *hoph'al* is not a form for which we have any evidence; but it may just have been because the form was unusual that MT vocalized it as *hiph'il*.

21b Since it is a word-for-word echo of v. 17, MT is more probable than the מֵהַר ("from Mount. . .'') which Gk presupposes (ἐξ ὄρους)

Form

Why v. 15a should be assigned to vv. 16f. was already explained on p. 37 above. The new rhetorical unit is linked with the preceding passage through the literary device of the deictic, or demonstrative כי (''Yes!''). The same rhetorical method is used in Amos 3:7; 5:4, 12 (see H. W. Wolff, *Joel/Amos*, BK 14/2, 273f. [Eng., *Joel and Amos*]). On the other hand the explanatory כי in v. 16a (''for'') confirms that v. 15a belongs to 16f. as a unified saying that is directed against ''all nations'' (vv. 15a, 16a) but which at the same time promises deliverance for those on Zion who have been spared (v. 17). Whereas in vv. 2-14, 15b it was mainly Edom that was addressed (in the 2nd person singular; see p. 37 above), here it is the people of Jerusalem (2nd person plural, v. 16a), with whom Obadiah associates himself in solidarity (see p. 46 above).

A further saying is loosely joined to the previous one through והיה, ''then.'' This saying is not couched in address form, nor is it formulated in the first person — the ''I'' of Yahweh (as in v. 16a). Nonetheless the final formula sets it clearly among the Yahweh sayings. Verse 18 shows that it is a separate saying through the fact that the house of Joseph is now parallel to the house of Jacob (v. 17b); but the two are no longer set over against ''all nations''; they are confronted with the house of Esau in particular.

In vv. 19f. a two-stage addition follows. It picks up וירשו ''they shall possess,'' from v. 17b three times, or even four (see textual note to v. 20b). It first of all, in v. 19, gives specific form to the new possessions of ''the house of Jacob'' which are promised. Verse 20 goes on to explain in addition how far the new occupation of the land by the exiles from the Northern Kingdom and by those from Jerusalem is going to extend. Both the new subjects and the mention of the southland (ערי הנגב, ''cities of the Negev''), which is quite new in kind, show that v. 20 is an addition to v. 19 and was probably made at a different time; like v. 18 and unlike v. 19 (v. 17), v. 20 is interested in the double history of the Northern and the Southern Kingdoms.

Verse 21 closes the book with a solemn three-stress tricola. The three brief cola are related to the three chief figures in the book — Jerusalem, Edom, and Yahweh. The message to the people delivered on Mount Zion was first mentioned in v. 17a, in connection with the threat to ''all nations.'' The final prosodic units now link this message with the threat to Edom (vv. 1bβ, 15b; cf. 18), but they subject it all to the royal rule of Yahweh, as in an eschatological hymn. The final saying, therefore, is by no means an interpretative addition, similar to that in vv. 19f. It leads up to a mountain peak, so to speak; and from this peak light shines out over the dark and uphill paths that lead up to it — those paths which the preceding words have described.

Setting

Very little convincing evidence can be brought to bear on the problems of *authorship*. Verses 15a, 16f. are directed against all nations, instead of against Edom. Yet this does not necessarily mean that the saying is not Obadiah's own, even though in his first speech he rallies not only Israel but also the nations against Edom (v. 1; cf. v. 7). For the law of retaliation (the *ius talionis*) is of equal importance in both passages (cf. vv. 16a, 17b with 15b and p. 56 above; the parallelism of the two כאשר ["just as"] clauses may actually have led to the transposition of vv. 15a and b). Moreover, in the exilic and postexilic period Edom is elsewhere too the very personification of Israel's enemies in the world of the nations: Isa. 34:2, 5ff.; Ezek. 36:5; Joel 3:2, 12, 19; Amos 9:12. More than any other text, Obadiah makes it comprehensible why from 587 onwards, Edom should have become the prototype of all the enemies of God's people (vv. 11-14 and pp. 53ff. above). The saying in v. 18 reverts directly to Obadiah's main theme, Edom, and states more clearly than v. 1 (see pp. 46f. above) that Israel itself is going to be Yahweh's instrument of judgment against Edom. Both sayings are linked with Obadiah's main discourse through the catchwords פליטה, "deliverance," "sparing," in v. 17a and שריד, "survivor," in v. 18b (cf. v. 14a,b). Where the content of the passage is concerned, the law of retaliation is again to the fore: Edom grudged Jerusalem survivors, and so no one will escape from Edom either. Calling the Judeans and the people of Jerusalem "the house of Jacob," in contrast to "the house of Esau" in vv. 17f., corresponds to the contrast between Esau and his "brother Jacob" in vv. 9f. (cf. v. 12). At the same time, the statements in the two sayings vv. 15a, 16f. and 18 are so different compared with the great speech in vv. 1-14, 15b that we must at the very least assign them to a different time. On the other hand, we cannot exclude the possibility that v. 21 originally constituted the close of the passage vv. 1-14, 15b (see p. 68 below), for there are no sufficiently cogent grounds for denying Obadiah the authorship of this verse (cf. W. Rudolph, KAT 13/2, 317f., and p. 22 above).

We have already seen that the Sitz im Leben (the situation in life) of Obadiah's main speech must be looked for in an assurance that prayer had been heard — an assurance proclaimed by the cultic prophet during lament ceremonies held in the ruins of the Jerusalem sanctuary during the exilic period (see p. 19 above). This will also have been the situation in which the three short sayings in vv. 15a, 16f., 18 and 21 were uttered. This is clearest in the case of the first of these three sayings, in which we find (in v. 16a) both the "I" of the divine utterances and the "you" with which the mourners are addressed; while the theme of the saying, above all, has been passed down in the framework of other national lament ceremonies (cf. Lam. 4:21; Isa. 51:17-23; also 64ff. below).

The two additions in vv. 19 and 20 initially served a literary purpose, being further expositions of v. 17b (see p. 62 above). In trying to arrive at a date for the statements in v. 20, we should bear the following points in mind. Homecomers from exile are expected, and we have hardly any evidence for this after the 5th century. A distinction is still made between those who have been deported from the Northern Kingdom of Israel and those who have been deported from Jerusalem; the latest writer who clearly does the same is Ezekiel (37:15ff.). Finally, the verses mention Judean deportees in Sepharad, in the western part of Asia Minor; and there is evidence for such deportees in this area in the 5th century (see pp. 67f. below). In view of all this, we shall hardly be able to assign v. 20, as the latest addition, to a later date than 400 B.C., while v. 19 must be assigned to the period between Obadiah's ministry in the early exilic period and 400; it is impossible to narrow down the date more closely than that.

B. Diebner and H. Schult ("Edom in alttestamentliche Texten der Makkabäerzeit" [1975]) would like to see Obadiah 19-21 as a prophecy after the event, dating from the period when the Hasmonean empire reached its greatest extent (cf. J. Wellhausen, *Die kleinen Propheten* [1963⁴] 213): "It stretched northwards about as far as Zarephath" (p. 13). "The accuracy of the territorial information" is thought to speak in favor of this date. But John Hyrcanus I (134-104 B.C.) thrust northwards only as far as Shechem and Samaria. It was only Aristobulus I (104-103) who then conquered parts of Galilee in addition. Neither he nor his successors ever penetrated further up the Mediterranean coast than the Carmel area, and certainly not as far as Tyre, let alone Zarephath; cf. Josephus, *Ant.* 13. 8-12 (§§230-347); M. Noth, *Geschichte Israels* (1969⁷) 346ff. [Eng. *History of Israel*, 1958]; B. Kanael, "Hasmonäer," *Biblisch-Historisches Handwörterbuch* 2, 650ff. (esp. map on 654); G. E. Wright and F. V. Filson, *Historical Atlas to the Bible* (1946), pl. XIIA. It must therefore be said that neither "the accuracy of the territorial information" nor the canonical history (cf. O. Kaiser, *Einleitung in das Alte Testament* [1975³] 278) are precisely in favor of a date at the end of the 2nd century B.C.

Commentary

[v. 15a]   The new saying begins with an announcement of the approach of the Day of Yahweh, which is directed against all nations. To proclaim the Day of Yahweh means proclaiming his victorious struggle (Zeph. 1:14-16; Joel 3:14; cf. 2:1f; also H. W. Wolff, *Joel/Amos*, BK 14/2, 38f. [Eng., *Joel and Amos*]). Here Edom recedes into the ranks of all Jerusalem's other enemies (cf. v. 11). The enemies who are specifically meant are not only the Babylonians but the neighbors who had profited materially by Israel's defeat, after 587. The preposition עַל ("upon") is an indication of the superior opposing forces (cf. Koehler and Baumgartner, *Lexicon* 704, No. 8).

[vv. 16-17]   The scope of the great declaration of war is made clear in v. 16. Israel is to know that all the nations will have to experience what God's people have already had to suffer. The prophet uses an image which we may assume was familiar to his congregation. Even earlier, in preexilic times, cultic prophecy had proclaimed to evildoers what they would have to drink: "the cup from Yahweh's right hand," the cup of his wrath and judgment (Hab. 2:16; Ps. 75:8; cf. 11:6; the image may have been taken over from ordeal procedures, cf. Num. 5:26ff. and J. Jeremias, *Kultprophetie und Gerichtsverkündigung in der späten Königszeit*, WMANT 35 [1970] 59, 136). The prophecy of judgment then probably termed Babylon first of all "the cup in Yahweh's hand" (Jer. 51:7; cf. W. Zimmerli, *Ezechiel*, BK 13 [1969] 551f; Eng. *Ezekiel* [1979]). At all events, Isa. 51:17-23 presupposes this "cup of his wrath," "the cup of insentience" or "stupefaction" (vv. 17, 22; RSV: "the bowl of staggering") which Jerusalem had to drink in 587

(vv. 19f.). Isaiah 51:17aβ-20 also shows how the saying about the cup of wrath became a part of the lament of the people of Jerusalem (cf. C. Westermann, ATD 19, 198f.; U. Kellermann, *Israel und Edom* [1975] 19f.; and Ps. 60:3). In vv. 21-23 the passage then takes up the assurance that the people's prayer has been heard, and proclaims that the cup has been taken away from Jerusalem and that it will pass into the hands of her tormentors. So Obad. 16a is really a concise summary of the message of Isa. 51:17-23, while the Isaiah passage is the most exact commentary on Obad. 16a. The theme of the handing on of the cup of desolation can be found in other passages as well: in Ezek. 23:31-33 Yahweh takes it out of Samaria's hand and puts it into the hand of her sister Jerusalem; in Lam. 4:21, in an oracle of assurance (vv. 21f.), the cup is passed on to Edom (cf. also Jer. 49:12). In Jer. 25:15, 17, 28 the cup of judgment is already sent to "all nations." We can therefore see from this brief survey that Obadiah is using the vocabulary of the lament liturgies. Israel has had to drink on Yahweh's *holy mountain*; and in this context we should think of the loss of the temple and the grief of the succeeding lament ceremonies among the ruins (see p. 42 above).

Similar distress is to come upon the nations. It will be worse than the distress of Jerusalem. The nations will have to drink "*perpetually*." The word used here, לעע ("swallowing down"), is a nonce usage and underlines the torture of having to drink without stopping. This torture ends with the loss of existence. The nations will drink themselves to death with God's cup of judgment, whereas on Mount Zion, in spite of the misery of the collapse, there is *sparing* (on פליטה see Joel 2:3; 3:5 and H. W. Wolff, *Joel/Amos*, BK 14/2, 53, 81f. [Eng., *Joel and Amos*]). Contrary to what the Edomites intended (v. 14), there is deliverance. What Obadiah has in mind here is primarily the remnant of the community, who still gather together for the services of lament. They can find fresh hope in the midst of Jerusalem's downfall. The "house of Jacob" in 17b means the Judeans and the people of Jerusalem who are left and who are still bound to Zion (17a) by ties of loyalty and affection. This is made clear from the language of vv. 10-12, as well as by the contrast with "the house of Joseph" in v. 18 (see below). They are going to "take possession of those 'who had possessed them' " (see textual note to v. 17c-c). This powerful saying is an exposition of what this threatened loss of existence (v. 16) is going to mean for the nations: they will no longer be themselves. They will be the subjects of the people of Zion.

[v. 18]   In the next saying, the tone becomes considerably sharper still. The saying differs from the previous one first of all because it mentions "the house of Joseph" as well as "the house of Jacob." The house of Joseph was the name given to the Northern Kingdom, Israel, after its leading tribe; Joseph is the tribal father of the central Palestinian tribes of Ephraim and Mannasseh (cf. Gen. 48:17-20; Josh. 17:17; and H. W. Wolff, BK 14/2, 282 [Eng., *Joel and Amos*]: the school of Amos calls the Northern Kingdom "the house of Joseph," Amos 5:6, 15; 6:6; cf. Judg. 1:22f., 35). For Obadiah, Joseph is the highest possible partner, together with Jacob, in the genealogy of the fathers of the tribes. Nowhere else in the Old Testament are "the house of Jacob" and "the house of Joseph" put side by side like this. But, substantially speaking, Isaiah (8:14) already groups together "both houses of Israel." Speaking to Edom, the exiled Ezekiel calls them "these two nations and these two countries" (35:10). In 37:16ff. he expresses the hope that they will be united again, and in this connection he also talks about "Joseph" as well as "Judah" (cf. Hos. 1:11). But apart from Obadiah, it is only Isa. 11:13, an early postexilic text (H. Wildberger's view: see *Jesaja 1-12*, BK 10/1 [1972] 467), that expects a new common initiative directed against the surrounding nations; this passage shows Ephraim united with Judah on the one side and, on the other, Edom arrayed with Philistines, "the people of the east," Moabites and Ammonites. The fact that Obadiah, in contrast, mentions only Edom is a pointed indication in favor of an early exilic date for the book.

What the reunited Israelites are going to undertake against the Edomites is expressed in an image which, though not new in itself, is used here in quite a new way. The picture of the raging fire that consumes straw is familiar in the Old Testament, at least from the time of Isaiah onwards (5:24; see H. Wildberger, BK 10/1, 196). In other passages the fire stands for Yahweh and his wrath (Isa. 10:17; 33:11; Exod. 15:7) or for the army he commands (Joel 2:5), while the straw is the people who reject Yahweh's Word (Isa. 5:24), the godless (Mal. 4:1), Babylon's astrologers (Isa. 47:14), or the nations as Israel's opponents in general (Exod. 15:7; Isa. 33:11; cf. Nah. 1:10). It is only in Obadiah that the image of *Israel* as Yahweh's instrument is used, and only here is it related to *Edom*. The image is carried through with poetic originality, with two parallel three-stress bicola (18a). An unusual feature of the language is that here the writer does not talk merely about the way the flames lick up the straw. He first tells how the stubble is set alight; דלק in Ps. 7:13 (as participle, cf. Koehler and Baumgartner, *Lexicon*, 3rd ed.) could mean the incendiary projectiles used to subdue fortified towns (cf. Amos 1:4 and H. W. Wolff, BK 14/2, 188 [Eng., *Joel and Amos*]). Here the metaphor is intended to show that the flames have an easy prey, to the point when everything is consumed. In this sense 18b proceeds from the image (18a) to the fact itself, and says tersely that no one belonging to the house of Esau will escape. ("The house of Esau" means the people of Edom, while "the mountains of Esau" is the name given to the region in which they lived.) This is the announcement of revenge for the already-censured behavior of the Edomites when the prisoners were carried off from Jerusalem (cf. v. 14). Earlier, vv. 9f. also threatened Edom with complete annihilation. Ezekiel 25:14 also says that Yahweh's "vengeance on Edom" will be put into the hands of the Israelites. In Ps. 137:7 Israel leaves revenge on the Edomites to its God (see p. 69 below). In a deeply impressive image, Obadiah testifies to the defeated community of those who had escaped by the skin of their teeth that their God is going to bring about a complete revolution in their present circumstances. The saying is explicitly clinched as being a saying of Yahweh's (cf. Ps. 60:6-8; Jer. 13:15). But it is probable that the phrase כי יהוה דבר, "for Yahweh has spoken," is actually the literary formula indicating the close of Obadiah's words, before vv. 19f. were added. On this function of the phrase cf. Joel 3:8, H. W. Wolff, BK 14/2, 89 [Eng., *Joel and Amos*], p. 22 above.

[v. 19] The augmenter offers a commentary on v. 17b by picking up the predicate ויר‍שׁו (''and shall take possession'') and answering the question: *what* will be newly possessed by ''the house of Jacob'' (together with ''the house of Joseph,'' v. 18a; cf. textual note to v. 19a)? As main catchword used for the possession of the land, ירש signalizes the new beginning of the era of salvation; cf. Gen. 15:7f.; Deut. 1:8; Amos 2:10; 9:12; also H. W. Wolff, BK 14/2, 206. The little remnant community of Judeans is allowed to expect first of all that they will again take possession of the southern region of the Negev and the hilly Shephelah in the west. Comments are added, explaining that the Negev is now, as ''the mountains of Esau,'' the region where the Edomites live (cf. 1 Macc. 5:65) and that the Shephelah is the land of the Philistines (see textual note to v. 19b-b). Towards the north, the house of Jacob (in accordance with the agreement made with the house of Joseph (v. 18; see pp. 64f. above) will occupy *Ephraim's* fields. In the light of the political conditions of the time, this region is then also declared to be Samaria's fields, because it had been known as the province of Samaria ever since its conquest by the Assyrians (see textual note to v. 19d-d). ''Benjamin'' was probably not mentioned in the addition in its original form (see textual note to 19e-e), though ''Gilead'' was; this is a way of announcing that the expansion will extend into the country east of the Jordan, south and north of the River Jabbok; cf. M. Noth, ''Das Land Gilead als Siedlungsgebiet israelitischer Sippen,'' *Paläs- tinajahrbuch* 37 (1941) 98-101 = *Aufsätze zur biblischen Landes- und Altertums- kunde* 1 (1971) 387-390. We should note that, as fulfillment of the promise in 17b, no more is initially expected than the immediately adjacent regions, the Negev, Shephelah, Ephraim, and Gilead, which were occupied by foreigners; and it is noteworthy above all that expectations do not extend any further towards the north — not as far as Galilee, for example. Israel's return to Carmel and Bashan, as well as to the fertile and well-wooded areas of Ephraim and Gilead, is already promised in Jer. 50:19. This suggests that the commentator of v. 19 did not write very much later than Obadiah himself.

[v. 20] The commentary in v. 20, on the other hand, must evidently be assigned to a later date. It reveals much more extensive views in every way than those cherished by the remnant of the Jerusalem community in the first years after the catastrophe of 587. Going beyond v. 19, it first of all asks who the people of Jacob's house are, that are going to possess the land anew. Here it apparently goes back to v. 17a, beyond v. 17b. It interprets the פליטה, ''the remnant'' or ''exemption,'' on Zion in the sense of Ezra 9:13 and Neh. 1:2, as being the people who survived in exile. Here it distinguishes between the early exiles from the Northern Kingdom and those from Jerusalem, thereby linking up with the distinction in v. 18 between the earlier Northern and Southern Kingdoms. The mention of a community of exiles from Jerusalem in *Sepharad* is particularly interesting. The name can be found with the same orthography (ספרד) in an Aramaic inscription from the necropolis at Sardes. This was discovered in 1916 and dates from the Persian period (H. Donner and W. Röllig, *Kanaanäische und Aramäische Inschriften* No. 260, 1. 2). The inscription names Sardes as the capital of the Persian satrapy of the same name, Sparda (= Sardes), in the western part of Asia Minor (Lydia). But we knew nothing of exiles from Judah in that area until in 1966 A. Dupont-Sommer was able to publish "Une inscription araméenne inédite d'époque perse trouvée à Daskyléion" (*Comptes Rendus de l'Académie des Inscriptions et Belles-Lettres* [1966] 44-57). Here a memorial stele attests the presence of a prosperous Jewish family in Dascylium in northwest Asia Minor, the satrapy bordering on Sparda (= Sepharad; cf. H. G. May, *Oxford Bible Atlas* [1974²] 82: E 2-3). F. M. Cross ("An Aramaic Inscription from Daskyleion," *BASOR* 184 [1966] 7-10) attributes the inscription to the 5th century B.C. (ca. 450). Probably these *gola*, or exiles, were people from Jerusalem who had come to Asia Minor from Babylon (E. Lipiński, "Obadiah 20" [1973] 370). Obadiah 20 shows that the inhabitants of Jerusalem knew that there was a quite considerable community of exiles in Sepharad. The new commentator in v. 20 therefore sees very extensive groups of survivors from ancient Israel waiting to possess the land anew.

He accordingly holds out the prospect of wider areas than does v. 19. Towards the north he points far beyond Ephraim into the region of "Canaanites as far as Zarephath." The word *Canaanites* is evidently used here in a narrower sense, not for the pre-Israelite inhabitants of Palestine, but for a group of people living especially on the Mediterranean coast north of Carmel — a group, broadly speaking, identical with the Phoenicians; cf. Isa. 23:11; Zeph. 2:5; and M. Noth, *Die Welt des Alten Testaments* (1962⁴) 47 (Eng., *The Old Testament World* [1966]); also D. R. Ap-Thomas, "The Phoenicians" (1973) 262. The mention of *Zarephath*, "which belongs to Sidon" (1 Kings 17:9f.) and which is situated between Tyre and Sidon, confirms this view. Our commentator therefore seems to see Galilee and Phoenicia as prepared for the homecomers from exile who had once belonged to the Northern Kingdom. The form of the promise in v. 20aα² is reminiscent of salvation history as Neh. 9:24 knows it. The Jerusalem *gola*, or exiles, from Sepharad are to receive "the cities of the Negev." Cities belonging to this area are mentioned in 2 Chron. 28:18, and one of them is named in Zech. 14:10 (Rimmon, 11 miles northeast of Beersheba). Were the deportees who were offered "cities of the Negev" privileged, compared with the others who, according to v. 19, were to receive the region of the Negev? At all events v. 20 presupposes v. 19.

[v. 21] The final verse takes the expectation of v. 17a further, in a more conciliatory direction than v. 18. Here too, the background is the question: what are "the delivered on Mount Zion" going to do? "They shall go up" is not an appropriate description for the occupation of the Negev, in view of the relative heights above sea level of the two areas. It fits in only with the ancient dwelling places of the Edomites, east of the Arabah. Perhaps Obadiah himself thought of this, as in v. 3 (see p. 48 above), in contrast to the commentators of vv. 19a and 20b. The aim of the procession, or "triumphal progress," is "to rule Mount Esau." According to the language of the book of Obadiah hitherto, הר עשׂו ("Mount Esau") would have to be interpreted here, as in vv. 8f. and 19, as the area in which the Edomites lived. The verse would then provide the answer to the question: "what is going to happen to the country of Edom after the loss of its inhabitants (v. 18)?'' (W. Rudolph, KAT 13/2, 317). This interpretation certainly does away with any possible tension between the expectation in vv. 18bα and 21aβ. But it is nevertheless improbable because שפט (''govern,'' ''rule'') is always applied to people, never to things. Probably הר עשׂו (''Mount Esau'') has been chosen here in order to highlight the contrast to הר ציון (''Mount Zion''; J. A. Thomson's suggestion). But the statement does not exclude the Edomite people; it includes them. This is the only explanation that makes sense of שפט (''govern,'' ''rule''). The word by no means implies oppression, let alone the complete annihilation announced in v. 18b. It at most means a ruler which includes the expiation of injustice, if not inclusion in a saving order (cf. Isa. 2:4; Ezek. 34:17; Ps. 96:13; and G. Liedke, *Gestalt und Bezeichnung alttestamentlicher Rechtssätze*, WMANT 39 [1971] 72; U. Kellermann, *Edom* [1975] 26: ''Verse 21 actually implies a kind of 'promise' for Edom''). The phrase is too brief to allow a definite decision. But it is certainly closer in feeling to v. 17b than to 18b. Above all, however, the saying about the ''going up'' fits in with the call to battle in v. 1bβ (see p. 22 above). עלה is the word that is most generally used in the call to battle for the moving up of troops: Jer. 46:9; 49:28, 31; 50:21; Isa. 21:2; Jer. 5:10; 6:4f.; Joel 3:9, 12; cf. R. Bach, *Aufforderungen* (1962) 63.

At all events, the remnant on Mount Zion who have been delivered are not intended to impose their own rule on Edom. The final sentence makes this unequivocally clear: ''The sovereignty shall belong to Yahweh.'' This fact alone explains why there are people on Mount Zion who have been delivered in the midst of the misery of Jerusalem's downfall, and why these people will contribute to the surmounting of injustice. The idea of Yahweh's kingship belongs as much to the Zion tradition as it does to the certainty of his rule over the whole earth (cf. Zech. 14:9; Pss. 47:7f.; 96:13; and frequently elsewhere), and especially the subjugation of Israel's enemies after Zion's chastisement has been ended (Zeph. 3:15). It is above all the Word about Yahweh's sovereignty, with all that this means, which holds good for a totally powerless, despondent, despised, and threatened community (also Mic. 4:6f.). In Ps. 22:28 the same acknowledgment of Yahweh's kingship in the world of the Gentile nations is part of the thanksgiving for deliverance of the person who had been the helpless victim of the pains of death.

Purpose

So the interpreter of the collection of sayings in vv. 15a, 16-21 is not permitted to forget Jerusalem's situation, as it is described in vv. 11-14. The prophetic cry of encouragement was uttered in the framework of the cult to assemblies gathered together for lamentation (see p. 63 above). It went out to a community that saw nothing but extinction ahead. This is the single presupposition of all the different sayings, and it is against this background that the tensions and differences in the substance of these sayings must be seen. These tensions and differences suggest that it was not only the two literary commentaries in vv. 19 and 20 which were written at a different time; the three prophetic sayings in 15a, 16f., 18, and 21 also belonged to different occasions in each given case. In the one saying, the threat of the many nations by which Jerusalem was surrounded concentrates the prophetic vision on all nations (vv. 15a, 16a); afterwards the outlook narrows down to the nearest enemy of all, Edom (vv. 18, 21). On the one occasion Edom is threatened with complete annihilation (v. 18); afterwards it is included in a new rule over the nations which is to be exercised by those who have been delivered on Mount Zion (cf. v. 21 with 17; U. Kellermann, *Edom* 28, would like to assign these various utterances to different tendencies and movements within "the national prophecy of salvation" — a "radical" group and a "moderate" one). On one occasion encouragement is addressed only to the remnant on Mount Zion (vv. 17, 21); then it applies equally to Judah and to what had once been the Northern Kingdom (see pp. 65f. above on v. 18), while in the addition in v. 20 the promise goes out even to the *gola*, or exiles, from both the Northern Kingdom and Jerusalem.

What is common to all the diverse sayings from this time of collapse is the resolute hope for a complete change in the situation. What is particularly striking is the consistent expectation that all Israel's oppressors will be overcome, an expectation that is joined with a lively insistence on the new gift of the land in the context of salvation history — land which is at present occupied by foreigners. We should note the catchwords ירש, "take possession" (vv. 17b, 19f.), עלה, "go up," and שפט "rule" (v. 21; see pp. 68f. above). The combination of the traditions about the gift of the land and the holy wars with the Zion tradition (vv. 15a, 17, 21) leads in the new expectation to an intensification of the old gifts given in the framework of salvation history, insofar as no other nation is going to have an independent existence beside Yahweh's people (vv. 16b, 17b, 18, 21). The path to this end is by way of "the day of Yahweh" (v. 15a), when God will bring about the victories in which the spoils will fall to his own people (v. 17b, cf. 18). But the goal is not the rule of the people who have been saved; the goal is the kingly rule of God himself (v. 21). It is this which will be brought about through the most bitter privations and enmities.

The only people who understood these words were probably the community which was prepared to be led along the path to this goal. How? First of all, in the midst of desolate confusion, the words awakened a hope, not only for Israel but also, in a different way, for her most immediate enemies and for all the nations. The words created a community which waits for a change in all conditions of domination, and the engendering of such a community is their purpose still. A second point: the sayings display different forms of hope. Jesus Christ, as the fulfiller of Israel's hope, has added hope in yet another, new form — hope in the form of his person, which sheds new light on the prophetic Word. The new Israel, which he does not cease to call, will be freed from all inclinations towards revenge and retaliation (cf. v. 18 with Rom. 12:14-21) and summoned to a "rule" which finds expression only in the form of ministry among men and women (Mark 10:42-45). Finally, the new call aims, not to distract attention from the ancient saying, but to quicken that attention. For the different prophetic sayings point out that in history not only God's people of old but his new people too participate in "a real movement into world history as a whole" (K. Barth, *Kirchliche Dogmatik* 4/3, 63f.; Eng., *Church Dogmatics* 4/3 [1961] 58) and that there is an indissoluble link between the history of Israel and the church on the one hand, and the history of the nations of the world on the other. In this interdependence humanity is moving towards the kingdom of God that is to come. On the way to this goal, and especially in discouraging situations, the church that listens to the Word will meditate on these sayings anew — the sayings about the drinking of the cup, the fire that consumes the straw, and the going up to the mountains of Esau. It will consider what these words have to say to it, in the discipleship of that Jesus to whom, as the One crucified, the sovereignty belongs.

THE PROPHET JONAH

Introduction

1. The Book of Jonah in the Canon

At the beginning of the second century B.C., the book of Sirach refers to Isaiah (48:22), Jeremiah (49:6f.), Ezekiel (49:8), and Job (49:9), and then goes on to mention the twelve prophets ("May the bones of the twelve prophets revive from where they lie" [49:10]). This summary can best be explained if we assume that "The Book of the Twelve Prophets" was already in existence at that time. The book of Jonah must therefore then already have been assigned to the prophetic writings, even though it differs from all the others; for this book is not a collection of prophetic sayings, interspersed with stories about the prophet. It is a self-contained story about the prophet with only a single, brief prophetic saying (3:4bβ). By that time, independent accounts of the lives of prophets had long come to seem just as worthy of transmission as the prophetic proclamation itself (cf. Isaiah 36-39; Jeremiah 37-43).

The book of Jonah was assigned fifth place in the Hebrew canon, probably for reasons of chronology and content. The editors knew from 2 Kings 14:23-25 that a prophet called Jonah had lived at the time of King Jeroboam II. And the superscriptions to the collections of sayings of Hosea and Amos name Jeroboam as one of the kings of the Northern Kingdom of Israel, describing him as a contemporary of King Uzziah of Judah. Hosea 1:1 adds the names of his Judaean successors: Jotham, Ahaz, and Hezekiah. Only these three are mentioned in Mic. 1:1. This makes the placing of the book before Micah comprehensible. But why does Obadiah comes first, immediately after Amos, although his sayings are just as undated as the book of Jonah? A point worth mentioning is that the prophet Obadiah was identified by the compilers and editors with the Obadiah who was steward, or ruler of the household, at Ahab's court in the time of Elijah (1 Kings 18:3ff.); and this Obadiah was earlier than the Jonah mentioned in 2 Kings 14:23ff. Content may provide another reason. With its opening ויהי ("now it once happened"), Jonah 1:1 might have been read as a sequel (but see the textual note to 1:1a below); and as such it may have been understood in the light of Obad. 1, which talks about a messenger sent among the nations. For Jonah's message, like Obadiah's, is a message to a foreign people.

If a link was assumed between the content of Obadiah and Jonah, this would make it understandable that the same sequence is to be found in the Septuagint, although otherwise the writings in the first half of the Book of the Twelve are there arranged differently. In the LXX, the earlier prophets seem to have been ordered according to the length of the books: Hosea, Amos, Micah, Joel, and then Obadiah. But Jonah still follows Obadiah, even though it is the longer of the two books. Perhaps the intention was also to set it apart from the earlier collections of sayings, as a narrative coda (like Isa. 36ff.). However, the decisive point was probably that in the sequence of the LXX Jonah moves up to a position immediately before Nahum, who — like Jonah — had to prophesy against Nineveh, according to 1:1.

As far as the interpretation of the book of Jonah is concerned, its inclusion in the Book of the Twelve according to Sir. 49:10 is a contribution towards a solution of the problem of date; for it means that Jonah cannot have been written after the end of the third century.

2. The Date of Composition

Although the history of the canon shows that the book of Jonah must have been written before the beginning of the second century, we must nonetheless exclude the presumption that, like the historical Jonah, it belongs to the preexilic period (see §1 above). Too many features clearly point to a postexilic date.

Here we may mention *the vocabulary* first of all. The little book shows disproportionately many words — and sometimes corresponding circumstances — which can be found only after the time of Ezekiel, but more especially in the latest Old Testament writings, such as Chronicles, Ecclesiastes, and the book of Daniel. We may think here of the relative clause with שֶׁ (1:7, 12; 4:10; see pp. 110f. below) and of words especially typical of the book of Jonah, such as words for "sailor": מַלָּח (1:5) and חֹבֵל (1:6; see p. 110 below), אֱלֹהֵי הַשָּׁמַיִם ("the God of heaven," 1:9: see p. 115 below), מנה *pi'el* ("appoint," 1:17; 4:6-8; see p. 132 below), the verb עמל for laborious work (4:10; see pp. 173-174 below) and the numeral רִבּוֹ (10,000, 4:11; see pp. 174-175 below). In addition there are a number of words which occur nowhere else at all in Old Testament Hebrew, although some of them recur repeatedly in late biblical and nonbiblical Aramaic texts: סְפִינָה ("ship," 1:5; see p. 110 below), עשׁת *hithpa'el* ("think," 1.6; see p. 110 below), קְרִיאָה ("message," 3:2), טַעַם ("taste," 3:7; see p. 152 below), קִיקָיוֹן ("a plant, 4:6f., 9f.) and חֲרִישִׁית ("sultry," 4:8; otherwise only in Qumran, 1QH VII.5). Not all these expressions have much weight as evidence. For example, in the case of special seafaring words, or specialist words used in the paradigm of the castor oil plant, a nonce usage in the Old Testament may be due to the rarity or uniqueness of the circumstances described (cf. also the pointer to direct influences from Phoenician in O. Loretz, *BZ* NF 5 [1961] 19-24.) However, the choice of particular characteristic expressions indisputably suggests the late postexilic era, rather than its earlier years — perhaps the same period as Ecclesiastes (cf. K. Marti, 247; O. Loretz, ibid., 25).

How far removed the narrator is from the historical realities of the preexilic era is shown by the uninhibited way he combines historical names. The addressee of his Jonah is no longer the eighth-century Jeroboam II (as was the historical Jonah's, according to 2 Kings 14:25). Jonah's message is now addressed to Nineveh, which entered Israel's orbit only when it became the capital of the Neo-Assyrian empire in the seventh century (see pp. 99-100 below). Again, Nineveh is viewed, not as the capital of a great empire, but as a huge city-state, with a constitution which is also reminiscent of the Persian period (3:6f.; see p. 152 below). The home of the historical Jonah, Gath-hepher, is never mentioned. The Jonah of our book is soon to be found in the port of Joppa, which was probably not Israelite at all in the eighth century, and which was not precisely the nearest port for a Galilean, but which was no doubt of interest for Jerusalem in postexilic times (1:3; see p. 102 below). An uninhibited juggling with geographical and historical facts like this is possible only if the main characters have become buried in the dust of the past. The historical distance between the book of Jonah and the preexilic period corresponds roughly to the distance between the stories in the book of Daniel and the period of the exile.

Only a consideration of thematic references can help us further towards a more precise date. These are as multifarious as they are boldly combined. Elijah's flight, his dialog with God, and his wish to die, as well as individual features of the framework of the Elijah stories (the ravens, the broom tree, the cave, the number of days involved) may have influenced the narrator, and seem already to have been in existence in their canonical form (cf. especially 4:8b with 1 Kings 19:4; see also p. 119 below). He is quite obviously familiar with the ideas and phraseology of a particular theology of repentance, familiar to us in the form of Deuteronomistic traditions about Jeremiah (cf. 3:8-10 with Jer. 18:7ff.; 26:3ff; and see p. 168 below). Even the combination in a single narrative of these two different types of reference is only conceivable well on into the postexilic period.

One clear milestone that helps towards a closer dating is the verbal echo in 3:9a; 4:2b of Joel 2:13b, 14a (see pp. 167f. below): the hope for Yahweh's merciful recall of his pronouncement of judgment on Jerusalem is exactly transferred to Nineveh and, with unheard-of skepticism, is used as an accusation against Yahweh; also noticeable is the interpretative echo of the saying about the merciful withdrawal (נחם 3:9f.; 4:2 = Joel 2:13f.) in the saying about Yahweh's pity (חוס 4:10f.; cf. Joel 2:17). It is very much more probable that the book of Jonah is picking up Joel than that Joel is an echo of Jonah. For the book of Jonah shows a developing reflection about the function of the saying of judgment directed against the Gentiles which is still unknown in Joel, but to which we find a comparable approach in Zech. 14:9, 16, for example. Jonah's connections with Joel are therefore definitely polemical ones. The two books are related in the variety of their dependence on earlier traditions (see BK 14/2, 4, 10f. [Eng., *Joel and Amos*]). But the book of Jonah must be assigned to a date at least somewhat later. Our study of Joel has shown that this means that the book of Jonah cannot have been written be-

fore the middle of the fourth century (see BK 14/2, 2ff.). At this period it is also
quite conceivable that the theme may have been influenced to some degree by the
universalistic theology of Psalm 145 (vv. 8f., 18f.; on 4:2 see p. 167 below), and
that the problems which tormented Malachi's listeners may also have lived on
(Mal. 2:17; 3:13ff.; see p. 168 below).

Perhaps we should even go beyond the late Persian period and consider a
date in the early Hellenistic era. This is suggested especially by the use of
nonbiblical sea motifs. These are worked up into variants of Greek saga material,
strangely reminiscent of old Indian stories. This is true of the "great fish," the
rescue through "being swallowed" and "vomited up," the discovery of the
guilty person through the casting of lots by the seamen during the storm, etc. (cf.
H. W. Wolff, *Studien,* 25f.). If the writer drew on inspiration of this kind for
chaps. 1f., this is more readily explicable after the campaigns of Alexander the
Great than before. In this case our book would have to be dated not earlier than the
last third of the fourth century. But we may even look for the author later still, in
the third century (see §5 below). This will be so if we go along with E.
Bickermann (*Four Strange Books of the Bible* [1967]) in detecting the mentality of
the Hellenistic period (which we also find reflected in the books of Ecclesiastes,
Daniel, and Esther), if we even, like A. Fáj (*Stoic Features*) discover an attitude
of mind close to the early Stoa, and if we see the book of Jonah as a particular kind
of "narrated dogmatics" (L. Schmidt, *De Deo*, 125). At the same time, the arguments do not permit any very certain dating. For the time being we can do no more
than say that a date in the early Hellenistic period is slightly more probable than
one in the late Persian era.

3. Literary Growth

As far as the history of the text is concerned, the Jonah story has in general been
transmitted as a unified whole. Only 1:8aβ is missing in a few early texts; and the
context also makes it clear that this is a later addition (see textual note on 1:8a-a).
The same cannot be maintained of 1:10bβ; stylistic features which have been put
forward as evidence are not completely cogent (see textual note on 1:10c-c and
pp. 116-117 below). Recent investigations of the narrative form tell even more
clearly against the widely accepted suggestion that 4:5 should be viewed as a fragment split off from chap. 3, and that the verse should accordingly be moved back
to follow directly on 3:4 (see p. 163 below).

Whether the psalm in 2:2-9 (with or without its introduction in 2:1) was
originally part of the prose narrative, however, is still a matter of lively controversy. Reasons and counterreasons must be examined in the exegesis (see below). A
decision must be guided by the answers to three questions. How is the language of
the psalm related to the language of the narrative, even if we set aside its poetic
character? How do the situation and main themes presupposed in the psalm relate
to the immediate and wider context? How does the portrait of Jonah given in the
psalm fit in with the picture we gain from the prose narrative as a whole? The answers which the text gives to these questions suggest that 2:2-9 is a later interpola-

tion and that 2:1 belongs to the same addition (see p. 130 below). It presents the reader with a Jonah who has repented in the most exemplary way — a Jonah we do not as yet find at the end of the ancient prose narrative. The interpolator has grafted this new devotional Jonah into the scene with the fish, which was to prove the most fascinating of all to later interpreters, as well as to literature and art (see pp. 132, 140-141 below).

The question about distinguishable stages of growth is also raised by two other passages in the prose narrative. The striking change in the name for God in chap. 4, and the repetition in 3:1f. of the wording of 1:1 have both given rise to attempts to solve these cruxes by the methods of literary criticism (see p. 164 below).

In Jonah's dialog with Yahweh in 4:2-4, 10f., God is invariably called *Yahweh*; in the scene with the castor oil plant (vv. 6-9), however, the narrator uses the word *God*, in a number of variations (in v. 6, the transition, the text uses *Yahweh-God*, in v. 7 *the God*, in vv. 8 and 9 *God*). If we add that at the end of the scene with the castor oil plant, vv. 8b-9a, the dialog in vv. 3f. is repeated almost word for word, and that the shadow of the booth in 5b, goes ill, from a narrative point of view, with the shadow of the castor oil plant in 6a, there would seem every reason to suppose that the scene with the castor oil plant was an independent fragment with a fixed form of its own which has been interpolated into the present context.

Yet it proves impossible to separate the fragment convincingly as literary source. If we detach vv. 10f., the plant scene is pointless. If we admit vv. 10f. we have arbitrarily to change *Yahweh* into *God*; and this means depriving ourselves of an essential reason for separating the dialog in vv. 2-4 on stylistic grounds, because of the *Yahweh*. But without this dialog the substance of vv. 10f. also remains incomprehensible. The question about the place to be assigned to v. 5 is equally difficult. According to all literary principles, the repetition of 3f. in 8b-9a enjoins us to assign v. 5 to the scene with the castor oil plant (cf. C. Kuhl, *ZAW* 64 [1952] 1-11; see pp. 164f. below). What speaks against this is the double shade in vv. 5b and 6a. If we assume that 5b is secondary, the difficulty of the double shadow would have been introduced by the interpolator himself; so its occurrence before 6a is even harder to explain.

The conclusion that emerges is that 4:1-11 must be viewed as, in the literary sense, a unified fragment into which previously shaped material has been fused in such a way that its existence remains disturbingly evident; but that at the same time it is impossible to separate this earlier material by the methods of literary criticism (see pp. 164f. below).

The same result emerges if we use literary criteria in an attempt to detach chaps. 1f. as a secondary expansion of chaps. 3f., because of the repetition of 1:1f. in 3:1f. (see p. 130 below).

On the one hand, it is impossible to overlook the differences between the two halves of the book. The very material used in the scenes at sea and the scenes in Nineveh derives from entirely different sources (see p. 164 below). But differences can also be seen in the theological thinking and language. In chaps. 1f. the narrator himself talks only about Yahweh. On the other hand, in 3:3b, 5 he talks about "God" or "the God" (3:10), switching from one to the other, just as he does in 4:7f. and just as he makes the Ninevites do (3:8f.; cf. 1:5f.). But the framework makes it quite clear, in chaps. 3f. too, that Yahweh is meant throughout (3:1-3a; 4:2, 4, 10). Chapter 1 describes in detail the way the heathen sailors turn from their gods to the Yahweh about whom Jonah speaks. The result is that they come to "fear Yahweh" (see p. 121 below). In chap. 3 neither the gods of Nineveh nor Jonah's God are specifically named. Here "belief in God" comes into being as the people turn from their wickedness and put their hope in the one who sent Jonah (see p. 150 below). An already existing train of theological ideas, not mentioned in chap. 1, shapes the description of the path to salvation (see p. 153 below).

But these distinctions do not permit the assumption that chaps. 3f. ever existed independently in their present form. Jonah's remark in 4:2a is a direct narrative link between the story of his flight and the scenes in Nineveh. There are unobtrusive little word links: Yahweh "appoints" his creatures to perform their services in both 1:17 and 4:6-8, and in both passages exerts a silent influence on his refractory messenger. The hope of the men at sea and the hope of the men in Nineveh is the same: "that we do not perish" (1:6; 3:9; cf. 1:14; 4:10; and see p. 154 below). But, above all, the scenes with the sailors and the scenes in Nineveh are linked, as composition, by their common framework — the framework of the three scenes where Yahweh and Jonah encounter one another (1:1-3; 1:17—3:3a; 4:1-11); and here the middle scene uses the recapitulation of 1:1f. in 3:1f. as an intensifying element. To what degree similar stylistic devices, and also the assimilation of different material in the book of Jonah, are variations on the rhetorical figure known as anaphora still has to be considered. At all events, it seems neither advisable nor possible to carry observations about the change in the name for God or the "recapitulation" of particular phraseology or sentence structures to the point where these can be used to distinguish between different sources. They must rather be integrated into an understanding of the narrative character of the prose which goes to make up the book.

4. The Narrative Character

An attempt to define the genre of the prose narrative of the book of Jonah is not merely tempting; it is also difficult. Why? Scholars waver in their designation. Some see the book as a prophet's biography, others as a legend; some describe it as a midrash, others again as a satire. The problems are due mainly to the protean character of the material and traditions that go to make up the book. Here we find learned theology side by side with original experiences, sacred texts beside dramatic stories, contemporary material flanked by the fabric of tradition. The narrator takes the risk of linking thrilling episodes from tales of the sea, such as are current coin in seaports, with an acknowledgment of faith in Yahweh as the creator of sea and land (1:9; see p. 115 below). He takes the name of a historical prophet and tells things about his behavior which resemble the things with which we are familiar in the stories about Elijah or Jeremiah — or which are deliberately contrasted with these (see p. 168 below). He introduces great liturgical texts (4:2) and theological precepts (3:8-10), only to interpret them the next moment in a completely new way through some fantastic happening (see p. 176 below).

What binds together this wealth of highly disparate material? We never lose sight of Jonah himself throughout the whole narrative. And yet we cannot detect any biographical or historical interest in Jonah as a person, or in the era in which he lived (see p. 99 below). The book differs from the historical memoranda in 2 Kings 14:23ff.; for here Jonah is merely very generally characterized as the type of "a Hebrew" who believes in Yahweh as "the God of heaven" (1:9). We therefore have to think in terms of a literary work of art.[1]

Does this mean that the book should be described as a legend (A. J. Jepsen's view — to take the most recent example — in "Anmerkungen zum Buche Jona," *Fest. W. Eichrodt* [1971] 299)? What speaks against this is not merely that the legend springs from that preoccupation of the spirit, in Jolles's phrase,[2] to which we give the name of *imitatio*, or emulation (A. Jolles, *Einfache Formen* [1929, 1968[4]] 34ff.), whereas Jonah is by no means presented as a model (though he is not shown either as precisely a figure to shock and repel); a more important reason is that what we have here is not really a story about Jonah at all. It is a story about Yahweh's dealings with Jonah. Yahweh has the first word (1:1f.) and the last (4:10f.). It is what he does that thrusts the story forward from phase to phase (1:4; 1:17; 3:1; 4:6ff.), even at the points where Jonah recedes completely into the background for the time being (1:15f.; 3:10).

If we ask what contemporaries would have called the book of Jonah (see pp. 77f. above), the only description that really comes into question is the midrash (cf. A. G. Wright, "The Literary Genre Midrash," *CBQ* 28 [1966]105-138, 417-457; H. W. Wolff, *Studien*, 56-68). A midrash is an investigation into something that is worth learning. According to 2 Chron. 13:22, a midrash contains "the ways and sayings" of a king, as these were written down by a prophet. The word can be used for "annals" (2 Chron. 24:27), but it can also be applied to the interpretation of some earlier teaching through a story (cf. O. Loretz, *BZ NF 5* [1961] 27, and W. Rudolph, HAT 1/21 [1955] 238f.). "Ways and sayings" is a description that accords very well with the essential methods of the book of Jonah, which may be summed up as narrative account and dialog. We might therefore see the book of Jonah as a midrash on 2 Kings 14:25; Jer. 18:8 (cf. Jonah 3:10 and A. G. Wright 431); or even on Exod. 34:6 (Joel 2:13f., cf. Jonah 3:9; 4:2). And yet this would be to lose sight of the story's specific artistic form.

---

1. J. G. Herder, *Briefe, das Studium der Theologie betreffend* (1790[2]), 135: "I wonder that no man has hitherto arrived at the hypothesis that the whole succession of events is to be received as a work of art, such as many see the history of Job, for example, to be. . ."; and 141: "If then this history, as work of art, be beautiful, pertinent, and of utility, why should we torment ourselves with difficulties as to whether it be also a true history, and in what way this might be possible?"

2. "Geistesbeschäftigung": Jolles sees the person as "preoccupied" by the "objectively acting" spirit (in the Hegelian sense) of a certain form. He may therefore be preoccupied, or possessed, by the spirit of the legend; cf. *Einfache Formen* 34, 56, and passim (trans.).

If we are trying to find a description for this singular account of what happens between Yahweh and Jonah which takes in the complex warp and woof of narrative and dialog, the novella seems to offer itself as the most appropriate genre (cf. W. Kayser, *Das sprachliche Kunstwerk*, 1963[2], 354ff.; H. W. Wolff, *Studien zum Jonabuch*, 32ff.); for the following characteristics of the novella apply to the story of Jonah exactly. A limited sequence of events is brought to a conclusion in the light of an opening incident. The progress of these events is by no means straightforward, but is crossed through by surprises. The tension that spans the story from beginning to end is preserved in its most concentrated form in what is unexpected. Every sentence has its place in the main happening. The sequence of scenes does not strictly follow the temporal sequence, as it does in a drama; the tension of the impending goal can carry an individual scene so far forward that the scene that follows has to cast back in time (see p. 163 below). And, like the leap in time (1:5b; 4:5), a change of place (1:3; 2:10) is also entirely possible within a scene in a novella. The essential point is that the main group of actors remains unchanged. All the individual scenes, from the opening onwards, are directed towards the conclusion of the limited series of events. If we define the novella as literary form in these terms, then the story of Jonah in the Old Testament is one of its earliest examples in the literature of the world. It can be compared only with the frame story of Job, and the little books of Ruth and Esther; and yet it is clearly distinguishable even from these in the artistic shaping of its scenes and characters.

The opening scene fulfills all the requirements of an exposition (see p. 96 below), for at the very beginning Yahweh's saying brings out Jonah's relationship to Nineveh as being the main theme of the story (1:1-3; see also pp. 103f. below). Jonah's thwarting of Yahweh's will leads to the scene with the sailors, in which, through his own failure, the reluctant messenger brings heathen to faith in Yahweh (1:4-15; see pp. 122f. below). Only after this purpose has been achieved in the second scene — after Jonah has been thrown into the sea — does Yahweh turn to his fugitive again. The third scene shows Yahweh alone with Jonah once more. Now, with the great fish and with the new word, he sets him on his way to Nineveh (1:17—3:3a; see pp. 140-142 below). There, in scene four, Jonah's threat that downfall is impending leads — again in an unexpected turn of events — to the great movement of repentance and to God's gracious withdrawal of the pronouncement of judgment (3:3b-10). Afterwards Jonah's anger at this act of mercy provokes Yahweh to contend with his messenger. The second and fourth scenes both brought the heathen to fear God (1:16) and to believe in him (3:5ff.), in each case (i.e., after 1:5a and 3:4) after a skillful branching out of the narrative (see H. W. Wolff, *Studien*, 30ff.). One of these branches of the story — the part dealing with the heathen — leads in both cases to "a happy end." But the other branch — Jonah's fate and his behavior — still remains open. The question raised in the first scene of all, and only temporarily surmounted in the third — the question, that is, about Jonah's affirmation of Yahweh's work among foreign nations — waits until the fifth scene for a satisfactory answer from Jonah; and we are still waiting for that answer at the end (4:1-11; see also pp. 176f. below).

And yet everything thrusts forward to this answer. Both the composition of the scenes in general and the sentence construction in general are designed to keep the reader in suspense, waiting for the dénouement. Consequently purpose clauses are frequent (infinitive with ל: 1:3a,b, 5aβ, 13a; 1:17; 3:4, 10b; 4:2a, 6a; consecutive imperfects: 1:6; 3:9; 1:7aβ, 12a; 4:5b). Chains of consecutive imperfects show the forward thrust of the action (1:3ff, 15f.; 3:5; 4:5, 7, 8). In the dialogs, imperatives (1:2, 6b, 7, 12; 3:2) and questions (1:6, 8, 11; 4:4, 9, 11) fulfill the same function. On the other hand, the descriptive sentences typical of the idyll are almost totally lacking; for these entice the reader to pause and linger. (Exceptions are 3:3b, which is intended to set the tone for the Nineveh scenes, and 4:11, which is designed to add reflective emphasis to the final question.) The reader has been prepared to expect some reaction to the final question; for earlier, in all the important happenings, the basic reaction by the people affected to what Yahweh does is reported immediately (1:5, 10, 16; 3:5; 4:1). But here, at the end, the reader is left without any reply to Yahweh's main question.

This already brings us face to face with the necessity of defining the genre novella more closely (cf. M. E. Andrews, ''Gattung and Intention of the Book of Jonah,'' *Orita* 1 [1967] 78-85). For the final open question shows the *didactic* character of the work even more forcibly than the questions scattered throughout the rest of the text (see above). This didactic purpose shows itself most strongly in the way important doctrinal statements are revolved and discussed. In chap. 1 it is the confession of faith in Yahweh, the God of heaven, as creator of sea and land (v. 9); in chap. 3 the Jeremian-Deuteronomistic progression that proclamations of judgment will graciously be withdrawn by Yahweh if they lead to the conversion of the people threatened (vv. 8-10; see pp. 154f. below); in chap. 4 the liturgical utterance (frequently found elsewhere) about Yahweh's mercy (v. 2b, in the form of Joel 2:13; see pp. 167f. below). These doctrinal statements largely determine the inner shaping of the chapters. L. Schmidt (*De Deo,* 113) therefore believes that the form of the narrative ''can best be characterized through the term *narrated dogmatics.*'' But — in view of the special character of our novella — to say this is to lay undue stress on the elements of wisdom theology which it contains. Nevertheless it is impossible to overlook the way in which key words belonging to the doctrinal statements run through the individual chapters. On ירא (''fear'') in chap. 1, see p. 121 below; on נחם (''repentance'') and its extension in חוס (''pity''; cf. 3:9, 10; 4:2 and 4:10-11) see p. 175 below. The word רעה (''evil'') actually pervades the whole narrative, for we find it both in the doctrinal statements taken up in chap. 3 and at the climax of the confessional utterance in 4:2 (see p. 167 below). At the beginning it characterizes Nineveh's wickedness (1:2), from which the city then turns away (3:8, 10a) and — in association with this — the disaster (thus first of all 1:7, 8) which Yahweh threatened (3:10b) but for which he is then sorry (4:2). It is this very resolve of Yahweh's which ultimately kindles Jonah's wickedness (4:1); and this sounds the keynote for the final chapter (see pp. 165f. below). The lesson which Yahweh teaches by way of the castor oil plant, with the aim of bringing his hard-hearted pupil to reason through experience of his power as creator, also belongs to the category of wisdom didactic.

Yet we should notice that these didactic features have been introduced quite unobtrusively into the art of novellistic narrative. The didacticism never forces itself on us, simply because the author is a humorist with a roguish mind. We may recognize the well-structured form of our narrative as belonging to the genre novella, and we may see that its aim is instructive; but the unique beauty of the story and its liberating power is to be found in its *comedy*. In no other book of the Bible do we find all the different varieties of the comic style so richly developed as here (cf. E. M. Good, *Irony in the Old Testament* [1965] 39-55; M. Burrows, "The Literary Category of the Book of Jonah," *Translating and Understanding the Old Testament: Essays in Honor of H. G. May*, ed. H. Frank and W. L. Reed [1970] 80-107).

In the first two scenes (chap. 1) *satire* is the prevailing comic mode. Jonah surrenders himself luxuriously to a profound slumber, while the sailors rouse to bustling activity. The heathen pray; it does not occur to the Hebrew to do so. He thinks that he can escape from Yahweh and has in the end to acknowledge and discover by experience that Yahweh is Lord of the sea as well. These contradictions are exposed with biting derision. The satirist mercilessly pillories the preposterous nature of Jonah's behavior. "Satire annihilates — irony educates" (A. Jolles, *Einfache Formen*, 1958[2], 255). The kindlier way of exposing what is open to censure is also already evident in chap. 1. The reader is cheered when Jonah is not merely exposed to ridicule in a somewhat bitter way, but when the irony of God's laughter also plays its part: the person who wants to flee his service can do no more than widen the scope of that service through his obduracy; and the man who seeks death for himself is saved by God after all. So even in the first scenes the annihilating satire already begins to change into liberating irony — the literary form of a restrained didacticism.

But first of all the writer of our novella introduces another comic device: *the grotesque*. This dominates the third and fourth scenes especially. The person who wanted to escape with the ship (at his own expense! 1:3) is brought back by "the great fish" (free of charge!) on God's orders. In coarsely comic terms and in the tersest sentences we are told how Jonah — who simply wanted to die (1:12) — is not merely swallowed up by the monster (1:17) but is vomited up onto dry land after three days and nights of a fantastic shipment (2:10). At this the reader's mild amusement turns into open laughter. The fourth scene is also heightened into the grotesque. This is not merely as a whole a counterpart to the ironization of Jerusalem's behavior according to Jeremiah 36 (see p. 136 below); here even the animals wear mourning and take part in the prayer and fasting.

"There are great works of art which begin as satire and end as irony — works of art where the writer first of all thinks that he will confront his subject with mockery, hoping to be able to resolve the matter without sympathy, but where he gradually realizes that he himself is profoundly involved with the thing he mocks, and that the victim he pierces so deeply with his mockery is his own self" (A. Jolles, *Einfache Formen* 256). The writer of the Jonah story goes through a similar process. In the final scene he arrives at an *irony* that is almost kindly. Of course the irony has an edge to it, when the furiously angry Jonah can be lifted out of his ''great ill-humor'' (4:1) into ''exceeding gladness'' simply by a little shade (v. 6). It remains satirical even when Jonah's inconsistency is exposed, his fury over God's pity with Nineveh being confronted with his own distress over the withered plant. His petty self-pity, when God's mercy is withdrawn from his own head, makes him just as tired of life as his ill-humor over God's pity for 120,000 people. And yet — the comedy of God's creation game with the castor oil plant has eased the tension over Jonah's own infamous behavior. Biting through the irony is, the modified repetition in 4:9 of the question in 4:4, ''Do you do well to be angry?'' namely, ''Do you do well to be angry for the plant?'' resolves the strain. And the final, highly didactic question in 4:10f., with its restrained irony, acts on the reader like a liberation: you are distressed about the short-lived plant — and yet you are not willing for me to be distressed about the great city. . . ''and so much cattle''? (see pp. 173f. below). Here the irony robs the lesson of its harshness. It has also served to keep the reader's attention alive to the very end (cf. A. Jolles, *Einfache Formen* 257f.).

Irony is a favorite device in all polemical and protest writing; and our writer has steeped his novella in it in a masterly way. The irony has shaped his indirect desire to teach a lesson into a form which liberates the reader's mind through wit and jest, so that the proper answer to the final question no longer has to occupy him unduly. ''When grape juice and milk, honey, rice and potatoes ferment, they produce something which stimulates and intoxicates'' (A. Jolles, *Einfache Formen* 261); and, in the same way, with our narrator humor is the yeast of the spirit which ferments the most widely varying material and teaching, turning it into new wine. The writer of our novella has made a caricature of Jonah, so that he can more easily free the reader who is in a similar state of mind from his fatal dilemma (4:8f.). The form of this ironically didactic novella therefore fits the message about God which it wants to convey — the message telling something of the history of that God's dealings with human beings.

5. The Narrator's Guiding Concern

What is the novella trying to do when it makes Jonah the caricature of a typical Hebrew, a type that may perhaps have been prevalent round about the early Hellenistic period (see §2 above)?

First of all, the story is evidently trying to arrive at an understanding of certain contemporary groups. The crisis of faith which these people were undergoing may be most clearly evident in the final question in 4:11, the enormous significance of which we discovered is to be found in the ironic didacticism of our narrator. Its underlying assumption is that there are men and women who are no longer able to understand Yahweh's forbearance with the great heathen powers to which Israel had been a prey for centuries. What troubles them particularly is a profound contradiction in Israel's traditions. On the one hand, Yahweh's unconditional threats of judgment against Israel's archenemies are still awaiting their fulfillment. On the other hand, Israel's age-old acknowledgment of Yahweh's mercy knows no frontiers (see p. 168 below). To proclaim the destruction of the brutal metropolis and at the very same time to believe that Yahweh will revoke his threat is a requirement that is becoming intolerable. Yahweh's incalculable pity (1:6; 3:9f.; 4:2b) seems to be calling in question his service of obedience. The old skepticism towards the prophetic proclamation is eating in more and more deeply (cf. Isa. 5:19; Jer. 5:12f.; Zeph. 1:12; Ezek. 12:22; Mal. 2:17f.). This skepticism also means that practical behavior is no longer guided by the confession of faith of old (cf. 1:3ff. with v. 9; also pp. 115f. below). Yahweh makes no distinction between Israel and foreigners. He persecutes his faint-hearted servant with the tempest (1:4ff.) and permits the bloodthirsty metropolis to escape completely unscathed. So, since serving Yahweh seems pointless, all that can be done is to wish for death (1:[5b], 12; 4:3, 8f.). It is to this kind of despairing theology and to just such a totally resigned piety that the narrator turns.

What does he have to say to these groups of people? He lures them out of their gloomy concern with themselves by ironically exposing the sullen dourness of their faith. Their behavior gives Yahweh endless trouble and labor (1:4; 1:17; 2:10; 3:1f.; 4:4, 6-11), and the writer shows them — sometimes with satirical exaggeration — how little bother Yahweh has with the Gentiles. What he lays before them is hope in narrative form. Prophetic promise is translated into terse scenes (see p. 157 below). The parallelism between scene two and scene four makes it plain that the path that brings the Gentiles to the God of the Hebrews can vary considerably. In the ship's crew there are men belonging to many different nations and religions, side by side. When Yahweh's tempest rises they make every conceivable effort to save themselves: prayer, skilled seamanship, the casting of lots and, after the lot has fallen on the unknown Hebrew passenger, his advice as well; and then they put forth their own efforts once more, finally turning to Yahweh in prayer (see pp. 122-124 below). Painstakingly and consistently, they find their way step by step to lasting trust in Jonah's God. The Ninevites are different. The huge city receives the brief message that its days are numbered. Afterwards, the narrator paints the picture of immediate and comprehensive repentance, with matchless self-humiliation, a resolute abandonment of every kind of raw brutality, and hope in the messenger's God (see pp. 156-157 below). The two scenes are alike only in that the foreigners depicted do not cause Yahweh any difficulty, once they have encountered his messenger. Yahweh's glory shines out in the wide world of the nations: with all of them he arrives at his goodly goal.

Although this does not come about without the help of his messenger, it is with this very messenger, and only with him, that Yahweh comes up against resistance. But, for the narrator, describing this resistance is not as important as showing how Yahweh is tirelessly concerned to overcome it. It would seem as if the writer already wishes to urge against Jonah the question that Paul was to put: "Is God the God of Jews only? Is he not the God of Gentiles also?" (Rom. 3:29). He wishes to bring about the assent of the religious egoist to Yahweh's pity for all human beings.

We have shown how the writer attempts to do this by way of narrative. To sum up the substance of his arguments is more difficult. For, skilled though he is in the creation of scenes and in the use of satire, grotesque, and irony as literary methods, our writer is not a systematic theologian. He can shift about in his application of different kinds of theological tenets, though without losing sight of his practical goal.

What is important throughout the narrative is his theology of creation. Yahweh hurls the storm on to the sea (1:4) in order to show Jonah the vainness of his flight, and at the same time to win wider groups of the heathen than had originally been envisaged. Yahweh orders up the great fish, as a drastic demonstration to Jonah that there is no way in which he can escape going to Nineveh. Finally, a whole series of other created things — the castor oil plant, the worm, and the east wind — must present themselves in rapid succession, in order to teach Jonah a final lesson. The narrator has recourse to a wisdom theology of creation for his own purposes (cf. Job 38f.; also G. von Rad, *Weisheit in Israel* [1970] 290ff. [Eng., *Wisdom in Israel*, 1972] and pp. 170ff. below).

Whereas in chap. 1 it is with the help of this theology that the sailors arrive at the fear of Yahweh (v. 9), in chap. 3 the writer brings into play a completely different doctrine. This proceeds from the Jeremian and Deuteronomistic perception that the real function of the word of judgment is to bring about the conversion of its listeners, and that after this conversion Yahweh will not allow the disaster to occur. This train of thought was well developed where Israel itself was concerned; but now the narrator boldly applies it to Nineveh, as a foreign people. The only comparable example is Jer. 18:7f. (see p. 154 below). The essential importance of repentance, as the outcome of the threat of judgment, is brought out by the narrator only in chap. 3. Astonishingly enough, he makes no further use of this idea at all in the final didactic dialog with Jonah in chap. 4. This is surprising, because it is after all precisely the pointer to the real function of the word of judgment (to bring about repentance) and stress that Nineveh really has repented, which could parry the reproach that Yahweh is unjust and incalculable.

Instead of this, chap. 4 has a different theological emphasis. This is certainly already led up to in 3:9 (similarly in 1:6); for there Yahweh's abandonment of his anger is expressly made dependent on his free act of decision; it is not viewed as the necessary consequence of repentance (see pp. 153f. below). Chapter 4 underlines the completely free nature of Yahweh's mercy. The cited confessional utterance in v. 2b already makes this point. Like 3:9a, it picks up the wording of Joel 2:13f. In this way the narrator makes it excitingly and provokingly clear that what is promised to Jerusalem in Joel's prophecy applies to strangers in exactly the same way (see pp. 153ff. below).

But stress on the free nature of Yahweh's pity is even more evident in the creation game which Yahweh plays with Jonah in vv. 6-9. Jonah rejoices over the shadow of the castor oil plant, and is correspondingly indignant over its rapid withering. And yet even in his obduracy he is forced to concede that he himself is wholly dependent on Yahweh's undeserved pity (see pp. 172f. below). It is surprising that the final question in vv. 10f. does not enter by so much as a single syllable into the idea of repentance as presupposition (although it is not explicitly denied). The reason for Yahweh's decision is to be found solely in his free mercy with his needy creatures (see pp. 174f. below). Here belief in creation and the the-ology of grace are splendidly united.

In this context, the final scene is so skillfully designed that when Jonah insists on Yahweh's free pity, he cannot really avoid simultaneously conceding to his God the forgiving mercy he has extended to the heathen. But the narrator leaves his readers to draw this harmonizing conclusion themselves. Even the most morosely obstinate of them can hardly do other than — in Jonah's stead — respond with gratitude to their God's final question. They are now intended to laugh over their own ill humor, and to rejoice in their God. What long-suffering love on Yahweh's part they themselves have experienced! In their egotistical self-righteousness they would long since have deserved to perish in the deadly flood that engulfed the fleeing Jonah. But now the God of Israel has glorified himself even in the utter failure of his messenger (G. von Rad, *Theologie des Alten Testaments* 2, 1975[6], 301 (Eng., *Old Testament Theology* 2, 1965).

In his addition in 2:1-9 (see pp. 133f. below), the psalmist perceives something of the fact that "God's mercy can turn the belly of hell into the womb of a new birth" (U. Steffen, *Mysterium* 106). Men and women who are resigned in faith should discern, full of hope for themselves and all human beings, that "deliverance belongs to Yahweh" (2:9b).

6. Literature

For literature on the minor prophets in general see above, pp. 23-27.

1. *Commentaries on Jonah:* P. Bergmann, *Jonah* (1885). T.T. Perowne, *Obadja and Jonah* (1898). J. Döller, *Das Buch Jonah* (1912). J. Halévy, *Le Livre de Jonas, RSEHA* 14 (1916) 1-49. D. Velutti-Zati, *Il sacro libro di Giona* (1916). D. T. Evans, *The Book of Jonah* (1925). T. H. Dodson, *The Book of Jonah* (1926). G. E. Hagemann, *The Prophet Jonah* (1927). D. Avanden Bosch, *Jona (1937).* T. E. Bird, *The Book of Jonah* (1938). N. H. Snaith, *The Book of Jonah* (1945). G. A. F. Knight, *Ruth and Jonah* (1950; rev.ed. 1956). J. Lindon, *Le livre de Jona traduit,* Editions de Minuit (1955) 7-63. E. Haller, *Die Erzählung von dem Propheten Jona:* Theol. Ex. 65 (1958; Gladbeck 1965[2]). H. Martin, *The Prophet Jonah: His Character and Mission to Nineveh,* Geneva Series of Commentaries (1958). H. Livings, *Jonah* (1974).

2. *General Studies on Jonah:* B. Wolf, *Die Geschichte des Propheten Jona* (1897). W. Simpson, *The Jonah Legend* (1899, 1971[2]). W. Volck, "Jonah, Prophet," *RE* 9 (1901) 338-340. T. K. Cheyne, "Jonah (Book)," *EB* 2 (1901) col. 2565-2571. A. Condamin, "Jonas," *DAFC* 2 (1915), col. 1546-1559. K. Budde, "Jonah," *JE* 7 (1925) 227-230. L. Dennefeld, "Le Livre de Jonas," *DThC* 8 (1925) 1497-1504. L. Stollberg, "Jona" (Diss., Halle, 1927). H. Gunkel, "Jonabuch," *RGG*[2] 3 (1929) 638-643. U. Cassuto, "Jona," *EJ* 9 (1932) 268-274. E. König, "Jonah," *Dictionary of the Bible* 2 (1942[11]) 744-753. J. Zmora, "Jonah ben 'Amittai," *Maḥbarot le-sifrut* 3 (1946) 62-64. A. Feuillet, "Jonas," *DBS* 4 (1949), col. 1104-1131. G. von Rad, "Der Prophet Jona" (1950), in *Gottes Wirken in Israel,* Vorträge zum AT, ed. O. H. Steck (1974) 65-78. J. S. Licht, "Sepher Jonah," *Enṣiqlopediyah Miqra'it* 3 (1958) col. 608-613. H. W. Wolff, *Die Bibel — Gotteswort oder Menschenwort? Dargestellt am Buch Jona* (1959); "Jonabuch," *RGG*[3] 3 (1959) 853-855. B. Hessler, "Jonas," *LThK* 5 (1960) 1113-1115. W. Neil, "Book of Jonah," *IDB* 2 (1962) 964-967. O. Loretz, *Gotteswort und menschliche Erfahrung: Jona, Ruth, Hoheslied und Qohelet* (1963). H. W. Wolff, *Studien zum*

Jonabuch (1964, 1975²). M. Sekine, "Jona, Jonabuch," *BHH* 2 (1964) 88lf. G. H. Cohn, "Book of Jonah," *EJ* 10 (1971) 169-173. D. Barsotti, *Jonas* (1974). L. Schmidt, *"De Deo": Studien zur Literarkritik und Theologie des Buches Jona, des Gesprächs zwischen Abraham und Jahwe in Gen 18,22ff. und von Hi 1*, BZAW 143 (1976).

3. *The Text:* W. Wright, *Jonah in Chald. Syr. Aeth. and Arab.* (1857). N. H. Snaith, *Notes on the Hebrew Text of Jonah* (1945). H. C. Youtie, "A Codex of Jonah: Berl. Sept. 18 and P.S.I.X 1164," *HThR* 38 (1945) 195-197. M. Stenzel, "Zum Vulgatatext des Canticum Jonae," *Bibl* 33 (1952) 356-362; "Altlateinische Canticatexte im Dodekapropheton," *ZNW* 46 (1955) 31-60 (54-60). A. Mallon, *Grammaire Copte* (1956⁴) 37- 43 (Bohairic version of the book of Jonah).

4. *Literary Problems:* K. Kohler, "The Original Form of the Book of Jonah," *Theological Review* 16 (1879) 139-144. W. Böhme, "Die Composition des Buches Jona," *ZAW* 7 (1887) 224-284. H. Winckler, "Zum Buche Jona," *Altorientalische Forschungen* 2, 2 (1900) 260-265. H. Schmidt, "Die Komposition des Buches Jona," *ZAW* 25 (1905) 285-310. E. Sievers, *Alttestamentliche Miszellen* (2, "Die Form des Jonabuches"), BVSAW. PH 57 (1905) 35-45. J. Döller, "Versumstellungen im Buche Jona," *Kath* 35 (1907) 313-317. G. M. Landes, "The 'Three Days and Three Nights' Motif in Jonah 2:1," *JBL* 86 (1967) 446-450; "The Kerygma of the Book of Jonah: The Contextual Interpretation of the Jonah Psalm," *Interp* 21 (1967) 3-31. E. G. Kraeling, "The Evolution of the Story of Jonah," *Hommages à A. Dupont-Sommer* (1971) 305-318. J. D. Magonet, "Form and Meaning: Studies in Literary Techniques in the Book of Jonah" (Diss. Heidelberg, 1973).

5. *Style and Form Criticism:* B. Gemser, "Die Humor van die OuT," *HTS* 8 (1951) 49-63. M. R. de Haan, *Jonah, Fact or Fiction?* (1957). J. A. Díaz, "Paralelos entre la narración de libro de Jonás y la parábola del hijo prodigo," *Bibl* 40 (1959) 632-640. N. Lohfink, "Jona ging zur Stadt hinaus (Jona 4,5)," *BZ* NF 5 (1961) 185-203. J. Schreiner, "Eigenart, Aufbau und Inhalt des Buches Jonas," *BiKi* 17 (1962) 8-14. A. Vaccari, "Il genere letterario del libro di Giona in recenti publicazione," *Divinitas* 6 (1962) 231-252. R. Weiss, " 'Al Sefer Jonah," *Maḥanaim* 60 (1962) 45-48. E. M. Good, *Jonah: The Absurdity of God: Irony in the OT* (1965) 39-55. R. Pesch, "Zur konzentrischen Struktur von Jona 1," *Bibl* 47 (1966) 577-581. P. L. Trible, "Studies in the Book of Jonah" (Diss. Columbia University, 1963, *Diss. Abstracts* 27 [1966/67] 2611). M. E. Andrew, "Gattung and Intention of the Book of Jonah," *Orita* 1 (1967) 13-18, 78- 85. G. H. Cohn, *Das Buch Jona im Lichte der biblischen Erzählkunst*, SSN 12 (1969). M. Burrows, "The Literary Category of the Book of Jonah," *Translating and Understanding the OT: Essays in Honor of H. G. May* (1970) 80-107.

6. *Sources and Tradition:* W. Erbt, *Elia, Elisa, Jona* (1907). H. Schmidt, *Jona. Eine Untersuchung zur vergleichenden Religionsgeschichte*, FRLANT 9 (1907). A. Feuillet, "Les sources du livre de Jonas," *RB* 54 (1947) 161- 186. H. W. Wolff, "Origin and Form of the Book of Jonah" (in Czech.), *KrR* 26 (1959 (111-116). O. Eissfeldt, "Amos und Jona in volkstümlicher Überlieferung: '. . . und fragten nach Jesus'," *Fests. E. Barnikol* (1964) 9-13 = *KlSchr* 4 (1968) 137-142. B. Hruška, *Poznámy k Jonášovi* ("Comments on Jonah," in Czech., *KrR* 32 (1965) 53-54. A. Fáj, "The Stoic Features of the 'Book of Jonah,'" *Annali dell' Istituto Orientale di Napoli* 34 (1974) 309-345.

7. *Authorship and Date:* K. Budde, "Vermutungen zum 'Midrasch des Buches der Könige,'" *ZAW* 12 (1892) 37-151, on Jonah: 40-43. H. Schmidt, "Absicht und Entstehungszeit des Buches Jona," *ThStKr* 79 (1906) 180-199. A. Thoma, "Die Entstehung des Büchleins Jona," *ThStKr* 84 (1911) 479-502. R. D. Wilson, "The Authenticity of Jonah," *PrincThR* 16 (1918) 280-298, 430-456. D. E. Hart-Davies, "The Book of Jonah in the Light of Assyrian Archeology," *Journal of the Transactions of the Victoria*

Institute 69 (1937) 230-249. M. D. Goldman, "Was the Book of Jonah Originally Written in Aramaic?" *ABR* 3 (1953) 49-50. J. J. Glück, "A Linguistic Criterion of the Book of Jonah," *OuTWP* 1967 (1971) 34-41.

8. *The Theology of the Book of Jonah:* P. Magnus, "The Book of Jonah," *The Hibbert Journal* 16 (1917/18) 429-442. A. D. Martin, *The Prophet Jonah: The Book and the Sign* (1927). D. E. Hart-Davies, *Jonah: Prophet and Patriot* (1932). F. Dijkema, "Het Boek Jona," *NThT* 25 (1936) 338-347. H. Junker, "Die religiöse Bedeutung des Buches Jona," *PastB* 41 (1940) 108-114. A. Feuillet, "Le sens du livre de Jonas," RB 54 (1947) 340-361. G. C. Aalders, *The Problem of the Book of Jonah* (1948). G. B. Stanton, "The Prophet Jonah and his Message," *BS* 108 (1951) 237-249, 363-376. B. Trépanier, "The Story of Jonas," *CBQ* 13 (1951) 8-16. S. H. Blank, " 'Doest Thou Well To Be Angry?' A Study in Self-Pity," *HUCA* 26 (1955) 29-41. H. Bardtke, "Der Erweckungsgedanke in der exilisch-nachexilischen Literatur des Alten Testaments," BZAW 77 (1958) 9-24. B. S. Childs, "Jonah: A Study in OT Hermeneutics," *SJTh* 11 (1958) 53-61. J. A. Díaz, "Difficultades que plantea la interpretación de la narración de Jonás como puramente didáctica y soluciones que se suelen dar," *EstBibl* 18 (1959) 357-374. H. W. Wolff, "The Jonah Event" (in Czech.), *KrR* 26 (1959) 72-78. J. Alonso, "Lección Teológica del Libro de Jonás," *Fests. Antonio Perez Goyena,* EstE Misc 35 (1960) 79-93. J. Steinmann, "Le livre de la consolation d'Israel," *Lectio divina* 28 (1960) 286-290. J. Fransen, "Le Livre de Jonas," *BiViChr* 40 (1961) 33-39. W. Vischer, "L'evangelo secondo il profeta Giona," *Protestantesimo* 16 (1961) 193-204. R. L. Díaz, "Misericordia divina y universalismo en el libro de Jonás," *MEAH* 11 (1962) 43-56. J. B. Schildenberger, "Der Sinn des Buches Jonas," *Erbe und Auftrag* 38 (1962) 93-102. K. H. Miskotte, *When the Gods Are Silent* (1967) 422-438. R. Weiss, "W-ānāh mippanäkā 'äbrāh," 'Orot 49 (1963) 28-33. P. A. H. de Boer, " 'Jona' Zoals er gezegd is over Jeremia," *Phoenix Bijbel Pockets Antwerp* (1964) 93- 102. Rdell'Oca, "El libro de Jonas," *RBiblArg* 26 (1964) 129-139. D. Zimmermann, "Has-sippur 'al ha-'iš Jonah," *Niv hak-kwutsah 12* (1964) 706-714. C. A. Keller, "Jonas: Le Portrait d'un prophète," *ThZ* 21 (1965) 329- 340. R. B. Y. Scott, "The Sign of Jonah: An Interpretation," *Interp* 19 (1965) 16-25. L. Fränkel, " 'And his mercy is over all his works.' On the Meaning of the Book of Jonah" (in Hebrew) *Ma'yānōt* 9 (1967) 193-207. G. von Rad, *Theologie des AT* 2 (1975⁶) 299-302 (Eng., *Old Testament Theology* 2, 1965). J. H. Stek, "The Message of the Book of Jonah," *Calvin Theological Journal* 4 (1969) 23-50. J. More, "The Prophet Jonah: The Story of an Intrapsychic Process," *American Imago* (Spring 1970) 3-11. J. H. Eybers, "The Purpose of the Book of Jonah," *Theologia Evangelica* 4 (1971) 211-222. H. J. Grünewald, "Das Buch Jona," *Udim* 2 (1971) 69-82. A. H. van Zyl, "The Preaching of the Book of Jonah," *OuTWP* 1967 (1971) 92-104. A. D. Cohen, "The Tragedy of Jonah," *Judaism* 21 (1972) 164-175. O. Kaiser, "Wirklichkeit, Möglichkeit und Vorurteil: Ein Beitrag zum Verständnis des Buches Jona," *EvTh* 33 (1973) 91-103. R. E. Clements, "The Purpose of the Book of Jonah," VT Suppl 28 (1975) 16-28.

9. *Individual Problems:* A. Rosenthal, *Das Buch Jonah metrisch übersetzt* (1899). M. Löwy, *Über das Buch Jona* (1892), J. Kennedy, *On the Book of Jonah* (1895). E. Seydl, "Das Jonalied," *ZKTh* 24 (1900) 187-193. P. Jensen, "Das Jonas-Problem," *DLZ* 28 (1907) 2629-2636. H. Wiesmann, "Einige Bemerkungen zum Buche Jona," *Kath* 38 (1908) 111-125. A. Abraham, *Die Schiffsterminologie des AT* (1914). R. D. Wilson, "מנה, 'To Appoint' in the OT," *PrincThR 16 (1918)* 645-654. A. Köster, *Das antike Seewesen* (1923) 45-55. Mayr, "Jonas im Bauche des Fisches," *ThPQ* 85 (1932) 829-832. I. B. Schaumberger, "Das Bussedikt des Königs von Nineve bei Jon. 3,7.8 in keilschriftlicher Beleuchtung," *Miscellanea Biblica edita a Pontificio Instituto Biblico ad celebrandum annum XXV ex quo conditum est Institutum* (1909 — VII. Maii — 1934) 123-134. T. Boman, "Jahve og Elohim i Jonaboken," *NTT* 37 (1936) 159-168. H. L. Jansen, "Har Jonaboken en enhetlig opbygning og en bestemt hovedtendens?" *NTT* 37

(1936) 145-158. S. Mowinckel, "Efterskrift til pastor Th. Bomans artikel," *NTT* 37 (1936) 164-168. S. D. Goitein, "Some Observations on Jonah," *JPOS* 17 (1937) 63-77. A. Salonen, *Die Wasserfahrzeuge in Babylonien* (1938). E. F. Weidner, "Das Archiv des *Mannu-Ki-Aššur,*" *AfO*Beiheft 6 (1940) 8-46. A. R. Johnson, "Jon 2,3-10: A Study in Cultic Phantasy," *Studies in OT Prophecy,* ed. H. H. Rowley (Fests. T. H. Robinson) (1950) 82-102. W. M. Valk, "Jonas and the 'Whale,' " *Scrip* 6 (1953) 46-49. H. H. Fingert, "Psychoanalytical Study of the Minor Prophet Jonah," *Psychoanalytical Review* 41 (1954) 55-65. F. Nötscher, "Zur Auferstehung nach drei Tagen," *Bibl* 35 (1954) 313-319. A. Parrot, "Nineve und das AT," *Bibel und Archäologie* 1 (1955) 111-169. J. H. Kennedy, *Studies in the Book of Jonah* (1956). S. D. Goitein, "Sefer Jonah," *'Ijunim lam-madrik w-lam-moreh* 23 (1956) 94-103. H. Rosin, *The Lord Is God (The Translation of the Divine Names and the Missionary Calling of the Church)* (1956) 6-33. W. Vycichil, "Jonas und der Walfisch," *Muséon* 69 (1956) 183-186. D. N. Freedman, "Jonah 1:4b," *JBL* 77 (1958) 161-162. S. Abramski, "Jonah ben 'Amittai," *Gazith* 17 (1959) 5-10. J. Bacharach, *Jonah Ben 'Amittai w'Eliyahu* (Jerusalem 1959). J. Heemrood, "Jonas und die Heiden," *HLa* 12 (1959) 33-35. R. Martin-Achard, "Israël et les nations," *Cahiers Théologiques* 42 (1959) 45-48. J. Möllerfeld, " 'Du bist ein gnädiger und barmherziger Gott' (Jonas 4,2)," *Geist und Leben* 33 (1960) 324-333. O. Loretz, "Herkunft und Sinn der Jonaerzählung," *BZ* NF 5 (1961) 18-29. M. Lawrence, "Ships, Monsters and Jonah," *AJA* 66 (1962) 289-296. U. Steffen, *Das Mysterium von Tod und Auferstehung (Formen und Wandlungen des Jona-Motivs)* (1963). Z. Soušek, "Nineve, Taršíš a Jonáš" (in Czech.), *KrR* 32 (1965) 147-148. H. W. Wolff, *Studien zum Jonabuch,* BiblStud 47 (1965, 1975²). P. Cintas, "Tarsis-Tartessos-Gadès," *Sem* 16 (1966) 5-37. K. Heinrich, *Parmenides und Jona* (1966). R. North, *Exégèse pratique des petits prophètes postexiliens: Bibliographie commentée 950 titres* (1969) 128-143. H. Bojorge, "Los significados posibles de lehassîl en Jonas 4,6," *Strom* 26 (1970) 77-87. F. D. Kidner, "The Distribution of Divine Names in Jonah," *Tyndale Bulletin* 21 (1970) 126-128. D. F. Rauber, "Jonah — The Prophet as Shlemiel," *BT* 49 (1970). W. Rudolph, "Jona: Archäologie und Altes Testament," *Fests. K. Galling* (1970) 233-239. A. Jepsen, "Anmerkungen zum Buche Jona: Wort — Gebot — Glaube," *Fests. W. Eichrodt* (1970) 297-305. J. L. Helberg, "Is Jonah in His Failure a Representative of the Prophets?" *OuTWP* 1967 (1971) 41-51. Avan-Selms, "Some Geographical Remarks on Jonah," *OuTWP* 1967 (1971) 83-92.

10. *The History of Interpretation:* Jerome, *Commentariorum in Jonam Prophetam,* MPL 25, 1171-1208. Theophylactus, *Expositio in Prophetam Jonam,* MPG 126, col. 905-968. K. Langosch, *Die Lieder des Archipoeta,* Reclam-Universal Bibliothek No. 8942 (1965) 52-59 ("Jonas redivivus"). Germanus II of Constantinople, *Homilia in Jonam Prophetam* (ed. under the name of John Chrysostom), MPG 49 (1862) 305-314. Pseudo-Tertullian, *Carmen de Jona et Nineve,* MPL 2 (1844) 1107-1114. M. Luther, *Der Prophet Jona ausgelegt* (1526), WA XIX (1897) 169-251; *Jona,* ed. G. Krause (1938). S. Poznanski, "Targoum Yerouschalmi et son commentaire sur le livre de Jonas," *RÉJ* 40 (1900) 130-153. F. Delitzsch, "Etwas über das Buch Jona und einige neue Auslegungen desselben," *ZLThK* 1 (1840) 112-126. P. Friedrichsen, *Kritische Übersicht der verschiedenen Ansichten über das Buch Jonas* (1841²). F. M. Abel, "Le culte de Jonas en Palestine," *JPOS* 2 (1922) 175-183. H. Speyer, *Die biblischen Erzählungen im Qoran* (1931; 1961²) 407-410. H. Lewy, *The Pseudo-Philonic De Jona I,* StD 7 (1936). B. Heller, "Yūnus," *EJ* (D)4 (1938) 1273 = B. Heller, "Yūnus b. Mattai," *HIsl* (1941) 811f. J. Jeremias, "Der Prophet Jonas," *ThWNT* 3 (1938) 410-413. J. Heuschen, "L'interprétation du livre de Jonas," *REcL* 35 (1948) 141-159. O. Komlós, *Jonah Legends,* ÉtOr P. Hirschler, ed. O. Komlós (Budapest 1950) 41-61 = "Jóna- Legendák," *Jubilee vol. B. Heller* (1941) 208-222. H. Greenberg, "Go to Nineveh," *The Inner Eye* (1953) 57-61. L. Ginzberg, *The Legends of the Jews* 4 (1954⁶) 239-253. A. Penna, "Andrea di S.Vittore/il suo commento in Giona," *Bibl* 12 (1955) 305-331. W. Werbeck,

RGG[3] 3 (1959) 855f. (and further literature there cited). C. Kopp, "Das Jonagrab in Meschhed," *Das Heilige Land* 103 (1960) 17-21. P. Antin, "Saint Cyprian et Jonas," *RB* 68 (1961) 412-414. E. Biser, "Zum frühchristlichen Verständnis des Buches Jona," *BiKi* 17 (1962) 19-21. A. M. Goldberg, "Jonas in der jüdischen Schriftauslegung," *BiKi* 17 (1962) 17f. H. Horst, "Israelitische Propheten im Koran," *ZRGG* 16 (1964) 42-57. K. H. Rengstorf, "Das Jona-'Zeichen,' " *ThWNT* 7 (1964) 231f. E. J. Bickermann, "Les deux erreurs du prophète Jonas," *RHPhR* 45 (1965) 232-264; *Four Strange Books of the Bible: Jonah/Daniel/Kohelet/Esther* (1967) 1-49. F. Weinreb, *Das Buch Jonah: Der Sinn des Buches Jonah nach der ältesten jüdischen Überlieferung* (1970). Y. M. Duval, *Le Livre de Jonas dans la Littérature Chrétienne Grecque et Latine* (1973) with further literature cited there on pp. 727-733.

11. *Aspects for Practical Theology:* J. Schoneveld, *God en zijn wereld: Het boek Jona* (n.d.). A. J. Wilson, "The Sign of the Prophet Jonah and Its Modern Confirmations," *PrincThR* 25 (1927) 630-642; 26 (1928) 618-621. E. Hirsch, *Das AT und die Predigt des Evangeliums* (1936) 49-67. R. Brunner, *Unterwegs mit Gott: Das Zeugnis des Propheten Jona* (1938). M. Ronner, *Das Buch Jona* (1947). W. C. Hay, *The Wideness of God's Mercy: A Study in the Book of Jonah,* Books of the Bible Series 6 (1952). J. Ellul, *Le Livre de Jonas: Foi et vie* (1952) 81-184. H. Hug, *Die Taube zu Nineve: Jona-Predigten* (1952). W. Stählin, "Das Zeichen des Jona," *Quatember* 22 (1957/58) 193-197. W. Kemner, *Jona: Ein Mann geht nach Nineve* (1960). M. L. Digges, "Jonah the Reluctant Prophet," *Worship* 36 (1961/62) 321-326. H. Gollwitzer, T. Jänicke, and F. W. Marquardt, *Das Buch Jona in Predigten: Nineve ist überall* (1962). O. Knoch, "Das Zeichen des Jonas," *BiKi* 17 (1962) 15f. W. Pfendsack, *Der lachende Fisch: Fünf Predigten über das Büchlein des Propheten Jona* (n.d. [1964]). H. Dietzfelbinger, *Jona, ein Knecht Gottes,* Bibelarbeit zum 12. Dt. Evang. Kirchentag 1965 (1966). S. Ben-Chorin, *Die Antwort des Jona: Zum Gestaltwandel Israels* (1966[2]). H. Werner, *Jona: Der Mann aus dem Ghetto* (1966). W. L. Bauks, *Jonah, the Reluctant Prophet,* Everyman's Bible Commentary Series (1968). E. Lange, *Die verbesserliche Welt: Möglichkeiten christlicher Rede erprobt an der Geschichte vom Propheten Jona* (1968). K. Gräve, "Das Zeichen des Jona," *Geist und Leben* 43 (1970) 87-90. P. W. Schäfer, *Und Gott redet: Jona '70* (1970). A. Haarbeck, *Unterwegs nach Nineve* (1972). C. Lewis, "Jonah, A Parable for Our Time," *Judaism* 21 (1972) 159-163. G. Bader, "Das Gebet Jonas: Eine Meditation," *ZThK* 70 (1973) 162-205. D. Hillis, "Jonah Speaks Again," Contemporary Discussion Series (1973). Helen Schüngel-Straumann, "Umgeworfene Gottesvorstellungen exemplarisch dargestellt an Jona 4,1-11," *Katechetische Blätter* 98 (1973) 745-752.

12. *Jonah in the Visual Arts:* O. Mitius, *Jonas auf den Denkmälern des christlichen Altertums* (1897). H. Leclercq, "Jonas," *Dictionnaire d'Archéologie Chrétienne et de Liturgie* 7,2 (1926) 2572-2631. F. Gerke, *Die christlichen Sarkophage der vorkonstantinischen Zeit* (1940) 38-51, 151-182. E. Stommel, "Zum Problem der frühchristlichen Jonasdarstellungen," with 3 illustrations, *JbAC* 1 (1958) 112-115, illustration 8. E. Lucchesi-Palli, "Jonas. Ikonographisch," *LThK* 5 (1960) col. 1115. H. Rosenau, "The Jonah Sarcophagus in the British Museum," *Journal of the British Archaeological Association* 24 (1961) 60-66.

13. *Jonah in Literature:* Robert Green and Thomas Lodge, *A Looking Glasse for London and England* (1594, 1932). Francis Quarles, *A Feast for Wormes Set Forth in a Poeme of the History of Jonah* (1620) = *The Complete Works in Prose and Verse of Francis Quarles* 2, ed. A. B. Grosart (1874, 1967[2]) 1-30. Martin Opitz, "Jonas," *Geistliche Poemata* (1638; Deutsche Neudrucke, 1975) 57-85. Anon., *Ninevitish Repentance* (1643). Zachary Boyd, *Historie of Jonah: Four Poems from "Zion's Flowers"* (1855). J. Ritchie, *The Prophet Jonah* (1860). János Arany, *Proféta lomb* (1877), John Thomas Beer, *The Prophet of Nineveh: A Drama in 3 Acts* (1877). A. P. Herbert, *The Book of Jonah* (1921). Max Deauville (pseud. of Maurice Duwez), *Jonas* (1923). Robert Gruntal, *Nathan, Jonah*

(1925, 1934[2]) = *Son of Amittai* (1925). A. C. Lichtenstein, *Yonah ben Amittai* (in Yiddish; 1929). M. Foner, *Jonah ben Amittai* (in Hebrew; 1930). James Bridie (pseud. of O. H. Mavor), *Jonah and the Whale* (1932). Zora Neale Hurston, *Jonah's Gourd Vine* (1934). Haakon Bugge Mahit, *Jonas* (1935). Harald Tandrup, *Jonah and the Voice* (1938). Babits Mihàly, *Jonás Könyve* (1940, 1963). James Bridie, *Jonah 3: The Sign of the Prophet Jonah* in his *Plays for Plain People* (1944). Paul Goodman, *Jonah* (1945). Robert Lee Frost, *A Masque of Mercy* (1947). Laurence Housman, *The Burden of Nineveh* in his *Old Testament Plays* (1950). Olov Hartman, *Profet och timmerman* (1954). Günter Rutenborn, *Das Zeichen des Jona* (1955). W. Mankowitz, *It Should Happen to a Dog* (1956). Albert Camus, *Jona ou l'Artiste au Travail: L'exile et le royaume* (1957, 1972). Aldous Huxley, "Jonah," *The Cherry Tree* (1959). Uwe Jonson, "Jonas zum Beispiel," *Das Atelier* 1, ed. Klaus Wagenbach, Fischer Bücherei 455 (1962) 132f. Stefan Andres, *Der Mann im Fisch* (novel, 1963). Klaus Peter Hertzsch, *Wie schön war die Stadt Nineve* (n.d.) 55-69 = *Der ganze Fisch war voll Gesang* (1969) 50-64.

14. *Jonah in Music; Oratorios and Cantatas:* Giacomo Carissini (1605-74), *Jona* (oratorio, rev. Ferdinand Hiller). Giovanni Battista Bassano, *Giona* (oratorio, 1689). Giovanni Battista Vitali (1644-1692), *Giona* (oratorio). Pasquale Anfossi (1727-1797), *Nineve Conversa* (oratorio). Lennox Berkeley, *Jonah* (oratorio, 1935). Hugo Chaim Adler, *Jonah* (cantata, 1943). Mario Castelnuovo-Tedesco, *Jonah* (oratorio, 1951). Vladimir Voegel, *Jona ging doch nach Nineve* (oratorio, 1958). B. Bayer, *EJ* 10 (1971) 176f. and the literature there cited.

The Strain
of Disobedience

Literature

S. D. Goitein, "Some Observations on Jonah," *JPOS* 17 (1937) 63-77. D. Harden, *The Phoenicians* (1962). M. Weiss, "Einiges über die Bauformen des Erzählens in der Bibel," *VT* 13 (1963) 456-475. M. Weippert, "Archäologischer Jahresbericht," *ZDPV* 80 (1964) 150-193. G. Garbini, "Tarsis e Gen 10,4," *BeO* 6 (1964) 13-19. J. M. Blazquez, *Tartessos y los origenes de la colonizacion fenicia en occidente* (1968). W. T. In der Smitten, "Zu Jona 1,2," *ZAW* 84 (1972) 95. K. Galling, "Der Weg der Phöniker nach Tarsis," *ZDPV* 88 (1972) 1-18, 140-181.

Text

1:1 Now it once happened[a] that Yahweh's word came to Jonah, Amittai's son. It ran:

2 "Set out, go to Nineveh, the great city, and preach[a] against it. Because[b] their wickedness[c] has risen up to me."

3 Then Jonah set out to flee to Tarshish,[a] away from Yahweh.[b] He went down to Joppa, found a ship that was going to Tarshish,[a] paid the price of it, and went on board, in order to go with them to Tarshish,[a] away from Yahweh.[b]

1a It is in this sense ויהי should be understood as opening phrase at the beginning of stories: cf. Josh. 1:1; Judg. 1:1; 13:2; 17:1; 19:1; 1 Sam. 1:1; 2 Sam. 1:1; Ruth 1:1; Esther 1:1. See also Meyer 3^3 §100 3b; W. Schneider, *Grammatik des biblischen Hebräisch* (1974) §54.2.2.1; also L. Schmidt, *De Deo,* 70f.

2a In der Smitten's proposed translation, "Cry out to it" seems unjustified.

2b It is more probable that here כי ("because") is introducing a causal clause (Vg *quia*) rather than an object clause ("that their wickedness has risen up to me"), firstly because this is not the message which Jonah is supposed to convey according to 3:4, and secondly because this conversation between Yahweh and Jonah about Nineveh fits in better with the theme of the book (cf. pp. 175f. below on 4:1ff.)

2c Gk reads ἡ κραυγὴ τῆς κακίας αὐτῆς "the crying of her wickedness," correctly understanding רעתם as meaning the wickedness of the Ninevites and not the disaster threatening them (Goiten's view, p. 72).

3a Targ לימא . . . בימא . . . לימא = "to sea") does not seem to know the name of the destination, either here or in Ezek. 27:12, 25 and frequently; but the name is given in Gen. 10:4.

3b Targ twice interprets מן קדם דיתנבי בשמא דיוי = "away from prophesying in God's name."

Form

The exciting compression of this opening scene leaves the reader breathless. Hardly has Yahweh given his commission to Jonah when it seems already doomed to failure — as far as Jonah's own intention is concerned. But according to the deliberate artistic shaping of the narrator, it is just this that leaves everything open. The history of Yahweh's dealings with the man who refuses to do what his God commands is only beginning. Formally speaking, *the self-contained compression* of the scene is shown in the balance between the utterance of Yahweh's word at the beginning (v. 1) and the reiterated "away from Yahweh" at the end (v. 3a,b). But at the same time the passage acts as an *exposition* opening the story. It presents the different arenas in which the scenes that follow are set: The Tarshish ship (cf. 1:4-16) and the city of Nineveh (3:3b-10), together with the people belonging to them (3rd person plural suffix in 2b [רעתם] and 3b [עמהם]), with whom Jonah is to be involved. But above all it brings out the main problem and prompts the reader to ask what is going to be the outcome of Yahweh's charge to Jonah, in view of his flight (cf. 2:1-3, 3a; 4:1-11). But as the problem forming the main thread of the story, it is presented at the beginning in narrative form, not in intellectual abstraction.

Stylistically, the passage falls into two parts. In vv. 1f. a single narrative verb (in the imperfect consecutive) introduces the divine saying that triggers off everything that follows (v. 1). The saying itself is expressed in direct speech with three imperatives (v. 2a) and a clause of reason (v. 2b; see pp.99-100 below). This solemn opening is followed in v. 3 by a series of five verbs in consecutive form, all of which have Jonah as subject. They report five wordless actions which follow one another with increasing rapidity, calm only returning with the last of the five. The clauses consist of six, two, four, two, and seven words respectively. In the first and last of these clauses, an infinitive with ל indicates the "purpose" character of the acts; this is foreshortened narrative. In both cases the goal is described in the same terms: "to get away from Yahweh." The repetition in the purpose clauses precisely emphasizes the problem: what is going to be the end of it all? So by way of the double declaration of intent, the silent acts become the response to Yahweh's word ("experienced speech"; cf. M. Weiss, pp. 461f., 464f.). And in the reader they evoke tense anticipation of what is to come.

Does the exposition already reveal the particular *genre* of this prose narrative? The introduction of different arenas for the action, together with different groups of actors, certainly makes the reader expect several scenes. But these scenes may be expected to concentrate on the tension between the explicit divine saying (vv. 1f.) and its human contradiction (v. 3), and to confine themselves to this. In this light, what is being heralded here is a problem novella. We may also notice that the divine command is furnished with a justification and that the reason for the human reaction is explained; that, furthermore, there is no sign of any historical interest (no period of history is in any way indicated); that Nineveh is described in the vaguest and most general terms ("great," "wicked," v. 2); and that Jonah's intention is outlined in quite basic categories ("away from Yahweh," v. 3a,b). In view of all this, we may take it that there is a didactic component in the story; and, in spite of all the narrative skill, we will see that entertainment is being pressed into the service of the elucidation of a problem, in which the reader himself can feel involved.

Yet even here the didacticism already takes a special form. Does not Jonah's overzealous activity in v. 3 have an almost comic effect, especially since his purpose — as he himself well knows (1:9) — cannot hope to succeed? In particular, does not the formulation that he "paid its price" (the price of the ship!) sound somewhat ironic? So, all in all, we should most probably look for *a satirical novella with a didactic purpose* (cf. M. Burrows, *Category*, 80-107).

Setting

Yet we still have to await the continuation. For when all is said and done, the first scene has no separate function of its own. It acts as preparation for the story as a whole. Varied though the raw material for the following scenes is, this material is all already gathered together in *the literary setting* of the opening scene. Apart from the general problem of Yahweh and Jonah, every scene is furnished with at least one catchword: the "great city," which belongs to 3:2a, 3b (cf. 4:11); the "flight from Yahweh" (belonging to 1:10; 4:2); "the ship" (from 1:5) and the commission of 1:1-2a, which is later repeated in 3:1-2a.

If we try to discover where the writer came from, we may notice that he is silent about Gath-hepher (Jonah's home, according to 2 Kings 14:25), which is in the Galilean mountains (see p. 102 below); but he mentions Joppa (v. 3b), the port most easily accessible from *Jerusalem,* though certainly not from Gath-hepher. In considering the author's period, it is worth mentioning that Tarshish ships are hardly mentioned at all in any securely datable texts earlier than Ezekiel (see p. 101 below), and that the formula for the confronting event of God's word (v. 1) also only becomes current coin from the sixth century onwards (see Wolff, *Joel/Amos* [Eng., *Joel and Amos]*).

Commentary

[1:1] The opening, which uses the phraseology of the formula for the confronting event of God's word, is certainly directly reminiscent of the vocabulary used in numerous title of collections of prophetic sayings (Hos. 1:1; Joel 1:1; Mic. 1:1; Zeph. 1:1; cf. Hag. 1:1; Zech. 1:1; see also J. D. Smart). But the difference is not merely that all of these (except Joel 1:1) offer more than simply the name of the prophet and his father. The essential distinction is that what we have here is

not a heading for prophetic sayings at all (דבר יהוה אשר היה אל "the word of Yahweh that came to . . .''); it is the phrase introducing a prose narrative. In its choice
of words and its structure it strikingly resembles the Elijah narratives, four of
whose individual fragments begin in exactly the same way: ויהי דבר־יהוה
אל . . . לאמר (קום לך) ("Now it once happened that . . . .''; 1 Kings 17:2f., 8f.
[18:1]; 21:17f. [28]). Jeremiah passages, such as 1:11, 13; 2:1f; 13:3f., begin
similarly. As we shall see, chap. 4 is even closer to the Elijah traditions (see p.
168 below), and chap. 3 to traditions about Jeremiah (see pp. 145f. below). But
even at this early point our narrator's literary and theological models become evident. (For detail about the formula for the confronting event of God's word, cf.
Zimmerli, *Ezechiel*, 88f. [Eng., *Ezekiel*].)

Who is Jonah? By calling him "Amittai's son,'' the narrator clearly
identifies him with the prophet from Gath-Hepher who, according to 2 Kings
14:25, was active as prophet of salvation in the Northern Kingdom of Israel under
Jeroboam II (787-747). The identification is plain, since the two names are found
only in these two Old Testament passages.

But why should he of all people be made the hero of this didactic and satirical novella? At the time of the neo-Assyrian empire, the historical Jonah had proclaimed to King Jeroboam—on the basis of Yahweh's compasssion upon Israel
(2 Kings 14:26)—that, in spite of his wickedness (v. 24) the ancient frontiers
would be restored (v. 25); and this then actually came about as a result of victorious wars (cf. vv. 25 and 28). These memoranda in 2 Kings 14:23-29 will have
been known to our postexilic writer. An Israelite prophet of salvation fitted his
story, for any such prophet was already per se a prophet of judgment for Israel's
enemies. He also knew that in the eighth century Assyria was Israel's chief enemy
(2 Kings 15:19f. and frequently elsewhere) and that Nineveh was Assyria's capital (see p. 99 below). Whether the relationship between divine pity and human
wickedness had already occupied his thoughts, as a consequence of the eighth-
century traditions (cf. 2 Kings 14:24) is something we cannot prove; but it may
well be deducible from the relationship between 3:8-10 and the Jeremiah traditions (see p. 153 below). As a typical prophet of salvation belonging to the time of
the long-past Assyrian hegemony, Jonah ben Amittai sufficed him; the name provided a peg on which to hang his didactic narrative. The less that was generally
known about the prophet, the more freely the author could tell his story. Other
postexilic writers chose the righteous Job or the wise Daniel as "heroes'' for their
stories in a similar way (cf. Ezek. 14:14; 28:3 with Job 1f.; Daniel 1ff.).

The satirist may also have found the name Jonah particularly suitable. Jonah means "dove.''[1] The names of about 40 different animals are applied to, or
associated with, human beings in the Old Testament. Most of them are not very
flattering nicknames, e.g., flea (Neh. 10:14 and frequently, cf. 1 Sam. 24:15),

---

1. Jonah is often associated with a dove in Christian art. A grave slab in Rome (in the Department of
Christian Art in the Lateran Museum) shows a dove hovering over the sea-dragon which is vomiting
Jonah up. On a sarcophagus fragment a dove is sitting on the foliage of the gourd under which Jonah is
lying (see pp. 170f. below). The Gebhard Bible (ca. 1100 A.D.) paraphrases the name Jonah as *colum-
ba pulcherrima*, "most beautiful dove'' (quoted in U. Steffen, *Mysterium*, 110, and F. Sühling, "Die
Taube als religiöses Symbol im christlichen Altertum,'' *RQ* 24 (1930) 234ff.

swine (1 Chron. 24:15; Neh. 10:20; Prov. 11:22), or mole (1 Chron. 11:30 cj. חֹלֶד and 2 Kings 22:14 חֻלְדָּה, the prophetess Hulda!); cf. Noth, *Personennamen* 229f. Hosea already compared his people with a dove (7:11): "Ephraim is like a dove, silly and without sense, calling to Egypt, going to Assyria." Jonah is just the same: he is supposed to go to Nineveh; he wants to go to Tarshish. Later Israel is often compared with a dove, for example in Targum Song of Sol. 2:14 or b. Shab. 130a (cf. G. A. F. Knight, *Ruth and Jonah*, 1956[2], 90f.). Other stories comparable from a literary point of view are quite clearly interested in the meaning of names. For example, in the little book of Ruth, Orpah (1:4, 14) means "the shrew," Mahlon means "the sickly one," and Chilion "the one who is infirm" (1:2, 5). The name Job itself probably means "the one to whom hostility is shown," and his three daughters are called "little dove," "cinnamon flower," and "cosmetics box" (42:14). Daniel means "God is judge." Like almost all these other names, Amittai only occurs once; it is probably "the abbreviation of a name built up by way of a nominal clause formed with אֱמֶת" (M. Noth, *Personennamen* 162), a name which is an acknowledgment of Yahweh's faithfulness. Our didactic writer would like the name itself to hint that his "hero" is fickle and capricious (like the dove Israel in Hos. 7:11), but that he is nonetheless a son of Yahweh's faithfulness. This is all the more possible since the writer does not expend so much as a single syllable on the period of the historical Jonah, on his home, or even on his occupation. When Jonah is later specifically asked about the commission he has been given (1:8), it is noticeable that he merely calls himself "a Hebrew" (1:9). So from the very beginning the reader is given hardly any chance to take up a detached attitude. (Cf. J. D. Magonet, *Form and Meaning* 209f.) Jonah as prophet and Jonah as a typical representative of Israel can hardly be separated from one another in the story.

[1:2]   This is also true if we consider the particular charge he is given. Nineveh has been stripped of every historical feature. It is presented as the archetype of "the great city" (Gen. 10:11f.; cf. Jdt. 1:1). For a more detailed discussion of its size, cf. the comments on 3:3b. It is of no particular interest to the narrator that for a single traveler on foot, the city lay unattainably far from Israel, on the east bank of the Tigris, further north even than the Great Zab River, opposite today's Al-Mawsil (Mosul). Its special importance as capital of the neo-Assyrian empire does not seem to be precisely known to the writer either; for at the time of the historical Jonah, Nineveh was not the capital at all. Ashurnasirpal II and Shalmaneser III had held court there for a time in the 9th century (cf. Weissbach, *RLA* 1: 218), but the city was only built up and fortified as imperial capital by Sennacherib, after 705. In 612 the city was destroyed by the Medes and Babylonians and never rebuilt. It was just because for him it belonged to the remote and primeval past that Nineveh seemed to our narrator to offer a suitable didactic example (see the comments on 3:6f.). Whereas all geographical and historical details are lacking, we are clearly told (though in sufficiently general terms) what makes the city a universal example: *the wickedness* of the people living in it. This is indicated by the 3rd person plural suffix (Gk αὐτῆς and Vg *eius* are grammatically congruent but less precise in their reference). Here the narrator could play on Israel's own historical memories, which recorded the neo-Assyrian power as being incomparably more brutal than the empires that followed, evoking terror and abhorrence (cf. Nah. 2:12-14; 3:1ff.; Nah. 3:19 also sums up the judgment in the word רעה ["evil"]; see below on 3:8). What is important is not any individual characteristic. The thing that matters is what continually recurs, in the present and in the future.

Jonah is to take the field "against" this great and dangerous Nineveh through his preaching. The Gk text translates here, as in 3:2 (אליה), κήρυξον ἐν αὐτῇ, "preach in her"; but the clause of reason that follows makes it seem probable that here the preposition על also implies opposition ("against"; cf. BrSynt §100b). On the other hand, this preposition gives extra force to the assumption that the following clause is not giving the substance of the message (see textual note to 2b) although Gk presupposes this in 3:2 (τὸ κήρυγμα τὸ ἔμπροσθεν ὃ ἐγὼ ἐλάλησα πρὸς σέ). Moreover, in the book of Jonah קרא ("cry") never by itself introduces direct or indirect speech; cf. 1:14; 3:2, 4). The causal clause is in accord with the narrator's general trend; for in the story Yahweh is more interested in Jonah than in Nineveh. Jonah is initially supposed to know only why he has to go to Nineveh. The fact that the wickedness of the Ninevites leaps to Yahweh's eye quite directly (similarly Lam. 1:22), and not merely (as in earlier texts) by way of a mediating cry that goes up from it (cf. Gen. 4:10; 18:21; 1 Sam. 5:13 and here Gk, see textual note to 2c) indicates Yahweh's intimate closeness to human beings in this novella. (The picture in Job 1f. is very different.)

[1:3] Jonah's commission is unambiguous, great, and full of danger. His response is both understandable and unusual. It is bound to rouse intense suspense in the reader; for he knows from the stories passed down about the prophets that the reaction to Yahweh's "Arise and go!" (קום לך) is simply "And he arose and went" (ויקם וילך; 1 Kings 17:10; cf. Jer. 13:5). It is true that Jonah also sets out (ויקם), just as we expect. But we are immediately shocked by his intention "to flee." And the actual goal enjoined on him, Nineveh, is at once three times contrasted with the actual goal of his flight, Tarshish. It is characteristic of the purposeful, ongoing narrative of our writer that he should report the intention immediately in the very first sentence (v. 3a); it is only afterwards, in four further clauses (v. 3b) that he describes the way in which Jonah tries to implement that intention. The reader is supposed to associate Tarshish with the notion of remotest distance — and a distance in the very opposite direction from Nineveh. Perhaps he is even supposed to have in mind the idea that knowledge of Yahweh has never penetrated to these remote parts; cf. Isa. 66:19.

Excursus: Tarshish

In both Gen. 10:4 and an inscription of Esarhaddon's (681-669; *ANET* 290, *Tar-si-si*) Cyprus and Tarshish are mentioned in a single breath (cf. C. Westermann, *Genesis 1-11*, 507f.). But it would not be admissible to deduce from this that Tarshish is to be identified with Tarsus in Cilicia, Asia Minor (Josephus, *Ant.* 9.10.2; G. Garbini). One factor that speaks especially against this identification is that in cuneiform script Tarsus is written differently *(Ta-ar-zu)* from Tarshish *(Tar-si-si)*. The juxtaposition of Tarshish and Cyprus points rather to the eastern and western Greek colonies in the Mediterranean world (cf. "sons of Javan" in Gen. 10:4). In *ANET* (290) the Esarhaddon text is not translated in full at the decisive point. It may be found in its correct form in R. Borger, *Die Inschriften Asarhaddons, AfO* Beiheft 9 (1956) pl. 1 and p. 78. The inscription runs, in English translation: "The kings [of the islands] in the midst of the sea are all of them, from Yadanana [and] Yaman, as far as Tar-si-si, beneath my feet." Here, that is to say, "the land of the Ionians" is mentioned between Cyprus (Yadanana) and Tarsisi. According to this, we ought to look for Tarshish west of that. K. H. Deller, to whom I am indebted for the translation of the inscription* and for detailed information about the cuneiform texts, thinks that a place in Spain is improbable. The "Spanish" solution is maintained by, among others (see below) P. Cintas, "Tarsis — Tartessos — Gadès," *Sem* 16 (1966) 5-37 (34). Cf. J. M. Blazques, pp. 16f.

Tarsus would have been reachable by a coastal vessel. The Tarshish ships are deep-sea vessels, which reach the furthest shores (cf. Ps. 72:10 and Isa. 60:9, as well as Isa. 66:19). But then we may perhaps think of Tartessos (Ταρτησσός), an Iberian foundation and later Greek colony in southwest Spain, at the mouth of the Guadalquivir, already mentioned by Herodotos (1:163). On the identity of Tarshish and Tartessos cf. A. Schulten, *Tartessos* (1950²) 25-30. On the precise site, probably a few miles north of the Baetis (i.e., Guadalquivir) estuary, see Schulten, 155-176; also J. M. Blazquez, 226-231. Tarshish is the destination of long voyages made not only by warships but by merchant vessels as well. As trading city (Ezek. 38:13), especially for silver, iron, tin, and lead (Jer. 10:9; Ezek. 27:12), Tarshish was familiar in Israel as well, probably through the intermediary of Phoenician Tyrians (Isa. 23:1, 6, 10, 14; Ezek. 27:25ff.). Other attempts at a localization accord less well with the Old Testament references to Tarshish; W. F. Albright, "New Light on the Early History of Phoenician Colonization," *BASOR* 83 (1941) 14-22 (21f.), thinks of Sardinia; a contrary view is taken by G. Garbini, H. Wildberger *(Jesaja 1-12,* BK 10/1, 110f.) and J. Lindblom, *ASTI* 4 (1965) 60f. B. *B. Bat.*38a and 39a calculates that a full year is necessary for a voyage to Spain. It is a place as extremely remote as this which the narrator has in mind. That is why the Tarshish ships supply all kinds of exotic rareties: 1 Kings 10:22 lists not only precious metals but also ivory (elephants' tusks), apes, and baboons; cf. M. Noth, *Könige I 1-16,* BK 9/1, 232f. Certainly, what is thought of here is in the first place Solomon's ocean-going ships, bound for foreign climes, which put out into the Indian Ocean — evidence of the fact that "Tarshish ships" had become the usual term for deep-sea vessels in general; cf. also 1 Kings 22:49. In Jonah's case we should think of a merchant ship — a "round" ship, as distinct from the "long" ships used for war; cf. Herodotos 1.163, where he talks about "round merchant ships" as well as the quinquerimes, the 50-oar ships; also reliefs in Karatepe and in Nineveh (mound of Kouyunjik) showing the deep-sea fleet belonging to King Luli of Sidon, where the ships depicted are furnished with both sails and oars ("Ruder-Segler," *BRL* 456; cf. D. Harden, p. 169 and plate 50; M. Weipert, 162, with the further literature there cited). In the Old Testament,

---

*I.e., into German (translator).

Tarshish ships are mentioned with any frequency only in exilic and postexilic times (Ezek. 27:25; Isa. 23:1-14; 60:9); 1 Kings 10:22 probably also goes back to narrative material current in the Deuteronomistic period (M. Noth, *Könige I 1-16*, BK 9/1, 208; cf. 1 Kings 22:49). Isaiah 2:16 and Ps. 48:7 may well be older.

In order to reach a Tarshish ship, Jonah goes to Joppa, which lies north-west of Jerusalem. (It is now the district of Tel Aviv called Jaffa.) We are not told where he came from. Gath-hepher, the hometown mentioned in 2 Kings 14:25, would suggest that the harbor of Tyre would have been a more probable destination, since Tyre was famous for its Tarshish ships (Ezek. 27:25ff.; Isa. 23:1ff.). But for the storyteller and his readers in Judah, Joppa was no doubt a better-known port, for it was here that cedarwood for Jerusalem was unloaded after it had been brought in by sea from Lebanon (Ezra 3:7; 2 Chron. 2:15). The only other mention of Joppa is in Josh. 19:46, where it is not an Israelite port at all. According to the so-called Taylor prism of Senacherib, in 701 the town belonged to the Philistine state of Ashkelon *(AOT* 353; *ANET* 287; *Von Sinuhe bis Nebukadnezar,* ed. A. Jepsen [1975] 174). This fact also speaks against any attempt to turn our novella into a historical work. Joppa suggested itself to the narrator because it was a place where sea stories were passed on by word of mouth — stories which he drew upon for the story that follows. For example, Pseudo-Skylax *(Geographi Graeci Minores* 1 [1855] 79) and Strabo (16.2.28 [C 759]) provide us with evidence that an offshoot of the Perseus and Andromeda saga was being told in Joppa in the 4th century. Even at that time there was a dispute about the location of the saga, some people believing that it had its setting in Ethiopia, i.e., on the Indian Ocean. On the history of the name Ethiopia and its connection with the coast of the Eritrean sea, cf. A. Dihle, "Umstrittene Daten," WAAFLNW 32 (1965) 65-79; on the subject itself, cf. H. W. Wolff, *Studien* 26ff.; M. Avi, "Jonah, Perseus and Andromeda at Joppa"(in Hebrew), *Yediot* 31 (1967) 203-210. More recent excavations have provided evidence that after the second half of the 5th century Joppa enjoyed an economic heyday and expansion. Pottery findings show that the city had trading connections with all the countries along the Mediterranean; cf. J. Kaplan, *The Archeology and History of Tel Aviv-Jaffa, BA* 35 (1972) 66-95, esp. 87.

Jonah's "descent" to Joppa is quickly followed by his finding of the ship, his payment of the price, and then his "descent" into the ship. The repeated וירד ("and went down") may be intended to stress the "descent," especially since a third ירד is to follow in v. 5b (cf. 2:6). (Gk distinguishes in v. 3b, using two different words, κατέβη ["went down]" and ἐνέβη ["embarked"], reverting to κατέβη in v. 5b.) The cost of a long voyage as far as the Straits of Gibraltar and beyond, and lasting almost a year, will have been no small matter. The obedient Elijah was looked after by his God even in time of drought (1 Kings 17:1-6); the disobedient messenger must pay dearly for his flight all by himself. The 3rd person feminine suffix in שְׂכָרָהּ has in this context to be related to the immediately preceding אָנִיָּה; in this way the impression is ironically conveyed that Jonah had to pay the price of the whole ship. The aim of his journey is reiterated at the end of v. 3b: "to escape from the face of Yahweh." Does this mean Yahweh's sphere of power? The idea that this was restricted to Israelite territory (1 Sam. 26:19; 2

Kings 5:17), or that it at least did not include "the furthest seas," is certainly not shared by the narrator, who believes that Yahweh has sole jurisdiction, even in Nineveh (v. 2). It can only be in irony that he imputes this notion to Jonah (cf. v. 9 and Ps. 139:9). We must interpret ברח/בוא מלפני יהוה ("to flee from the face of Yahweh") to mean that it was Jonah's declared intention to escape from Yahweh's service. The phrase is used in contrast to the phrase familiar from the Elijah and Jeremiah traditions, עמד לפני "to stand before" God (1 Kings 17:1; 18:15; Jer. 15:19; cf. 2 Kings 3:14; 5:16; and W. Rudolph's comment on this passage). The wordless abrogation of prophetic obedience, with the unattainable purpose of escaping Yahweh's grasp, can only be understood as the opening of a satire.

Purpose

The narrator has achieved the purpose of this exposition if he has made the reader ask himself how Yahweh is going to proceed. He has certainly no wish to see this question narrowed down to the problem of how Yahweh will prove his power over against Jonah's plan to flee (Ludwig Schmidt's view: *De Deo* 72). This opening scene certainly already makes it clear that the real subject of the story is Yahweh; for his word and his name begin and end the passage. Yet for that very reason the reader does not merely ask what the result of Jonah's disobedience is going to be. He asks at the same time about the future of Yahweh's commission. The tension between Yahweh and Jonah emerges as the main theme; but the motifs that drive it forward are to be found in the relationship to Nineveh, and to the ship's crew as well. So the reader looks ahead: what is going to happen to the charge Yahweh has given for Nineveh, now that Jonah has evaded it by taking passage with the crew of the Tarshish ship?

Jonah is presented as a person faced with the divine claim; Nineveh is shown as pattern example of the great and wicked world; and Tarshish is the place that symbolizes remoteness from God. Since all historical details are lacking, and since Nineveh and Tarshish will have been as familiar to the story's first readers as Moscow and New York to readers today, we may deduce that — by permitting no more detachment than is offered by a mirror held in front of one's own face — the narrator is throwing down a challenge to the vacillating faith of particular devout groups.

The Missionary Fruits
of a Flight from God

Literature

D. N. Freedman, "Jonah 1:4b," *JBL* 77 (1958) 161-162. J. Lindblom, "Lot-Casting in the Old Testament," *VT* 12 (1962) 164-178. D. K. Andrews, "Yahwe the God of the Heavens: The Seed of Wisdom," *Fests. T. J. Meek* (1964) 45-57. M. Weiss, "Weiteres über die Bauformen des Erzählens in der Bibel," *Bibl* 46 (1965) 181-206. R. Pesch, "Zur konzentrischen Struktur von Jona 1," *Bibl* 47 (1966) 577-581. M. Wagner, *Die lexikalischen und grammatikalischen Aramaismen im alttestamentlichen Hebräisch*," *ZAW* Beiheft 96 (1966). M. Weippert, *Die Landnahme der israelitischen Stämme*, FRLANT 92 (1967). W. J. Hornitz, "Another Interpretation of Jonah I 12," *VT* 23 (1973) 370-372. L. C. Allen, *The Greek Chronicles*, *VT* Suppl. 27 (1974).

Text

1:4 Then Yahweh threw a (great)[a] wind upon the sea, so that[b] great waves sprang up in the sea. When[c] the ship threatened[d] to break up,[e]

5 the seamen became afraid. Each of them cried to his god. They threw the cargo[a] which was in the ship into the sea, in order to lighten the vessel. But Jonah had gone down[b] to the lowest part[c] of the ship,[d] had lain down, and was fast asleep[e]

6 when[a] the captain[b] came and said to him: "How can you sleep! Get up! Call to your god! Perhaps the god will concern himself[c] about us, so that we do not perish."

7 Then they said to one another: "Come! We will cast lots, so that we may discover on whose account[a] this evil has befallen us." They cast lots, and the lot fell on Jonah.

8 Then they said to him: "Just tell us [a](why this evil has befallen us,)[a] what your occupation is, where you come from, what your country is, and from what people you come."

9 He said to them: "I am a Hebrew[a] and I fear[b] Yahweh, the God of heaven, who made the sea and the dry land."

10 Then the men became exceedingly frightened and said to him: "What

have you done!"[a] For the men had discovered that he was fleeing, away from[b] Yahweh; [c]for he had told them so.[c]

11 They said to him: "What shall we do with you, so that[a] the sea leaves us in peace?" For the sea was raging more and more violently.[b]

12 He said to them: "Take me and throw me into the sea! Then the sea will leave you in peace. For I am certain that it is because of me[a] that this tremendous storm (is raging) over you."

13 But the men bent to their oars,[a] in order to reach land again, but they were not able to do so. For the sea was raging more and more violently against them.[b]

14 Then they called[a] to Yahweh and said: "O[b] Yahweh! Do not let us perish because of the life of this man, and do not burden us with blood that is shed unjustly.[c] For you are Yahweh; you do as it pleases you."

15 Then they took Jonah and threw him into the sea. Then the sea stopped roaring.[a]

16 So the men arrived at great fear before[a] Yahweh. They offered Yahweh[b] a sacrifice,[c] and made vows.

4a Gk πνεῦμα and Targ רוח (both, "wind") leave גדולה, "great," untranslated. Is the shorter text the original reading, or is it rather a later (secondary) intentional reminiscence of Gen. 1:2? σ´ supports MT.

4b After the series of events which are related in v. 3 in the imperfect consecutive (narrative form), the next imperfect consecutive appears in v. 4aβ as a result clause; in v. 4aα its presupposition is stressed as being such through inversion of the subject and the (emphatic) perfect; the subject (Yahweh) is emphasized through its position at the beginning. Cf. Gen. 4:1; 22:1 aβ, b; 36:2-4 and BrSynt §122m.

4c V. 4b acts as preliminary clause to the narrative verbs which follow in 5a (with inversion of the subject and verb in the perfect) in the same way as v. 4aα does to 4aβ; see textual note to v. 4b. The circumstance of the threatening shipwreck is the presupposition for the human reactions.

4d חשב *pi'el* ("threaten") is otherwise never used of lifeless things; but the same may be said of זעף ("to be angry") in v. 15. So this is not a sufficient reason for a conjectural emendation such as חבה (from חוב, D. N. Freedman's suggestion, on the model of Dan. 1:10), especially since any such emendation destroys the alliteration (חשבה להשבר). Gk ἐκινδύνευεν, Vg *periclitabatur*, "was in danger," and Targ בעיא, "was about to," give the same sense as MT.

4e Infinitive *niph'al*, literally "to be broken."

5a Literally "the containers," which initially meant the jars, amphorae, etc., which were used for transporting goods; but Gk, ἐκβολὴν ἐποιήσαντο τῶν σκευῶν ("they jettisoned the tackle") seems to have thought of parts of the ship's gear; cf. Acts 27:19 and 112 below.

5b The inverted perfect clause with pluperfect meaning in 5b draws Jonah into the events on board ship (v. 6) by first of all catching up with what he had done after 1:3.

5c Cf. Amos 6:10 and Wolff, *Joel/Amos*, BK 14/2, 328 (Eng., *Joel and Amos*).

5d The word for ship used in vv. 3, 4, 5a (אניה) is replaced here by ספינה, which is quite frequent in Aramaic but which appears only here in the Old Testament; it means the decked-in ship (ספן = "cover"; cf. M. Wagner, 88) and here probably more precisely the lower deck (Ehrlich 5:264; G. H. Cohn, "Jonah," 13). See 112-113 below.

5e Gk translates the word for a deep sleep (Gen. 2:21; Judg. 4:21; Job 4:13) freely as ἔρρεγχεν, "he was snoring."

6a See textual note to 1:5b.

6b Literally, "the head of the crew"; Targ רב ספניא "the captain of the ship"; Gk πρῳρεύς, Vg *gubernator,* "helmsman" or "mate." But חֹבֵל means the sailor who ties together (II חבל) the ship's ropes (חֶבֶל). Like מַלָּח ("seaman," v. 5) the word occurs only in this passage and in Ezek. 27:8f., 27-29.

6c עשׁת *hithpa'el* is an Aramaism (cf. Dan. 6:4 and M. Wagner, 93: "show himself mindful"); Gk διασώσῃ, "save," Targ יתרחם, "have mercy," interpret freely, whereas Vg *recogitet,* "think again," is an accurate rendering of the sense of the word.

7a The form consists of four elements: the preposition בְּ, the relative pronoun שֶׁ, the preposition לְ, and the interrogative pronoun מִי. The relative pronoun שֶׁ is proto-Semitic, and in Hebrew was largely superseded by אֲשֶׁר (cf. 1:8); it only came into frequent use once more under Aramaic influence (also in 4:10); cf. M. Wagner, pp. 110f. The preposition לְ is inserted before the following pronominal suffix (cf. 1:12) and before interrogative pronouns (cf. Song of Sol. 1:7), as here.

8a-a V. 8aβ is a secondary interpolation; it is missing in MT^MSS Gk^BSV and frequently elsewhere; the lot has already supplied the answer to the question (v. 7, W. Rudolph). As prefix to the four terse questions that follow, it is both clumsy and superfluous. (For a different view cf. R. Pesch, 579.) The addition probably derives from a marginal gloss to v. 7aα, designed to replace the relative pronoun שֶׁ by אשׁר (see textual note to 7a above) and later absorbed into the text from the margin, but at the wrong point. Targ בדיל מא, presupposes בַּאֲשֶׁר לָמָה; i.e., it asks "why?" not "who?" which — since the person has already been determined through the lot — makes better sense.

9a Gk δοῦλος κυρίου ("servant of the Lord") misreads the ר in the word עברי, "Hebrew," as ד and interprets י as an abbreviation of the Tetragrammaton (עֶבֶד יהוה = "Yahweh's servant"); cf. L. C. Allen, 81). Targ יהודאה, "Judean," and Vg *Hebraeus* confirm MT.

9b The noun clause with participial predicate is to be understood as "durative present," representing something firm and abiding; cf. Ges-K §140e; Joüon, *Gr* §121c; Meyer³ 3 §104,2b.

10a Frequent expression of aghast questioning about a culpable event (neuter demonstrative pronoun, זֹאת "this" or "that"; cf. Gen. 3:13); an answer is not necessarily expected (cf. Gen. 12:18; 26:10).

10b Targ interprets as in 1:3; see textual note to v. 3b above.

10c-c The consensus in the transmission does not make an elimination of the final clause justifiable (as proposed by Wellhausen, Bewer, Nowack, BHS, and others), even though a third כִּי clause in v. 10b is stylistically unpleasing.

11a Here the imperfect of consequence (with ו copula), as already in 1:6bβ, 7aβ and in v. 12aβ, shows the forward-thrusting style, which heightens the tension (Ges-K §165a).

11b הלך, active participle of "go," as relative verb with adverbial function, expresses the continued heightening of the activity described through the second participle; cf. Ges-K §113u; BrSynt §93g and Exod. 19:19; 1 Sam. 17:41; 2 Sam. 3:1.

12a See textual note to v. 7a above.

13a Literally, "bored through" i.e., they tried to work their way through the waves with their oars.

13b See textual note to v. 11b above.

14a Gk ἀνεβόησαν and Vg *clamaverunt* translate קרא here and in 3:8 "cry," just as they do זעק in 1:5; but in 1:6 they take ἐπικαλοῦ and *invoca* respectively ("call upon").

14b The call is compounded of the cry of elemental terror אָה as opening of the complaint; see H. W. Wolff, *Joel/Amos,* BK 14/2, 25 (Eng., *Joel and Amos)* and the emphatic particle נָא (cf. E. Jenni, *THAT* 1:73f.; less probable: אַל + נָא = "don't!"; but see Gk μηδαμῶς (literally, "by no means!"). Targ קביל בעותנא paraphrases "hear our plea!"; similarly Vg *quaesumus.*

14c This and Joel 3:19 are the only occasions in the Old Testament when נקיא is written with א -metatheticum, the purpose of which is to show that the preceding י is to be read as a vowel letter (frequent in Qumran). On the translation see p. 120 below.

15a Literally, "Then the sea stood away from its raging." On עמד מן in the sense of "cease," cf. Gen. 29:35; 30:9; also textual note on 1:4e.

16a After the "inner object" the "external object" is introduced with the accusative.

16b In Gk^s ליהוה (the divine name) was originally untranslated.

16c Targ ואמרו לדבחא דיבח expands: "they promised to make sacrifices," because this seemed possible only after the return to land.

Form

With v. 4 a new scene opens. Now the place of action is the ship on the high seas, and new actors appear on the stage: the sailors. Both scene and dramatis personae take us up to v. 16. But the narrator makes a clear link with the scene that opened the story. The new intervention represented by Yahweh's action (v. 4a) can only be understood as response to Jonah's attempted flight; and, in the same way, the narrator presupposes that v. 3b has already made us familiar with the ship mentioned in v. 4b. Verse 10b picks up word for word the motive prompting Jonah's voyage, which has already been stressed in v. 3b: מלפני יהוה (ברח), "to get away from Yahweh." Here the problem of guilt already indicated in vv. 1-3 is developed further, as it has been from v. 7 onwards; and it is followed up more directly still in what follows (vv. 12, 14). It finds its provisional solution when Jonah is thrown into the sea (v. 15a). But this is simultaneously the preparation for a further scene; for the reader is bound to ask: what is going to happen to Jonah, and to the commission he was given in 1:2?

But before a third scene begins (2:1ff.) the scene on board ship is completed, first of all, in a way which displays to the full the stylistic skill of the writer. For after Jonah has gone overboard (v. 15a), so that his appearance on the scene (introduced in v. 5b) has been wound up, the fate of the sailors and their behavior is described in a brief final tableau (vv. 15b-16). In this way the conclusion of the scene is made to correspond precisely to its brief opening (vv. 4-5a). Yet the correspondence also outlines a great change. In v. 4 Yahweh hurls the storm on to the sea; in v. 15b the sea quiets down. In v. 5a the sailors are frightened and cry to their gods; in v. 16 they come to fear Yahweh greatly and bring him thank offerings and vows. In the scene's great central section (vv. 5b-15a) it is not Yahweh who confronts the sailors, as in the "frame" section — it is Jonah; and it is in this section that the cause of the great transformation is presented. And here at the center is Jonah's acknowledgment in v. 9, in which we find the three key words of the frame scenes: Yahweh, fear (of him), and the sea. Yet another catchword links the central section with the opening scene: טול *hiph'il,* "throw." After Yahweh "threw" the storm on to the sea (v. 4), the sailors first of all vainly "threw" cargo overboard (v. 5a); it is only after Jonah has demanded that they "throw" him into the sea that they actually make the "throw" which calms the sea (v. 15).

His *purposeful drive* does not allow the narrator any time to linger over a description. Just as already in v. 3, in vv. 5aβ and 13a purpose clauses (infinitive with ל) link actions directly with their intention; and in the same way imperfect verbs of result open up the perspective into the future (vv. 7a, 12a, cf. 6b and

14a). But it is above all questions which thrust the story so powerfully forward (vv. 6a, 7a, 8b, 10a, 11a). So the reader remains in a state of tense expectation.

This drive results in some lacunae in the action — points that are simply leapt over, as the story moves forward. For example, the reader never discovers whether Jonah makes the prayer demanded of him or not (v. 6), or whether he tells the sailors what his commission was, and where he came from (v. 8). The preeminent interest in the sequence of events described at any given moment, and especially their effect on the people involved, means that the storyteller has to go back and pick up happenings belonging to a previous point in time. For example, after the outbreak of the storm we are told about the effect on the sailors first of all (vv. 4- 5a). When Jonah is introduced into the scene, the narrator has first to add that he had meanwhile lain down to sleep (v. 5b). In such cases these "afterthoughts" are clearly indicated by inversion of the subject and the verb, which is in the perfect tense. In v. 10b we find a similar explanatory "afterthought" in the perfect tense, since here, after Jonah's acknowledgment in v. 9, the effect on the sailors is described for the first time only in v. 10a.

We should notice the difference between the flow of events and the flow of the narrative, if we want to see how the scenes are built up and shaped. On the one hand, Jonah's behavior in the ship is picked up in v. 5b, so that it can be incorporated (v. 6) into the stormy events on deck (vv. 4-5a); but then, from v. 15a, in a countermovement, the story divides into two different streams. After the seamen and Jonah separate, the story's purposeful sequence of events in vv. 5b-15a is first of all followed by two parallel happenings. In vv. 15b-16 Yahweh's history with the ship's heathen crew arrives at a happy and final end. This also completes the scene on board ship. What has meanwhile been happening to Jonah is reported only in a new scene, from 2:1 onwards. Yahweh's history with Jonah is by no means at an end.

The weaving together of the two strands (with v. 5b) and their subsequent separation (after v. 15a) shows the writer's architectural artistry. In addition, in this scene the genre novella displays some other particular characteristics. The throng of direct and indirect questions which we have already noticed (see p. 108 above) also has a didactic side. These questions emphasize the answers which are particularly important for the main theological problems in the novella — answers which explain the reason for the storm (v. 12) and thereby take on a direct didactic function for the heathen involved (v. 9). But this instruction is clothed in satire. How the narrator laughs at a Hebrew who takes great pains to flee from his God, and in the very process, and quite against his will, brings non- Israelites to believe in this God! How ludicrous he makes this good-for-nothing sleepyhead, in contrast to the crew, with their eager zeal to be saved! Here a piece of ironic protest literature has taken shape, aimed at an Israel which thinks it can evade its charge in the world.

Setting

There are no comparable models in the Old Testament. It is true that we occasionally hear about the "breaking" (שׁבר, cf. v. 4), or foundering, of Tarshish ships

(Ps. 48:7; 1 Kings 22:49 = 2 Chron. 20:37). But it is in only two texts that we find more than a single motif also belonging to Jonah 1: Psalm 107:23-32 mentions "ships" on "the sea" (v. 23; Jonah 1:4), the "sea storm" (רוּחַ סְעָרָה, v. 25; Jonah 1:4), the "crying out" of the petitioner (צעק, v. 28; זעק, Jonah 1:5) and the "coming to rest" of the sea (v. 30; Jonah 1:11f., שׁתק). Ezekiel 27:25-28 is somewhat closer still to our Jonah text. (On the expansion of the section belonging to the lament over Tyre [vv. 26, 28] by the prose text [vv. 25, 27] cf. W. Zimmerli, *Ezechiel,* BK 13/2 [1969] 634ff. [Eng., *Ezekiel: A Commentary,* vol. 2 (1979), commentary on 27:1-36: "Form"]). Here we find "the ships of Tarshish" (v. 25) which are "wrecked" by "the east wind" on "the high seas" (v. 26). In addition, the two groups of seamen, מַלָּחִים and חֹבְלִים, which are mentioned in Jonah 1:5f. also occur (v. 27), as well as their "crying out for help" (זעק, v. 28). It is noticeable that motifs and words also found in Psalm 107 and Ezekiel 27 appear only at the beginning of the scene. More particularly, the seamen are later no longer described in specialized terms, as they are in vv. 5f.; they are afterwards simply called "the men" (vv. 10ab, 13, 16). Another noticeable point is that, just when the danger of shipwreck is most acute, a question and answer game develops, as if the men concerned were meeting in an oasis (vv. 8ff.)! This may indeed be part of the satire with which the writer clothes his theological concern; but it is surely also related to the fact that experiences at sea were remote from the narrator's own experience, as they were for Israel as a whole. A quarrel on board ship occurs in the Greek saga about the musician Arion (ca. 620 B.C.). Sailors wanted to throw him overboard, so that they could seize his treasure. After cunning negotiations and threats of murder, Arion throws himself into the sea, in full minstrel's attire, but is saved by a dolphin (Herodotus 1.23f.; cf. H. Schmidt, *Jona* [1907] 98ff.). However, it is impossible to show that our writer has drawn directly on any other texts in or outside the Old Testament. He has picked up and freely adapted narrative material of the kind particularly likely to be current in a port like Joppa, but which had already been passed down in biblical texts.

    Some linguistic peculiarities point to the Persian period, in which "imperial Aramaic," the official language of the royal chancery, was widely used. It is true that we already find מלח (v. 5) and חבל (v. 6) in Ezekiel (27:8f., 27-29); but neither word is found anywhere else in the Old Testament. On the other hand מלח is frequent in Aramaic texts (cf. Jean and Hoftijzer, *DIS* 152; M. Wagner *Aramaismen* [1966] 76f.). חבל, "the tier of ropes," is only occasionally found in Phoenician texts (Jean and Hoftijzer, *DIS* 81). ספינה (v. 5), for a decked-in ship, is also a nonce use in the Old Testament, the usual word for ship being אניה, (which is frequent in Jonah as well [1:3, 4, 5]. On the other hand ספינה is widespread in Aramaic (cf. Jean and Hoftijzer, *DIS* 196; M. Wagner, p. 88). Wagner (p. 117) counts שׁתק (vv. 11f.), "become calm," among the Aramaisms; and in fact it may be found not merely in Old Aramaic *(KAI* 222, B, 8), but several times in imperial Aramaic as well (Jean and Hoftijzer, *DIS* 322; see p. 117 below). On עשׁת, "to remember someone, think of someone" (v. 6) cf. Wagner, p. 93. The repeatedly used relative pronoun שֶׁ in vv. 7, 12 (cf. 4:10) clearly points to Aramaic influence; comparable combinations with שֶׁ can be found mainly in the Song of

Solomon and Ecclesiastes (cf. Ges-K §36; Wagner, 110f.). All in all, therefore, this scene too can best be explained as belonging to the postexilic period.

Commentary

[1:4]   The exposition ended with emphasis on the repetition of Jonah's intention: "to get away from Yahweh." Now the new scene begins — in a counterstroke — with equal stress on the subject, which is placed in front of the verb for emphasis: "But Yahweh." The ship has long since reached the open sea (vv. 5, 13). But the narrator was not concerned to tell how it put out to sea from Joppa, and what arrangements Jonah made for himself. The most necessary points will be picked up later (v. 5b). It is not the course of events as such that is the narrator's guiding concern; it is the question about the relationship between God and human beings.

How does Yahweh react to Jonah's flight? He "throws" the wind on to the sea, just as Saul "throws" his javelin (טול *hiph'il* 1 Sam. 18:11; 20:33). What result does this have? The result is a סער־גדול. Here this cannot mean the storm of wind, as it generally does (Jer. 23:19; Ps. 83:15; cf. L. Schmidt, *De Deo* [1976] 65 n. 40). For in the first place the throwing of the wind and the rising of the סער are presented as cause and effect (see textual note on v. 4b). Secondly, the wind is thrown "onto the sea" (אל־הים), but the סער arises "in the sea" (בים). Thirdly, the verbal use of סער ("to rage" or "to be violent") in vv. 11b, 13b shows that the sea itself is the subject. Accordingly, here סער means the rough sea, the great waves that have been whipped up. The sailors are in danger, not through the force of the wind as such, but through the waves that break "over" them (cf. v. 12b הסער . . . עליכם "the storm . . . over them"). Verse 4b describes the state of acute danger. For the syntax see textual note on v. 4c. On חשב ("threaten") see the textual note on v. 4e. שבר is the usual word for shipwreck (1 Kings 22:49; Ezek. 27:26; Ps. 48:7).

[1:5]   Here Jonah is not initially mentioned at all. The new scene is marked, not merely by the new place of action, but also by new actors. In this context מלחים ("seamen") means the whole ship's company; the merchants may be included (Ezek. 27:9), though they can also be mentioned separately (Ezek. 27:27). In Ezek. 27:29 the מלחים constitute a special part of the crew, apart from the oarsmen and the חבלים, "the sailors who tie the ropes." Here probably all the sailors are meant, in spite of the following רב החבל (v. 6), "the captain of the crew," who is mentioned separately afterwards (see p. 113 below). They become frightened of the raging elements and the threatening shipwreck. This "fear" results in utter insecurity, as a consequence of which they try to press the gods into service, and also themselves employ every technical device to ward off the danger; cf. 1 Sam. 28:5ff.

The writer reports the mental reaction before he describes the individual measures. Fear first of all evokes the imploring religious complaint. The narrator makes "everyone cry to his god." This indicates that people from all over the

known world are assembled on the ship. It is almost a miniature edition of a metropolis like the Nineveh that Jonah wished to escape. Each of these people certainly puts his hope in his god, but Yahweh is known to none of them, although
the reader already knows that it is Yahweh who is the sole author of the storm. The
religious cry of each of the sailors is supplemented by seamanship. Just as Yahweh "threw" the wind "onto the sea" (v. 4a) so they in their turn now "throw"
receptacles "into the sea"; the original text links the same verb (טול *hiph'il*,
"throw") with the same preposition (אל־הים, "onto the sea"). Yahweh's acts
challenge human beings to corresponding acts. But what the crew do now is not as
yet the thing at which Yahweh is really aiming (cf. vv. 12a, 15a). Yahweh has Jonah in mind, but the seamen think of כלים, receptacles. The word can certainly
also mean equipment or gear (KBL[3]). But it is only in the very last resort that anyone would throw overboard parts of the ship's gear (e.g., sections of the rigging,
or oars) which would be an important factor in survival. Before that one would get
rid of the cargo, just as the sailors do in Acts 27:18f., 38; cf. E. Haenchen, *Die
Apostelgeschichte,* KEK 3 (1968[15]) 628. This being so, we should interpret כלים
as containers designed for the transportation of goods, especially earthenware receptacles such as amphorae — perhaps baskets as well; cf. O. Loretz, *Gotteswort
und menschliche Erfahrung* (1963) 193. Containers of this kind would also be
more likely to be described as being "in the ship" than gear belonging to the ship
itself. The aim of the action is "to lighten" the ship. The shallower the draught,
the fewer the waves that would break over the deck, and the easier the emergency
landing on some beach. So we may briefly sum up the efforts which the heathen
sailors exert by saying: they pray and they work.

Jonah does neither. Before the narrator can bring him into the scene (v. 6)
he has to catch up with what has been happening to the Hebrew ever since he went
on board at Joppa (v. 3). The only thing that seems worthy of report is that he had
taken himself off forthwith to the innermost part of the ship, in order to lie down
and sleep. This is the third time that we have been told about Jonah's "descent"
(ירד; cf. vv. 3bα.β). He is going down further and further. The person who inserted the psalm may have already discerned the direction leading to death (2:6f.), to
which the disobedient man or woman, like the fool, "descends"; cf. Prov. 5:5
and the frequent association of ירד with death, the grave, and the underworld (1
Sam. 26:10; Ps. 22:29; Job 33:24). The sequel also suggests that there is a metaphorical echo here: Jonah goes down into "the lowest part of the ship." In Isa.
14:15 ירכתי־בור means the lowest depths of the grave, and is parallel to the underworld (שְׁאוֹל) as the end of the "descent"; cf. textual note to v. 5c above. Since
here the word ספינה is used for ship — as we saw, a nonce usage in the Old Testament — we will be supposed to think of the decked-in part of the interior of the
ship (ספן, "cover," Hag. 1:4; 1 Kings 6:9); cf. already A. B. Ehrlich,
Randglossen zur hebräischen Bibel (1-7, 1908-14) 5:264, and textual note to 5d
above. The connection between "going down" and "lying down" (שׁכב) is often
found in metaphorical language about death; cf. Ezek. 32:21, 27-30; Ps. 88:4f. A
first indication of the death wish which Jonah utters in 4:3, 8 will be deliberate, in
accordance with the narrator's intention, especially since Elijah too "lies down"

with the same wish, according to 1 Kings 19:4f. But for the moment Jonah merely falls into a deep sleep, resembling complete stupor (רדם *niph'al*; Ps. 76:6; cf. Gen. 2:21), a sleep which can be a preliminary stage to death (Judg. 4:21). In the context, the satire in 5b is obvious: the vain activity of the seamen (v. 5a) is contrasted with Jonah's complete passivity, although he is the only one who has put them all in danger and he is the only one who can avert that danger.

[1:6] So then the captain approaches him. The word רב means the leader. It may be the highest court official (Esther 1:8; Dan. 1:3) or the commander-in-chief of troops (Jer. 39:3, 13). Here it is the head of the ship's crew. חֹבֵל is the collective word for the sailors as a whole; cf. חֹבְלִים in Ezek. 27:8, 27-29 and textual note to v. 6b above; etymologically the word is related to חֶבֶל ("rope," "cable") and to תַּחְבֻּלֹת ("helmsman's art"; Prov. 1:5; 12:5); according to Ezek. 27:8 the sailors to whom this word is applied belong to the חֲכָמִים, i.e., to the experienced experts (cf. G. von Rad, *Weisheit in Israel* [1970] 34f. [Eng., *Wisdom in Israel,* 1972]). These are the men who understand how to manage the ropes, set the sails, and navigate. If חֹבֵל was originally applied to especially competent seamen, the designation "captain" used here is particularly understandable. He approaches Jonah with the indignant question: what is he about, to go fast asleep? נרדם ("lie asleep," "snore") picks up the catchword from v. 5b, thereby stressing the purpose of Jonah's previous behavior — to absent himself totally from the human community of shared living and shared danger. The captain's words to him make it indirectly clear that the possibilities open to the sailors, both religious and technical, have now been exhausted. The only thing that has not yet been tried is the religion of the unknown passenger. קום קרא ("Get up! Cry out for help!"), the narrator makes the captain go on, as if this were an echo of Yahweh's words to Jonah in v. 2a. But he is to "cry out for help" to his God (קרא is the word also used in 1:14 and 3:8 for "pray"; cf. 1:5 זעק, "call" [for help]). The captain's hope is vague ("perhaps!"); after all, for him "the god" of this foreigner is no more than one of the many who have already been appealed to in vain. (On עשׁת *hithpa'el* see the textual note to v. 6c.) All the same, Jonah's prayer is now the only possibility "so that we do not perish." So rescue is in fact expected. The purpose clause ולא נאבד ("so that we do not perish") is a key phrase which is taken up in 1:14 by the sailors and is exactly repeated in Nineveh, in 3:9. The voyage — designed by Jonah to be a flight — increasingly proves to be a prelude to what happens in Nineveh. The reader must content himself with the information about the captain's despair and his hope.

[1:7] The narrator makes Jonah, even now, say nothing at all, as if he were still in that death-like slumber. Not a single word of prayer crosses his lips. Nor does the sequel allow us to suppose that Jonah prayed; for in that case he would surely have already admitted his guilt, and it would have been unnecessary for the sailors to cast lots (cf. R. Pesch, "Zur konzentrischen Struktur," 579). For the time being Jonah remains on the run, "away from Yahweh" (v. 3). So the next step is the consultation between the sailors, the result of which is that they will let the lots decide. The narrator already knows — and for his sailors too it is a foregone conclusion — that someone on board is personally responsible for the disaster; the reason why they cast lots is to discover who the responsible person is (aβ). We are not told anything about the exact method used. At all events, a number of lots is required, and probably more than two (as in 1 Sam. 14:38-42); this is also presupposed in Josh. 7:14-18; 1Sam. 10:20f. Did the lots really ''fall,'' after they had been cast, or is this an archaic turn of speech, and was the actual method perhaps to ''draw'' lots out of some receptacle (in Prov. 16:33 ''the lap'' formed by a garment)? This remains as obscure as the material used for the lots themselves (stones? wood?), or the way in which the guilty person was marked out by one of the lots (cf. Lindblom). Narrator and readers evidently have in mind a familiar procedure, which they think would be applicable even on board ship during a storm at sea. The result is unambiguous. Jonah is the guilty person.

[1:8]   But instead of immediately treating him as such, the sailors put four questions to him (on aβ see textual note to v. 8a) — questions which are generally asked when two people meet for the first time (Josh. 9:8; Judg. 19:17; 2 Kings 20:14). Only the question about his מְלָאכָה (''his work,'' or ''the business he has in hand'') might possibly be a question, not about his occupation generally, but about his special task (*לאך, ''send,'' KBL[3] 488) and the reason for his ''business trip''; cf. Ps. 107:23; Prov. 22:29 and W. F. Albright, ''Specimen of Late Ugaritic Prose,'' *BASOR* 150 (1958) 36-38 (38,n.14). It is unlikely that the narrator would have meant the word as used by the sailors to bear the meaning ''cultic activity'' (i.e., religion) — the meaning it has in Ezra 2:69; Neh. 7:69f.; 11:12 (cf. L. Schmidt, *De Deo* 64); this meaning fits neither the context nor the type of language used in the novella. The other questions — the place where he was last, his home, and his nation — seem to us inappropriate, in the midst of tumultuous seas and in the light of Jonah's guilt, which has now been determined. Is it part of the writer's irony to expect a biographical sketch in this situation (cf. E. M. Good, *Irony* [1965] 44)? Is he in this way trying to stress that, for the sailors too, everything now depends on getting to know their traveling companion? Apparently there is no survival for the sailors which leaves Jonah out of account. It is clearly Jonah who has brought all these others into deadly peril; and it is equally clear that these heathen sailors are anything but examples of heedless violence. They talk — no, they inquire — where we should surely simply expect a judicial sentence to be carried out.

[1:9]   But Jonah answers the fourth question only — the question about his nationality; he does not reply to the second or the third, let alone to the first question, about his commission, which is the most awkward of all. ''I am a Hebrew.'' In the Old Testament, עברי, ''Hebrew,'' is found especially often on the lips of foreigners, or is used towards foreigners, especially Egyptians (Gen. 40:15; 41:12; Exod. 1:16; and frequently) and Philistines (1 Sam. 4:6, 9; 13:3; and frequently). In our passage, the word certainly does not have a sociological meaning. It is used in a purely ethnological sense, as is general linguistic usage after the end of the Old

Testament period; cf. G. von Rad, *ThWNT* 3:359; K. Koch, "Die Hebräer vom Auszug aus Ägypten bis zum Großreich Davids," *VT* 19 (1969) 37-81 (43f.); M. Weippert, *Landnahme* (1967) 84-88. Is the term *Israelite* avoided because this would more readily have suggested a reference to Israel's particular salvation history? Hardly, for this reference is suggested even more explicitly by the name of Yahweh that follows. A more important point is that here too the title *prophet* does not appear where we might expect to find it, even more than we did in v. 1; see pp. 98f. above. "A Hebrew" is a description in which the readers addressed by the author can more easily recognize themselves; and the same is true of the acknowledgment that follows, which does not say anything whatsoever about Jonah's special charge, let alone about his misdemeanor. However, in the acknowledgment, the "I" of this particular Hebrew is immediately followed by the name *Yahweh*, although no question tending in that direction has been put. And on this confrontation everything depends, from vv. 1-3 onwards. In the sentence that follows the name *Yahweh* takes the emphatic position, ahead of the verb, as it does in the opening of the scene (v. 4a). For the first time the Name is pronounced on the ship. But who is Yahweh? Jonah adds two explanations.

First, he adds the phrase in apposition, "the God of heaven." In the Old Testament Yahweh is called the God of heaven in 19 other passages (e.g., 2 Chron. 36:23; Ps. 136:26; Ezra 1:2—Gen. 24:3, 7 is not included in the count). Seventeen of these 19 passages are to be found in the books of Ezra, Nehemiah, and Daniel (e.g., Neh. 1:4, 5; 2:4), and no less than 12 of them are in Aramaic (אֱלָהּ שְׁמַיָּא, e.g., Dan. 2:18; Ezra 5:11; 7:12). We also find the phrase 9 times in the Aramaic Elephantine papyri (A. Cowley, *Aramaic Papyri of the Fifth Century B.C.* [1923], e.g., 30:2, 28; 31:27). The phrase is therefore typical of the Persian period and we should probably look for its origin in the diplomatic language of the court chancery; cf. Ezra 6:9f.; 7:21 and D. K. Andrews, "Yahwe" 51f., even if we have no evidence that the predicate was ever applied to Ahura Mazda. The Jews may have contrasted Yahweh as "the God of heaven" with *Ba'al- Šamēm* (cf. O. Eissfeldt, *"Ba'alšamēm* und Jahwe," *ZAW* 57 [1939] 1-31 = *Kleine Schriften* 2:171-198). Persian tolerance may perhaps have conceded this divine title to the Jews. Since it was used in dealings with foreigners, it is here too an appropriate phrase in conversation with foreign seamen. Jonah is proclaiming that his God is not a local or national deity; he is the God who is purely and simply superior to all others.

The second explanation, or declaration, which Jonah adds to the name *Yahweh* introduces the relative clause "who has made the sea and the dry land." This clause makes it unmistakably clear that the sea is at Yahweh's sole command, since he is its Creator (cf. Ps. 89:9). This is the first indication, even though in highly restrained terms, that there is some connection or other between Jonah and the storm. The fact that the sea is mentioned before the dry land, puts the stress in exactly the right place. A confessional formula with precisely this wording is not otherwise known to us. However, we have no examples of the phrase in the reverse order either. But in fact, from the Priestly writing's account of the creation and the Israelites' passage through the sea onwards, it is made clear that Yahweh, because he is the one who commands the floods, is also the one who creates the dry land (Gen. 1:9f.; Exod. 14:16; Ps. 66:6; Neh. 9:11). Psalm 95:5 is particularly close to Jonah's declaration, because in both passages Yahweh is said to "have made" the sea (עשׂה). Elsewhere, in referring to Yahweh's power as Creator, the texts always simultaneously testify to his goodness and his will to save. Here it is initially merely his jurisdiction that is mentioned — the fact that this is his sphere of competence. It is an acknowledgment that is made through the words of his still refractory messenger.

Jonah acknowledges his personal adherence to his God through his declaration אני ירא ("I fear . . ."). This is the center of the sentence. It divides the second declaration from the first, thus stressing the relative clause. Here ירא has the conventionalized, technical meaning "worship," and means hardly anything more than "religious affiliation" (J. Becker, "Gottesfurcht im Alten Testament," *Analecta Biblica* 25 [1965] 176); cf., even earlier, 1 Kings 18:3, 12 and S. Plath, *Furcht Gottes* (1962) 52. By mentioning Yahweh, the official "God of heaven" in the Persian empire, Jonah is announcing his official "religion," with no more than a very impersonal pointer to its crucial significance. Here Jonah's ירא is far removed from the acknowledgment of the sailors in v. 5: there is no trace here of that elemental dread of destruction. He certainly "fears" Yahweh, but without any of the reverence which repents of the attempt at flight, and acknowledges his guilt before his God. He has still turned away from Yahweh's face, in spite of what he knows about God — indeed in spite of his experience of helplessness on his flight. He does no more than simply let the heathen sailors know with whom they have to do.

[1:10]   When they learn this, their complete uncertainty (v. 5) turns into a "great fear." The narrator stresses the mental reaction by adding to the verb the (internal, absolute) object, derived from the same root (BrSynt §92a; Meyer[3] 3 §105.4); it is in accordance with his narrative concern that he should have a particular liking for this construction (cf. vv. 16a; 4:1a, 6b), and in these cases he regularly calls the psychological emotion "great." In v. 10 the "great fear" is certainly not yet directly related to Yahweh, as it is afterwards, in v. 16; but after Jonah's declaration in v. 9, it does already clearly tend in this direction. Dread of the uncanny elements (v. 5) has become an "informed" fear, which begins to see through the reason for the storm. The cry which immediately follows (αβ) lends this fear concrete form. For the question "What have you done?" (also found in Gen. 3:13; 12:18; 26:10; 29:25; Exod. 14:11; Judg. 15:11) is a cry of terror springing from knowledge (b) rather than an inquiry requiring an answer. מה ("What?") is frequently used, not as an interrogative pronoun, but as an expression of astonished surprise (Gen. 28:17; Num. 24:5; Ezek. 19:2; Ps. 119:97; Job 26:2), which is the presupposition for the actual inquiry that can then follow (Gen. 12:18; 29:25; cf. Judg. 15:11). Here זאת (the demonstrative pronoun, "this") points to an already specifically known happening (Gen. 3:13; Exod. 14:5, 11; Judg. 2:2), in this case to the flight from Yahweh, which is then mentioned in the same words already used in v. 3.

Where have "the men" (as the sailors are simply called from now on) derived their "knowledge"? Did Jonah tell them, as the transmitted text says (bβ)? Or have they deduced it all by themselves from what Jonah says in v. 9, in which case we should have to view bβ as a later, interpolated gloss (see textual note to v. 10c-c)? A later interpolation of this kind would not be unusual in our text, as we already saw from v. 8aβ (see textual note to v. 8a-a). Moreover, the three successive clauses introduced by the particle כי are awkward stylistically. But from a narrative point of view, the cry of horror, "What have you done?" is more understandable if it is the response to direct information given by Jonah than it would be if it were based on an intellectual conclusion drawn by the sailors. הגיד belongs to the narrator's style (v. 8a). Something said is not always expressed in direct speech, even in the immediate context; cf. vv. 5a and 16b. The triple כי has three different functions; it first of all introduces the whole explanation; then an object clause; and finally a clause of reason. The parenthetic explanation after the event shows as a whole the "perspectivist" method of narrative, in which the temporal succession of facts is subordinated to the guiding concern (cf. N. Lohfink, *BZ* NF 5 [1961] 193-195). The shift in the narrative sequence, over against the sequence of time, emphasizes both the sailors' fear in 10a and Jonah's actual admission in 10b. In this way the agitated to-and-fro between crew and passenger is brought out with especial clarity.

[1:11] In v. 11 the seamen again put a genuine question, with a fourth, helplessly perplexed מה ("What?"), following on vv. 6, 8, and 10. What is to be done with Jonah? And how can they survive in the ever more tempestuous sea? This is now one and the same question. But it cannot be answered in terms of seamanship. It can only be answered by Jonah himself; for only he knows Yahweh's will. The formulation of the question: "What shall we do with you?" already shows that the sailors will have to act as instruments of Yahweh's will, if they do not want to perish together with Jonah. Their purpose is clear: "that the sea leaves us in peace" (see textual note to 11a). Apart from Jonah 1:11, 12, שתק is found only in Ps. 107:30 and Prov. 26:20, and really means "to quiet down," as the double preposition in our passage also shows (מן, "away from," shows the distance; על, "above," the towering up of the waves: that the sea comes to rest "away from over us").

Excursus: שתק *(štq)*

P. J. van Zijl, "Baal," *AOAT* 10 [1972] 20ff., conjectures that שתק as *šafʿel* form with causative meaning is derived from a possible Ugaritic root *tky* (C. H. Gordon, *Ugaritic Textbook,* Analecta Orienta 38 [1965] 137, 18, 34; Hebr. תקה?); but the word offered in evidence is interpreted differently by Gordon and others; cf. Gordon, *UT* 414 No. 1143: *yqy*. The suggested meaning of the Hebrew does not speak in favor of derivation from a causative form with preformative ש from the root תקה; we should be more inclined to think of the relationship between שתק and שקט (transposition, or metathesis, of two radicals; cf. KBL).

The narrator underlines the urgency of the question put to Jonah through the indication that the danger is still constantly increasing; on 11b cf. textual note 11b; on סער see p. 110 above.

[1:12] Jonah's swift reply is precisely directed towards the wish "that the sea should calm down" (cf. v. 12aβ with 11aβ). Does this show a generous spirit, and a readiness to sacrifice himself? The first thing to notice about his injunction, "Take me and throw me into the sea," is that it picks up the catchword from v. 4a: Yahweh "threw" the storm, which was not averted when the sailors "threw" the cargo into the sea (v. 5). Now Jonah himself enjoins the only "throw" that is adequate to the situation. Is he intending to obey Yahweh, or is the crucial recapitulation of the keyword הטיל ("throw") an ironical reflection of his obstinacy? (Cf. E. M. Good, *Irony* [1965] 45, and J. D. Magonet, *Form* [1973] 162.) The reason he gives in 12b for his advice certainly represents a step forwards, compared with what he has said hitherto: in v. 9 he described his God Yahweh as the one who disposes over the sea; according to v. 10 he had admitted that he was running away from Yahweh; only now does he explicitly associate the wild sea with his guilt. But how? "I know," he says, and in what he says to the sailors reminds them of what they have long since known, ever since the lots were cast (7aβb). We do not hear a single word of prayer; there is no confession of guilt before God; no imploring plea that he and all the rest should be saved (cf. v. 5a), no inquiry about God's will (cf. v. 14), let alone any vow of obedience (cf. v. 16b). We hear only one thing: he wants to die. He thus prolongs the line of development which we already detected in v. 5b (see above) and which is going to determine the very last of all his utterances, in 4:3, 8. If we compare Jonah's behavior with that of the sailors, it becomes clear that our satirist is painting him as intractable, unmoved in the face of Yahweh's will, and now — as he thinks — finally seeking refuge from him in death. Only the actual circumstances differ here from the circumstances in 4:3, 8; but we should not assume that there is any essential difference between the plea in 1:12 and the plea in 4:3, 8 if only because in 4:2f. (v. 2a) Jonah's motive is revealed for what it was at the very beginning, in chap. 1 (contrary to G. M. Landes, *Interp 21* [1967] 22f.).

To try to discover the word אֳנִי, "the ship" or its crew, in אני in 12b (W. J. Hornitz, "Another Interpretation") seems wholly wide of the mark. In the first place, in the Old Testament the word אֳנִי is otherwise only used in a collective sense, for "the fleet" (see KBL[3] 69); secondly, in Jonah especially the individual ship is called אניה (vv. 4f.), but not in the sense of its crew (cf. Meyer[3] 2 §42.7); thirdly, MT and most versions provide unanimous evidence for the meaning "I."

[1:13] The sequel is the best evidence of all that the narrator does not intend to depict Jonah as anything but mulishly refractory. The sailors — who have hitherto been presented as exemplary — show themselves disinclined to comply with Jonah's instructions. Instead they put forth all their most skillful seamanship (cf. v. 5a), now exerting themselves to the utmost as oarsmen. In Ezek. 8:8; 12:5, 7, 12

חתר means the breaking through of a wall (cf. Amos 9:2). Here it is the walls of the waves that have to be bored through. Sails are no help in this storm, and in fact they have to be struck. So "the men" have to lean on their oars in order to bring the ship "back to land." No object is given for שוב *hiph'il* ("bring back"). Since this follows immediately after v. 12, we ought to think of Jonah especially, rather than the ship and its crew as a whole: the man who has chosen death is to arrive at the path of obedience. This would mean that the crew would be saved also. Just as the sea is the place of flight and judgment, so the dry land is the place of salvation and the place where the assignment on Nineveh's behalf has to be fulfilled. Yahweh alone disposes over both land and sea (v. 9b). The divine satire so wills it that Jonah succeeds in arriving on land, not through "the men's" attempts at rescue, but only through his fall to his death (2:11). The men's efforts to reach land were in vain: "they were not able to do so. For the sea raged against them more violently than ever." עליהם "against them": this addition indicates that the situation has worsened again since v. 11b. The description of the storm is now heightened for a third time, if we start from the first mention, in v. 4, of the "rough sea" resulting from the tempest. Now the waves are running deliberately "counter" to the (good) intentions of the sailors.

[1:14] Although their attempt fails, they still do not yet comply with Jonah's strange and sinister death wish. Just as in v. 5 labor was added to prayer, so now (though the order is reversed) hard work is supplemented by prayer. But here it is prayer to Yahweh and it is cited in detail, word for word — the longest passage of direct speech in the whole scene. In spite of his flight, and through his flight, Jonah has convinced these adherents of a foreign religion that this is the only God to whom appeal can be made. The word אנה, as an expression of "distress," "terrified dismay," is used to open a plea of lament (cf. C. Hardmeier, "Kritik der Formgeschichte," diss. Heidelberg [1975] 190f. and textual note to v. 14b above). This is the way people cry when they are in danger of death: 2 Kings 20:3 = Isa. 38:3; Ps. 116:4, 16; Dan. 9:4; Neh. 1:5, 11; cf. also 4:2 and p. 166 below. So here too the first plea that follows is: "Do not let us perish!" The echo of v. 6bβ is unmistakable. They plead with Yahweh for succor, as the captain had vainly expected Jonah to do. Thus Israel's prerogative is exposed to bitter ridicule. Danger threatens בנפש ("because of the nepheš") "of this man." In this context נפש does not mean Jonah's (wrong) mental attitude; it means his actual "life"; cf. H. W. Wolff, *Anthropologie des Alten Testaments* (1973) 37-40 (Eng., *Anthropology of the Old Testament* [1974] 18-20). ב could mean "together with" (as it does in Jer. 41:15 and frequently elsewhere; cf. BrSynt §106 b). But it is more probably a causal ב, as in vv. 7a, 12b; Gen. 18:28 and frequently (KBL³ 101 [19]).

This meaning ("because of the life of this man") is brought out by the following request: "Give not innocent blood over us!" Here formal Israelite legal terminology has been taken over; cf. the wording of Deut. 21:8; Jer. 26:15; K. Koch, "Sein Blut bleibe auf seinem Haupt," *VT* 12 (1962) 396-416 = WdF 125 (1972) 432-456; J. D. Magonet, *Form* (1973) 125ff., 203f.; L. Schmidt, *De Deo* (1976) 77-80. "Innocent blood" always refers to the (shedding of the) blood of a slain person or of someone who is about to be slain (cf. Deut. 21:8) — in this case, that is to say, Jonah's blood, not the blood of the sailors (cf. H. W. Wolff, *Anthropologie,* 100 [Eng., *Anthropology* 61f.]: דם = "shed blood"). Uncertainty can only arise because it is called "innocent." For Jonah has finally, in v. 12, himself admitted his guilt, which has been known to the sailors ever since the lots were cast (v. 7; cf. comments above). This being so, נקיא can only refer to the behavior of the men with regard to (the shedding of) Jonah's blood. What worries them is that the nature of the slaying which Jonah expects, according to v. 12, is not a punishment that accords with his guilt — that is to say, they are afraid that Yahweh might expect a different kind of expiation, rather than that they should throw Jonah into the sea. In this case Yahweh would lay an irresponsible shedding of blood to their charge, as guilt (irresponsible because not really appropriate to Jonah's guilt). דם נקיא therefore means "unjustly shed blood"; accordingly נתן על means "requite," "charge against." The difficulty in understanding the phrase is due to the fact that — in order to show the correctly Yahwistic way they are behaving — the narrator puts into the sailors' mouths phrases belonging to Israelite tradition (Deut. 21:8). The ironic undertone becomes perceptible when we remember Jonah's antitype, Jeremiah, and the words of Jer. 26:15: "If you put me to death, you will bring innocent blood upon yourselves." There a true prophet warns a wicked people (Jerusalem!) against shedding his innocent blood. Here good non-Israelites, who are face to face with a prophet who is not good at all, pray that they should not acquire guilt through his death. Only a satirist switches roles like this, in order to convey a humiliating lesson to his readers.

What is the meaning of the clause of reason in 14b which closes the prayer after the imploring petition: "For you are Yahweh; you do as pleases you"? First of all we must recognize this sentence too as part of a quotation. It corresponds almost exactly to Ps. 115:3 and 135:6; and in fact the sentence in Ps. 135:6 is explicitly related to Yahweh's free disposal over the sea. The confirmatory perfect (a perfect denoting an existing state) should be understood as a present with an iterative meaning. In both psalms, the confession of faith contrasts Yahweh with other, impotent gods (135:5) and idols (115:4-7); for this and the following passage cf. L. Schmidt, *De Deo* (1976) 78ff. In the sailors' prayer this hymnal phrase of adoration is introduced by כי אתה ("because you"), thereby acquiring the function of an expression of trust within the prayer of lament; cf. Ps. 22:3, 9; 86:5; 143:10. In this way — through the prayer in general and through its individual phrases — the narrator depicts the sailors (up to now heathen) as people who turn to Yahweh like model Israelites, at least where Jonah's affairs are concerned, and when they are in danger of shipwreck.

[1:15] Only now do the sailors comply with Jonah's request (v. 12). The two acts with which they have retarded the action and increased the tension permit no alternative (v. 13), and have also relieved their consciences (v. 14). In v. 15a the narrator picks up the words from Jonah's own injunction in v. 12a; whereas Jonah acts contrary to Yahweh's word, the sailors comply exactly with Jonah's command. "They took Jonah and threw him into the sea." This is the fourth time that we meet the word הֵטִיל; and this is the correct ''throw'' at which Yahweh's ''throw'' in v. 4 was apparently aimed, unlike the vain ''throw'' in v. 5. Here the sailors faithfully carry out Jonah's instructions; for them, he is and remains the only person who knows what Yahweh's will is, even though he himself has been disobedient. This is the sole advantage he has over them. Yahweh still passes on his unambiguous word to the heathen only through the mediation of the Hebrew. Even after their prayer (v. 14), they do not wait for Yahweh to speak to them directly.

The narrator immediately shows that they have acted rightly: ''Then the sea stood still from its raging.'' On עמד מן see textual note v. 15a. The word זַעְפּוֹ can be both a substantive (''fury,'' ''rage,'' Septuagint ἐκ τοῦ σάλου αὐτῆς) and an infinitive (''to rage,'' ''to storm''); Gen. 29:35; 30:9 suggests that the verbal meaning is more probable. The style of the passage also suggests action (cf. vv. 4b, 11b, 13b). The roaring of the sea ceases. The prayer for rescue has been heard.

[1:16] Readers are not supposed to concern themselves as yet with what is going to happen to Jonah, even though this question keeps them in a state of suspense. They are supposed to learn first of all what is going to happen to the petitioners who have brought about the turn of events. Three statements bring their story to an end — a story which is in sharpest contrast to the story of Jonah up to now. Whereas Jonah sinks into the sea, thereby apparently achieving his goal (to get out of Yahweh's sight) the sailors come to ''fear Yahweh greatly.'' The essential thing that has come about through the prayer in v. 14 is now reduced to the formula יְרֵא אֶת־יְהוָה, ''fear before Yahweh.'' We meet this phrase on Jonah's lips in v. 9. Now it describes the sailors' new attitude. But whereas in Jonah's case it was no more than a verbal acknowledgment, here the phrase sums up the sailors' whole behavior. Where the sailors are concerned, Yahweh has achieved his good purpose. Their helpless ''fear'' in v. 5 because of the storm, and their ''great fear'' because of what they learn from Jonah in v. 10, has now turned into ''great fear before Yahweh'' because of the confirmation of what Jonah has said through the stilling of the storm. Though it has a narrative form, the statement reminds us of the phrase ''fear of Yahweh'' which, in the Elohist and in the wisdom writings, is not merely the term for worship, in the sense of a permanent religious affiliation, but even more describes a living relationship of obedience and trust; cf. Gen. 22:12; Exod. 20:20; Prov. 1:7; Ps. 111:10; and H. W. Wolff in *EvTh* 29 (1969) 62ff. = *Gesammelte Studien* (1973²), 405ff; G. von Rad, *Weisheit in Israel* (1970) 91ff. (Eng., *Wisdom in Israel* [1972]).

Again the narrator describes concrete action only after he has depicted fundamental psychological reactions (as in vv. 5a and 10f.). First of all, the men sacrifice. The word זבח is a reference to the thank offering described in Lev. 7:12 (cf. here K. Ellinger, *Leviticus,* HAT 1/4 [1966] 99f.) and mentioned in Ps. 107:22 directly before the psalmist's description of danger at sea, the themes of which are echoed in the account in v. 4f. (see p. 110 above). The narrator evidently means us to suppose that the sacrifice was offered to Yahweh immediately, on board ship (differently Targ, see textual note to v. 16c). But telling other people about the divine rescue was a regular part of the celebration of a thank offering (Ps. 22:22; 66:16; and F. Crüsemann, *Studien zur Formgeschichte von Hymnus und Danklied,* WMANT 32 [1969] 263-284). The vows which we are told were made as the second act may point to this part of the celebration of the thank offering. Here they do not refer to the offering as fulfillment of a vow, as they do in Ps. 50:14; 66:13; 116:17f.; the vows are only paid by the sailors after the sacrifice, and they could mean the narration — after a safe landing — of how they have been rescued by Yahweh, as an indispensable part of the feast of thanksgiving (L. Schmidt's view; cf. *De Deo* 80f.). But it is more probable that the vows point to a lasting bond of trust with Yahweh. This is the way they are also understood in Ps. 61:8, apart from the specific thank offering: "I will sing praises to thy name, as I pay my vows day after day." So, through Jonah's flight, worshipers of strange gods have become people who "fear Yahweh"; cf. Ps. 103:11, 13, 17; also Ps. 103:8, with Jonah 4:2 (see pp. 167f. below).

Purpose

The particular significance of the scene 1:4-16 has to do with the "success" of Jonah's flight. This is in no way dependent on Jonah himself; it is determined by Yahweh. His name opens events (v. 4a); he is at the center of Jonah's confession of faith (v. 9); the last sentence of all refers to him (v. 16). Jonah enters the scene late (v. 5b) and is taken off the stage before the scene ends (v. 15a). The sailors are on the scene before Jonah and after him. Their reaction to Yahweh's actions with respect to Jonah is therefore in the foreground of the narrative, initially. Yahweh acts exclusively through the storm at sea (v. 4), which builds up and dominates all human activities (vv. 11b, 13b) until it has achieved its goal; the purposefulness of this divine activity is brought out through the keyword "throw" (vv. 4a, 5a, 12a, 15a). It is only after the "throw" of the storm has led to Jonah's being thrown into the sea that the sea calms down (v. 15b). Although they are adherents of a foreign religion, the sailors, in an exemplary manner, submit to what Yahweh does. By way of an awestruck inquiry into Yahweh's will, they pass from their elemental fear to a trustful bond with him; cf. the "growing phrases" (J. D. Magonet, *Form* 46-51, and p. 121 above):

וייראו (v. 5);

את־יהוה . . . אני ירא (v. 9);

וייראו האנשים יראה גדולה (v. 10);

וייראו האנשים יראה גדולה את־יהוה (v. 16).

Through Jonah's declaration and directive (vv. 9, 12), they find their way to Yahweh. The path is a hard one. The narrator shows the exemplary fashion in which these heathen pursue it, unlike Jonah. Jonah sinks luxuriously into a deep sleep while the sailors exert themselves to the utmost (v. 5). Jonah offers an ice-cold, verbal acknowledgment of Yahweh (v. 9), and at the same time pertinaciously insists on running away from him (see p. 116 above), whereas the crew endeavors painstakingly and meticulously to conform to Yahweh's will (vv. 11-14). Jonah flees from the task of speaking the truth to the great city of Nineveh, while the seamen exert all their powers on behalf of this one passenger (v. 13). They pray, they implore, they give thanks (vv. 14, 16), whereas Jonah does not allow himself to be moved to a single prayer (v. 6) and strives only to get away from Yahweh. Jonah acknowledges only Yahweh's power as creator (v. 9) — and experiences it with irresistible force. The seamen implore his will to save — and it is that which they experience (vv. 6, 14, 16). Jonah desires death. The sailors desire life. So, in his own way, the narrator testifies: "I am sought by those who did not ask for me; I am found by those who did not seek me" (Isa. 65:1; cf. also 1 Kings 8:41-43; Isa. 2:2-5; 56:6f.). Paul could echo this experience, where the Israel of his own day was concerned (Rom. 10:20). A Christian church which is too much wrapped up in itself can be surprised by the same experience at any time. Through the medium of satiric narrative, our storyteller teaches that the God of Jonah, the Hebrew, is able to find among completely strange people the obedience and trust which his own messenger denied him.

But this is only the foreground, and the special contribution made by the scene with the sailors. In the background Yahweh's history with Jonah continues. The person who is trying to escape from Yahweh (vv. 3, 10) has never for a single moment escaped Yahweh's eyes or his grasp. It is in his very failure that Yahweh uses him for his service. The laughter over the escapee echoes ironically through the whole story; but through that very fact Israel is clearly taught that she cannot escape her election. We should fundamentally misinterpret the character of this chapter if we were to see here merely support for a wisdom theology of creation, teaching the inescapable will to power of the God of heaven (cf. L. Schmidt, *De Deo* 82-84). It is certainly true that there is no echo here of the typical great election traditions; the influence of wisdom thinking is clear (see pp. 109f. above), and Yahweh's power as creator is strongly stressed (v. 9). But although for the heathen sailors the Creator's power is visible in the guise of their rescue (vv. 6, 14-16), the part that Jonah plays in the matter makes the specifically Israelite function clearer still. It is only through Jonah that the seamen learn that Yahweh is the author of the storm. It is through the Hebrew voice and through no other that Yahweh reveals himself. And the threat of shipwreck only arises at all because the Hebrew is unwilling to fulfill his duties as messenger among strangers and foreigners. The self-revelation of God in Israel and Israel's election to God's service as messenger in the Gentile world is the essential presupposition of the story, and it is carried through consistently throughout the whole narrative.* The satire merely lends spice to the bitter teaching. The heathen are undoubtedly more humane, more active, wiser, and also more devout. And Jonah is undoubtedly exposed to ridicule. And yet it is only he who can tell the others how they have to be-

---

*According to Jewish tradition, there were representatives of all the 70 nations on board; cf. O. Komlós, "Jonah Legends," *ÉtOr* P. Hirschler, ed. O. Komlós (1950) 50; cf. also A. Fáj, "Stoic Features" 337.

have. Much though he would prefer another course, there is nothing else he can do. In the New Testament Peter would like to stand aloof — and is declared a rock; ''Irony could go no further, don't you think?'' was Albert Camus' comment *(The Fall* [1957] 116). The smile of many a Christian group may well die away on their lips, even during this second scene in the book of Jonah. But would it not be better if they had an ear for the laughter of the One who dwells in heaven over Christian attempts to escape, over fits of somnolence and wishes that one were dead? In the face of the misery round about them, should these Christians not in all honesty denounce themselves? And if they are quite justly thrown into the waves, they may then perhaps remember that this second scene is followed by a third.

Swallowed and Vomited Up

Literature

R. D. Wilson, "מנה, 'To Appoint' in the Old Testament," *PrincThR* 16 (1918) 645-654. J. Begrich, "Der Satzstil im Fünfer," *Zeitschrift für Semitistik und verwandte Gebiete* 9 (1934), 169-209 = his *Gesammelte Studien,* ThB 21 (1964) 132-167; A. R. Johnson, "Jon. 2.3-10: A Study in Cultic Phantasy," in H. H. Rowley, ed., *Studies in Old Testament Prophecy: Fests. T. H. Robinson* (1950) 82-102. M. Stenzel, "Altlateinische Canticatexte im Dodekapropheton," *ZNW* 46 (1955) 31-60 (54-60). J. B. Bauer, "Drei Tage," *Bibl* 39 (1958) 354-358. F. Nötscher, "Zur Auferstehung nach drei Tagen," *Bonner Biblische Beiträge* 17 (1962) 231-236. U. Steffen, *Das Mysterium von Tod und Auferstehung: Formen und Wandlungen des Jona-Motifs* (1963). G. M. Landes, "The Kerygma of the Book of Jonah," *Interp* 21 (1967) 3-31; also his "The 'Three Days and Three Nights' Motif in Jonah 2.1," *JBL* 86 (1967) 446-450. F. Crüsemann, *Studien zur Formgeschichte von Hymnus und Danklied in Israel,* WMANT 32 (1969). W. Rudolph, "Jona," in *Archäologie und Altes Testament: Fests. K. Galling* (1970) 233-239. J. D. Magonet, "Form and Meaning: Studies in Literary Techniques in the Book of Jonah," diss. Heidelberg (1973). G. Bader, "Das Gebet Jonas: Eine Meditation," *ZThK* 70 (1973) 162-205.

Text

2:1 [1:17] Meanwhile, Yahweh had appointed[a] a great fish to swallow up Jonah. Jonah was in the belly of the fish[b] three days and[b] three nights.

2 [2:1] Then Jonah prayed to Yahweh his God out of the belly of the fish,

3 [2] saying:
Out of[a] my affliction I called to Yahweh,[b] and he heard me.
　I cried for help out of the belly of the underworld, you
　　　　　did hear my voice.

4 [3] You did throw me into the heart[a] [the depths][b] of the seas, so
　　　　　that[c] the flood surrounded me.
　All your breakers and billows swept over me.

5 [4] So then I said: I am cast off,[a] away from your eyes [presence].

125

"How"[b] can I again look upon your holy temple?

6 [5] Waters closed round me up to my throat,[a] the primeval sea surrounded me.

Seaweed[b] was twisted round my head

7 [6]   at the roots of the mountains.[a]

I had descended into the land which [b] (was to close) its bars behind me for ever.

And yet you have brought my life out of the grave, Yahweh my God!

8 [7] When I myself,[a] despairing of myself, thought[b] of Yahweh,

then my imploring lament came to you, into your holy temple.

9 [8] Those who worship[a] unfounded Nothingness[b] forsake their help.[c]

10 [9] But I will sacrifice to you with a loud song of thanksgiving.

What I vowed I will fulfill. Deliverance belongs to Yahweh.

11 [10] Then Yahweh spoke to the fish, and it vomited up Jonah onto the dry land.

3:1 After that Yahweh's word came to Jonah a second time. It ran:

2 "Set out, go to Nineveh, the great city, and[a] preach to it the message[b] which I (now)[c] tell you!"

3 Then Jonah set out and went to Nineveh, in accordance with Yahweh's word.

1a [17a] As far as events are concerned, this goes back in time, catching up with what has already happened; the perfect-tense clauses in 1:5b and 10b served the same purpose. But the imperfect construction is more immediately connected with the narrative's dividing point in 15a, as a parallel action to 1:15b-16b; cf. 3:6 and 4:5. On the possibility of translating the imperfect by a pluperfect, cf. the comments on Hebrew syntax in R. Meyer[3] 2 §§62.63 and 3:100, and especially N. Lohfink, *BZ* NF 5 (1961) 191f.

1b-b [17 b-b] The phrase τρεῖς ἡμέρας καὶ ("three days and") is not translated in the Latin version of Gk (La[c], 5th century) or (in some cases) in the Sahidic (Upper Egyptian) translation. In the belly of the fish there is only night.

3a [2a] Gk (ἐν, "in") assimilates to the situation, as in Ps. 119:1 (MT, Ps. 120:1 בַּצָּרָתָה).

3b [2b] Gk adds τὸν θεόν μου, "my God," probably echoing v. 2a (1a); cf. 7b (6b).

4a [3a] "The heart of the seas" generally means the (unsearchable) open "high seas" (Prov. 23:34; 30; 19: Ezek. 27:4, 26), but then also the (unfathomable) "depths of the sea" (Ps. 46:2; Ezek. 28:8); cf. H. W. Wolff, *Anthropologie* (1973) 72 (Eng., Anthropology [1974] 43).

4b [3b] מצולה definitely means the depths of the sea (Mic. 7:19; Zech. 1:8; Ps. 68:22; 69:2, 15; 107:24; Job 41:22) and in this sense is understandable as a subsequent and additional interpretation of the more equivocal "heart of the seas," first of all noted in the margin of a manuscript and hence without the preposition which is actually indispensable in the context. For another view cf. G. M. Landes, *Interp* 21 (1967) 6, n. 13. M. Buber interprets the word as subject ("The maelstrom has thrown me into the heart of the seas"). This certainly explains the lack of a preposition, but in the light of v. 5a (4a) Yahweh is the more probable subject of v. 4a (3a). Rhythmically too, מצולה is an excrescence in the middle of regular five-stress lines.

4c [3c] The inversion should be understood as a clause of result, describing the new state of affairs.

5a [4a] See p. 135 below.

5b [4b] θ'(πως, "how") presupposes אֵיךְ and, in the context of the relation of the psalmist's extremity, is more probable than an expression of tenacious defiance or longing, which is what MT suggests; for אַךְ should be understood as a particle of restriction or antithesis; cf. N. H. Snaith, "The meaning of the Hebrew אַךְ," *VT* 14 (1964) 221-225 and H. W. Wolff, *Hosea*, BK 14/1 (1976³) 90, 94 (Eng., *Hosea: A Commentary* [1974] 73f., 76). The translation "Yet I should like once more . . ." (W. Rudolph) hardly renders the text's original meaning either, because יסף *hiph'il* with the infinitive signifies (unbroken) "continuation"; cf. Gen. 4:12; Exod. 5:7; Amos 7:8. The misreading of the original אֵיךְ as אַךְ can have been due to the similarity between v. 5a (4a) and Ps. 31:22a and its continuation with the adversative אָכֵן in v. 22b.

6a [5a] Targ (עד מותא, "to the death") is a correct interpretation: this is a matter of (life and) death; cf. H. W. Wolff, *Anthropologie* 29f. (Eng., *Anthropology* 14f.).

6b [5b] MT "reeds" stands for sea plants in general. Gk (ἐσχάτη) misread the word as סוֹף ("end"); cf. σ' απεραντος ("unlimited"). Targ (ימא דסוף) and α' (ερυθρα, "red") are thinking of the "Reed Sea" (Red Sea; Vg. *pelagus*, "sea"), since סוף ("reeds") occurs far and away most often in this connotation.

7a [6a] The two first words in v. 7 (6) should be added to v. 6b (5b), in order to complete the five-stress line; in addition the following ירדתי ("I descended") has its own determination of place in הארץ ("the land"); so also Vg.

7b [6b] The Septuagint already recognized the asyndetic relative clause (i.e., without a conjunction) (εἰς γῆν ἧς οἱ μοχλοὶ αὐτῆς, "into the land, the bars of which").

8a [7a] Here נפשׁ stands for the person in his mood of despondency or despair; cf. H. W. Wolff, *Anthropologie* 36, 41f. (Eng., *Anthropology* 17f., 21f.).

8b [7b] The construction with the perfect preceding the imperfect indicates the precondition for the following action.

9a [8a] שׁמר *pi'el* participle occurs only here; a change, in line with Ps. 31:6 (הַשֹּׁמְרִים) is not justifiable, if only because MT is supported by α' (αποφυλασσοντων), where απο points to a מִן, which has been misunderstood as a preposition. The *pi'el* form indicates repeated, intensified action.

9b [9a] Here worthless idols are meant, as in Ps. 31:6. In Deut. 32:21 הֲבָלִים ("baals" or "idols") stands parallel to לֹא־אֵל ("non-god"). Gk (μάταια καὶ ψευδῆ, "what is vain and deceptive") breaks up the compound construction; differently Ps. 30:6 (ματαιότητας διὰ κενῆς, "empty speculations").

9c [8c] Although the third person plural suffix means "people," here חסד stands for the true God in his merciful faithfulness; cf. Ps. 144:2.

3:2a Leningradensis offers the choice of pronouncing the copula as *u* or *wi*.

2b This word occurs frequently in late Hebrew, but in the Old Testament only here. Gk. κατὰ τὸ κήρυγμα τὸ ἔμπροσθεν, "according to the message commanded previously," will be a free interpretation based on this text's previous understanding of 1:2b as being the content of the message. Cf. pp. 99f. above.

2c The participial clause means the present or the immediately impending future. The Vg. translation *loquor*, "I speak," is therefore correct. Gk ἐλάλησα is wrong, in accordance with its implicit reference to the mistaken interpretation in 1:2; cf. textual note to 3:2b.

Form

The new scene is both shaped and *limited* by what Yahweh now does with Jonah, and by his new address to him. The story of the seamen has been brought to a happy end (1:16);* and Nineveh has not yet become the scene of the action, as it does in 3:3b. Now the reader finds Jonah alone with his God once more, as in 1:1-3. The fact that no one else is present — that the encounter takes place between Yahweh and Jonah alone — gives this scene its self-contained character. It is clearly structured through the change in the place of action. First of all, Yahweh acts silently on Jonah at sea, through the fish (2:1, 11); here the satire with which chap. 1 has made us familiar shows him from the humorous, ironical angle. Afterwards he speaks to Jonah again, this time on dry land (3:1-3a).

Whether Jonah's prayer is the work of the prose narrator is questionable. G. H. Cohn, "Jonah" (1969) 93f., O. Kaiser, EvTh 33 (1973) 97f., and — in particular detail — J. D. Magonet, *Form* (1973) 65-98, have all pleaded for a single authorship, pointing out that elsewhere too a hymn of thanksgiving is introduced in the function of the lament (compare וַתִּתְפַּלֵּל as introduction to Hannah's hymn of thanksgiving in 1 Sam. 2:1 with Jonah 2:2). According to this view, the psalm has been conceived for the story's particular situation, since it begins with an account of the psalmist's distress instead of with words of praise, such as normally introduce a hymn of thanksgiving; moreover, the description of the desperate situation continues to dominate the whole (up to v. 8a), while in vv. 4 and 6f. the particular danger at sea is clearly referred to in a way that finds no parallel in any of the other psalms that have come down to us. In addition, the prayer "is a mixture of quotations and innovations, just like the rest of the story" (Kaiser, 97). G. H. Cohn and especially J. D. Magonet try to support the identity of the author of psalm and story by producing evidence of a similar choice of vocabulary and stylistic devices; but their observations do not provide sufficiently cogent arguments for the desired conclusion.

Even the reminder of Hannah's prayer in 1 Samuel 2 speaks in favor of an interpolator rather than against; for on the one hand, in the book of Samuel we have been told previously that the request has been heard (1 Sam. 1:27); so a hymn of thanksgiving is appropriate. What is more, this hymn of thanksgiving is also now thought by scholars to have been introduced into the narrative complex at a later stage (cf. H. J. Stoebe, KAT 8/1 [1973] 106f.). It is only through the theme of the barren woman who after all bears children (2:5b) that it is linked with the context (1:5ff.), in which the theme is formulated in quite a different way. Anyone who points to the song of Hezekiah in Isa. 38:9-20 (Magonet) is also confronted with a later addition, unknown to the parallel text in 2 Kings 20 (cf. O. Kaiser, ATD 18 [1973] 320ff.). So, later interpolations of this kind are by no means rare.

Three different groups of observations suggest that our psalm was not incorporated in the text by the original narrator.

---

*Here and in the following sections on chapter 2 references have been given to verses in the numbering in which they appear in the Hebrew text. The reader can readily discover the English equivalent (which follows the numbering of the Septuagint) by reference to the preceding two sections (text and textual commentary), in which both numberings are given.

1. *The situation* of the psalm does not fit the context. In his distress (vv. 3-7), his prayer of lament (תפלה, v. 8b), his gratitude that his prayer has been granted (vv. 3, 6b, 8b), and his vow (v. 10b), the petitioner looks back to what has already taken place. He is now in the temple, where he had longed to be when he was in the sea (vv. 5b, 8b) and is bringing his hymn of gratitude (תודה, v. 10a) as a thank offering before God and as a way of telling the assembled congregation of his deliverance. That is why he does not merely speak *to* Yahweh (vv. 3b-5, 7b, 8b) but also *about* him (vv. 3a, 8a, 9, 10b). This "double direction" of the discourse is characteristic of the song of thanksgiving after deliverance; and the same may be said of the narration which looks back over past distress, tells of the prayer for relief and its answer (vv. 3-8), instructs fellow worshipers (vv. 9, 10b), and draws attention to the sacrifice that has been vowed (v. 10b); cf. F. Crüsemann, 247ff., 264ff. All in all, therefore, this song is better fitted for the temple than for the fish's belly.

2. *The language* of the psalm is different from that of the narrative (cf. also G. M. Landes, *Interp* 21 [1967]). We should compare especially the prayers in the story (1:14; 4:2f.). They are genuine prayers of lament ("O Yahweh!"); they are addressed to God alone and never talk *about* him; they fit precisely into the events of the story; they pick up important groups of words out of the context (cf. 1:14aα with 1:6bβ; 4:2a with 1:3 and 4:2b with 3:9f.); and they have the same prose form as the surrounding material. The psalm, on the other hand, describes the petitioner's distress in completely different words from those which 1:4 — 2:1 would lead us to expect. The only word echoed is the word "sea" (1:4f., 12, 15); but even that is only used in its poetic variant "heart of the seas" (2:4). There is no mention of the storm and the roaring of the sea, or of Jonah's flight and the great fish; nor is there any confession of guilt or any plea. The narrator's favorite word "great" (גדול, 14 times in 39 verses) does not occur a single time in 2:2-10. Instead of the prose cry of distress, what we read here is the formal language of the temple. It comes as no surprise to find that there are no Aramaisms in the passage; for it is closely linked with older transmitted psalm material, though it changes this to some degree, and expands it with an eye to the story that is being told (see the detailed analysis, pp. 133ff. below). The addition is therefore probably no older than the story itself (for another view cf. C. A. Keller, 278); cf. G. M. Landes, *Interp* 21 [1967] 16, whose comparison of the structure of 2:2-10 and 4:2-3 disguises the essential differences. Landes's valuable observations show that the psalm and the prose narrative may have been harmonized at a later stage, and certainly demonstrate the sensitive way in which the psalmist enters into the mood of the story; but these observations are unable to substantiate the probability that this was originally a unified conception with a unified language.

Excursus: Structure and Rhythm of the Psalm of Jonah

The *rhythmic* of the psalm shows unusual artistry. The poem consists exclusively of five-stress lines (on v. 4a see textual note to 2:4b). J. Begrich has investigated "the sentence style in the five-stress line" (cf. his "Satzstil im Fünfer," 1934/1964). In our psalm the most frequent pattern is the five-stress line consisting of a single sentence (Begrich, 136), with some degree of logical break after the third stress, and with a simultaneous pause in the rhythm: vv. 4b, 5b, 6b-7aα, 7b, 8a, b, 9, 10aα. In a few cases a five-stress line contains two different statements (Begrich 140f.; vv. 3b, 10aβ-b) or it may be two synonymous and parallel ones (Begrich 145; vv. 4a, 6a). When the rhythmical principle (3 + 2 stresses) does not match the logical break we use the word *enjambment* (Begrich 140f.); thus v. 4a consists logically of 4 + 1 stresses, vv. 5a and 7aαβ 2 + 3 stresses. As a rule two lines of five stresses each are linked into a single prosodic unit, there being therefore seven such units in all. Two exceptions from this rule are worth noting. In the fifth prosodic unit (v. 7aαβb) the two five-stress lines are in antithesis to one another. This is the moment when the psalmist reports the turning point in his distress. The seventh prosodic unit consists of three lines, the first of them (v. 9) being in antithesis to the two synonymous lines that follow (v. 10; Begrich 157). This indicates a final heightening and intensification, which culminates in the brief and succinct confessional statement in v. 10b.

3. *The Jonah* of the psalm is a different person from the Jonah of the story. That is why von Rad talked about the psalm's ''psychologically unconvincing'' character: ''These pious words of humble thanksgiving simply do not fit the mulish Jonah, who afterwards behaves in an even more incredible way than he did before'' (''Jona 3,'' in *Gottes Wirken in Israel* [1974] 76f.; Eng., *God at Work in Israel* [1980]). Even when, in the following passage, the narrator can talk about an obedient Jonah for a time, his ''hero'' remains as coldly reserved and taciturn as he was in chap. 1. But at the end his initial reluctance actually builds up to a sulky defiance that makes him want to die rather than submit. No, the man in the psalm, who prostrates himself before God in thanksgiving, and rejoices at being able to tell his brothers what he has experienced, is quite a different person — a later person. He has grasped the bitter teaching of the satire in his own way.

Verse 2a must also be assigned to the psalmist, as has been generally realized, from K. Marti to W. Rudolph — not merely 2b, as A. Jepsen thought possible (''Anmerkungen'' [1970] 297). In v. 2b we stumble over the form of the word used for the fish (דגה instead of דג, as vv. 1 and 11), for this is otherwise used only in a collective sense. In v. 2a the phrase ''Yahweh his God'' is also disconcerting, since there is nothing comparable in the rest of the story, although the phrase does occur in the psalm (v. 7b: ''Yahweh, my God''). Also, the fact that ''Jonah'' and ''the belly of the fish'' are repeated in v. 2, immediately after they have been mentioned in v. 1b, does not accord with the narrator's spare, economical style; cf. 4:1f.; 3:3; 1:3 and L. Schmidt, *De Deo* (1976) 56. In 1 Sam. 2:1 and Isa. 38:9 the transitional sentences are also the work of the interpolator. So the only part of the third scene that can be ascribed to the original story is initially 2:1, 11 and 3:1-3a.

But 3:1 brings us face to face with a new problem. Were chaps. 3f. and 1 originally a single literary unit at all? The sea story and the story about Nineveh's conversion are miles apart, as far as the history and background of the narrative material goes: about that there is no controversy. But do we not already find literary joins in 3:1-3a? The repetition of 1:1-2a in 3:1-2a could suggest that chaps. 1-2 were added at a later state; cf. C. Kuhl, ''Die 'Wiederaufnahme' — ein literarkritisches Prinzip?'' *ZAW* 64 (1952) 1-11 (esp. 10). The growth of the frame story in the book of Job can be traced from similar phenomena; cf. 1:6ff with 2:1ff. and F. Horst, *Job*, BK 16/1[3] (1974) IX, 22f. The word שנית interpolated in

Jonah 3:1 could show the literary "growth rings" as it does in Gen. 22:15 (cf. v. 11). Do we not also detect signs of a different narrator in a number of significant little linguistic details, immediately after the story has been taken up again? It begins with the different preposition קרא אליה, "cried out to" (3:2b) instead of קרא עליה (1:2b; but cf. pp. 139f. below); and — more strikingly still — as the story goes on אלהים (Elohim) is often used as the name for God (3:3b, 10; 4:6-9), whereas chaps. 1-2 use יהוה (Yahweh) throughout (cf. L. Schmidt, *De Deo* 18ff.).

But are these observations enough for us to reconstruct two separate literary strata? L. Schmidt *(De Deo* 18-47) works out a basic stratum to which he believes the following passages belong: 1:2; 3:3a (without "in accordance with Yahweh's word"), 3:3b-10; 4:1, 5a, 6aα (without "Yahweh"), 4:6b-11 (with Elohim instead of Yahweh in v. 10). At all events, it is impossible to overlook the formative power of the later narrator, to whom we owe the book in its present form. In 4:2 he has linked the narrative material of chap. 1 with chaps. 3f.; he, Yahweh's witness of chap. 1, lets Jonah go to Nineveh in 3:3a "in accordance with Yahweh's word." In 2:1 he says that Yahweh "appointed" the fish, as (Yahweh) Elohim "appointed" the created things in 4:6-8. So all that we can establish with any degree of certainty is that the narrator whose work we read today has independently fused together traditional material that had already taken on more or less fixed shape. Whether it had already been given literary form before him remains uncertain. At all events we lack the indisputably cogent arguments and distinguishing criteria with which we were able to support the assumption that 2:2-10 is a literary interpolation (see p. 128 above).

Setting

Our detailed interpretation will have to start from the assumption that the scenes in 1:1-3 and 1:4-16 find their continuation in 2:1, 11 and 3:1- 3a. We shall try to discover more particularly where earlier material has been absorbed and how it has been handled. The "fish" theme (2:1, 11) may have been prompted by the tales current in ports like Joppa; see U. Steffen, *Mysterium* (1963) 89; H. W. Wolff, *Studien* (1964, 1975[2]) 20-28; and L. Schmidt, *De Deo* (1976) 57-59.

The question about the psalm's origin and its introduction (2:2-10) is a subject that has to be treated separately from this. It is uncertain whether the psalm ever existed independently in its present form; cf. O. Kaiser, "Wirklichkeit" (1973) 97. It is noticeable that individual lines certainly pick up sentences from psalms that have come down to us, either exactly (for v. 4b cf. Ps. 42:7b) or approximately (for v. 3a cf.,Ps. 120:1; for v. 5a cf. Ps. 31:22a). This may be said more often still of part-sentences (cf. the detailed commentary). But this very fact could show the interpolator's independent attempt to put together a suitable poem out of separate traditional elements. That would explain why the frequent references to distress at sea which we find here are not found in any other psalms (vv. 4, 6f.). It could be the reason why the psalm begins with an account of the psalmist's distress, and addresses Yahweh directly, even at points where other psalms of thanksgiving speak *about* him (see p. 129 above). But the link with traditional material still influences the writer more strongly than his inclination to pick up specific themes belonging to the story — Jonah's flight, for example, or the fish. Perhaps the interpolator himself composed the psalm. In this case he would of course have been later than the narrator (for another view see O. Eissfeldt, *Einleitung in das Alte Testament* [1964³], 548; G. M. Landes, *Interp* 21 [1967] 30: "It was carefully selected for this purpose from some other source"; cf. p. 134 below). The Jonah whom this writer presents is a transformed Jonah. He reacts quite differently from the Jonah of chap. 4. He has taken events to heart, and so becomes a teacher of the congregation (2:9, 10b), which the Jonah of the story certainly is not. For the place of the psalm in the narrative, see also pp. 140f. below.

Commentary

2:1　The last thing the narrator has told us about Jonah was that the sailors threw him into the sea (1:15a). When he comes back to his "hero," it is again — as it was after Jonah's flight in 1:3-4 — in order that he can tell what Yahweh now does with him. Once more Yahweh makes use of dumb nature — earlier the storm, now the fish. Wisdom thinking has made this theologian familiar with Yahweh's playful dealings with his creatures (Prov. 8:30f.; cf. G. Bader, "Das Gebet Jonas" 162). He translates this into humorous narrative. Yahweh *"appoints"* the fish, as human beings employ servants (Dan. 1:11; cf. *pu'al* 1 Chron. 9:29) or "allot" food (Dan. 1:5, 10; cf. "nights of misery" in Job 7:3). In *qal* מנה means "count" or "number off" (Gen. 13:16; Ps. 90:12, and frequently elsewhere) and therefore in the *pi'el* form "apportion" or "designate," in the case of people "employ" or "nominate"; cf. R. D. Wilson, E. Jenni *Pi'el* (1969) 213, and 4:6-8. In its *pi'el* form, this word too belongs to later, Aramaic-influenced literature; cf. p. 76 above and M. Wagner, *Aramaismen* (1966) 78.

For Jonah, Yahweh employs a "great fish." Landlubbers like the Israelites were unable to define the beast any more closely. The Septuagint (κῆτος) may already be thinking of a whale or shark. On the coast people told stories about legendary heroes such as Heracles or Perseus who climbed into the mouth of a sea monster, killed it from within, and then emerged from the slain beast again. The hero of the Jason saga is devoured by a dragon. He frees himself by means of a magic ointment, which makes the beast so sick that it spews Jason out (cf. H. W. Wolff, *Studien* [1964, 1975²] 24). Inspired by tales like this, our narrator gives himself a free hand. In his story neither the sea monster nor the "hero" develop any independent activity. Yahweh commands the beast to swallow Jonah (as he later commands it to vomit Jonah up, v. 11). In the language of the psalms, בלע, "devour," always means acute danger, indeed often annihilation; cf. Jer. 51:34; Ps. 21:9; 35:25; 69:15; 106:17; 124:3; Lam. 2:2, 5, 8, 16; at this point the reader is by no means intended to think in terms of rescue (for a different view cf. G. M. Landes, JBL 86 [1967]).

Jonah's helplessness is further underlined by the feature that he had to spend *"three days and three nights in the fish's belly."* This particular statement

of time may undoubtedly have been prompted by myths and sagas. The "black,
moon" (new moon) rests for three days in heaven before the sharp sword of the
moon's sickle acts as a reminder that the monster by whom the moon was devoured was slit up from within. The messenger of the gods seeks for help "three
days and three nights" after Inanna had descended into "the land of no return"
(cf. *ANET* 52-57). Heracles "sprang into the mouth of the monster, killed it from
within, and, as some say, emerged as victor from the dead beast's body only_after
three days" (U. Steffen, *Mysterium* [1963] 41; cf. H. W. Wolff, *Studien* 22ff.).
Our narrator mentions this period of time because it is relatively long; cf. 3:3b; 1
Sam. 30:12; Esther 4:16; Luke 2:46; J. B. Bauer, "Drei Tage" (1958) 356, and
G. M. Landes, *Interp* 21 (1967) 11f. After so long a period there is hardly any
hope of survival (Luke 24:21). The great fish, the devouring, and the three days
and three nights in no way hint at any rescue operation; on the contrary. It is not
until v. 11 that the writer indicates that during this period of time the great fish
with its passenger had to cover the distance which the Tarshish ship had been driv-
en off course on its way to its far-off destination, in spite of the sailors' efforts to
row in the opposite direction (1:13). What is more important is that the length of
Jonah's stay in the fish's belly is already fixed in 1b. The point in time when Jonah
will be rescued and brought to land is not determined by any prayer. It is Yahweh's free disposal which creates the presuppositions that make it possible for his
stubborn messenger to take up his mission again. The fact that the vehicle is a
wholly fantastic one is something which the interpreter must not try to rationalize
away. With humor as his instrument, the narrator confronts Jonah's miscalculated
flight (1:3) with the incalculable potentialities of his God; cf. G. Quell, "Das
Phänomen des Wunders im Alten Testament," *Fests. W. Rudolph* (1961) 274f.

[2:2]   An interpolator (see pp. 128f. above) has inserted the psalm at the very
point where the story describes the length of Jonah's stay in the fish's belly; and he
introduces this psalm as an imploring complaint (פלל *hithpo'el,* as 4:2). That he
did not initially intend it to be understood as a hymn of thanksgiving emerges from
the circumstance that in 2b — picking up v. 1b — he explicitly stresses that the
prayer was spoken "out of the belly of the fish"; and this indication of place is immediately explained at the beginning of the psalm as meaning that it is the place of
"distress," indeed "the belly of the underworld"; ממעי הדגה, "out of the fish-
belly," in v. 2 corresponds to מצרה, "out of my distress," and מבטן שאול, "out
of the belly [or womb] of Sheol," in v. 3. The prayer is therefore intended first of
all to bring out Jonah's complete helplessness and so, at the same time, his
readiness to turn at last to the God from whom he has tried to escape. The interpolator invites readers who have understood the Jonah satire to share this attitude.

[2:3]   His psalm clearly shows the influence of the traditional language of the
psalms. The first five-stress line corresponds almost exactly to Ps. 120:1; it is an
account of the kind typically incorporated in a psalm of thanksgiving; cf. Ps.
118:5; 34:4; 138:3; 18:6; but it is not preceded by an utterance of praise, as in Ps.
118:1-4; 34:1-3; 138:1-2; 18:1f. In this respect it resembles Ps. 120:1, which re-

mains a complaint pure and simple, even as it goes on. Two small features which differentiate Ps. 120:1 from the opening of the Jonah psalm are worth noting. The phrase בַּצָּרָתָה לִּי ("*in* my distress") turns into מצרה לי ("*out of* my distress"). The assimilation to v. 2b, ממעי הדגה ("out of the fish-belly") will be intentional; cf. the comment above. Secondly, קראתי, "I called," is carried up to the very beginning of the psalm and is therefore emphasized. This too may well be intentional. Jonah has finally called upon Yahweh, as the captain had vainly begged him to do in 1:6 (קְרָא אֶל־אֱלֹהֶיךָ, "call to your god!") and as the sailors had long since done (1:14 וַיִּקְרְאוּ אֶל־יהוה, "they called to Yahweh"). For the interpolator, the cry of prayer cannot be separated from the answer. The new Jonah speaks in the second five-stress line also (v. 3b). In the psalms passed down to us, we do not find any parallel in this case as close as the one we found for v. 3a. But the poet is probably borrowing from traditional material here too; for it is only that which makes the transition to v. 3b (where Yahweh is addressed directly) comprehensible. The statement that the plea now rises to God "from the belly of the underworld" could be seen as a deliberate interpretation of the situation in which the prayer is uttered: "out of the belly of the fish" (v. 2b). The word שְׁאוֹל, "Sheol," the underworld, is an echo of the theme of Ps. 18:5, just as later vv. 4a and 6a echo Ps. 18:4f. At latest, the words "I implored, thou didst hear my voice" are a reminiscence of traditional material; for the change in the direction of the address (see p. 129 above) coincides with the echo of Ps. 31:22b (שָׁמַעְתָּ קוֹל תַּחֲנוּנַי בְּשַׁוְּעִי, "Thou didst hear the voice of my supplication when I cried to thee"), for in what follows the influence of Ps. 31:22a on v. 5a is unmistakable. We can therefore see that there is considerable reliance here on the traditional language of the psalms, which is slightly adapted to the context of the story. In the process of this adaptation, Jonah's particular lot, in the fish's belly, has become a more general human fate; and his trouble has already been completely surmounted.

[2:4]   Verse 4a does not, either, borrow words and viewpoints from 1:4—2:1; it draws on psalms that were already familiar. In the Jonah story, the seamen throw Jonah into the sea; in the psalm, it is Yahweh — the subject of the address — who himself casts Jonah into the waves. In 1:12, 15 this "hurling" or throwing is called הֵטִיל אֶל־הַיָּם, in accordance with 1:4f.; in the psalm the word used is הִשְׁלִיךְ, as often elsewhere in the psalter (Ps. 102:10; 51:11; 71:8; and frequently). On the other hand טוּל *hi̊phil* does not occur in the psalter at all. "The heart of the sea" also replaces the language of the prose narrator (יָם, 1:4f., 9, 12, 15) by the elevated language of the psalms (Ps. 46:2; see textual note to v. 4a and b). In the phraseology of the psalms, "the flood" (נהר) which encompasses the petitioner is more reminiscent of the mythical underground rivers of chaos and death which belong to the underworld (Isa. 44:27; Ps. 24:2; 93:3) rather than the Mediterranean, especially since the whole passage (vv. 3-6) repeatedly echoes the mood and language of Ps. 18:4f. The subject of the "encompassing" (סבב) in Psalm 18 are "the cords of the underworld" rather than the floods; cf. C. Barth, *Die Errettung vom Tode* (1947) 85f. In Ugaritic texts dealing with mythical material, *ym* and *nhr* are frequently used parallel to one another, as synonyms; cf. especially in C. H.

Gordon, *Ugaritic Textbook* 68, Analecta Orienta 38 (1965) 12-17, 19f., 22, 25, 27, 29f. (= CTA 2 IV), cf. 129, 7-9 (= CTA 2 III) and 51 II, 6-7 (= CTA 4 II). See textual note on v. 4b for a view contrary to W. Rudolph's reading of v. 4a. The fact that v. 4b agrees exactly with Ps. 42:7b is not a reason to put it down as a later addition (C. A. Keller, W. Rudolph). It rather confirms the considerable dependency on already familiar complaints and songs of thanksgiving. The circumstance that, as we have seen, the lines are grouped into prosodic units also lends support to the view that the five-stress line was an original component of the Jonah psalm. Verse 4 describes only the past distress (as do vv. 5-7a); it does not also refer to the fact that the prayer has already been granted, according to v. 3. The distress to which the psalmist testifies in v. 3 is now described more precisely as the distress of someone who is drowning; and the petitioner also confesses to his God that no one other than God himself delivered him over to the waters (aα.b). In the three statements (aα.β.b) the reader sees the deadly peril mounting.

[2:5]   Verse 5 makes this danger clear by quoting the original complaint. This is frequent practice in songs of thanksgiving: אני אמרתי (''I said'') is also used as introduction in Ps. 31:22; 41:4; 116:11; Isa. 38:10; cf. Lam. 3:54. Even apart from the introductory formula, the quotation itself (aβ) is reminiscent of the wording of Ps. 31:22a (v. 22b was already echoed in 3b). The verb used there נִגְרַזְתִּי (''I am cut off'') almost sounds like נגרשתי; two manuscripts even offer this saying out of Jonah 2 as reading in Psalm 31. It is also possible that the original reading in both passages (as well as in Lam. 3:54) was נִגְרַזְתִּי (L. Delekat's view, *VT* 14 [1964] 11). Otherwise all that is missing in v. 5a compared with Ps. 31:22a is בְחָפְזִי, ''in my alarm.'' The omission could have had factual reasons. The petitioner in Psalm 31 talks about his frightened scurrying away, as if he were someone who was being persecuted (v. 15); this does not fit the drowning theme. Moreover, rhythmically the omission makes the regular five-stress line possible (cf. p. 130 above). Again we see that our poet takes over already existing phraseology as exactly as he can (for example, he borrows from Ps. 42:7b word for word in 4b), but makes slight alterations for the sake of the meaning (as in v. 3a; Ps. 120:1; cf. p. 134 above). In the context 5a explains the deadly danger as exclusion from Yahweh's presence (''cast away from your sight''; cf. H. W. Wolff, *Anthropologie des Alten Testaments* [1973] 160-162 [Eng. *Anthropology of the Old Testament* (1974) 106-107]; the prose narrator would say מִלִּפְנֵי יהוה ''away from Yahweh,'' 1:3ab). How could the petitioner be sure of the end of this rejection? Through the fact that he was allowed to see Yahweh's holy temple again. This is what he longs for in 5b; see textual note to v. 5a above. היכל קדשׁך, ''your holy temple,'' means the sanctuary at Jerusalem (Ps. 79:1). It is the place of Yahweh's (scrutinizing) eyes (cf. Ps. 11:4 for the parallelism of the utterances in 5a and b). The person who can reach the sanctuary has arrived at the place where he can offer the song of thanksgiving (Ps. 138:1f.; cf. Ps. 138:3 with 3a; cf. p. 134 above). At the time of the complaint quoted, the petitioner was far away from it.

[2:6-7]   The floods ''surround'' him. The word אפף is found only in psalms (18:4; 40:12; 116:3; 2 Sam. 22:5). In the same form (''they surrounded me'') the verb in Ps. 18:4 and 116:3 has as its subject "cords of death" (חֶבְלֵי־מָוֶת) and in 2 Sam. 22:5 "breakers of death" (מִשְׁבְּרֵי־מָוֶת), cf. מִשְׁבָּרֶיךָ in v. 4b = Ps. 42:7b). But here the subject is the phrase familiar from Ps. 69:1, "water"which "reaches up to the neck" (cf. textual note to v. 6a above). As in v. 4, the deadly peril of the drowning man builds up in three sentences (aα.β.b). The "flood" that encompassed him in v. 4a has now become "the primeval sea"; Ps. 42:7a talked about תהום, "the deep," parallel to 7b, the sentence which we found again word for word in 4b; cf. also Ps. 88:17. For the nonmythical use of תהום in the Old Testament as a whole, cf. C. Westermann, BK 1/1, 145ff., Eng., *Genesis 1-11* (1984) 104ff. The psalmist is fascinated by the notion of mighty masses of water and their imprisoning effect (סבב, "encircle," אפף, "surround," "encompass"); the story (1:4 — 2:1) lets him linger on this idea. So in vv. 6b-7a, at the climax of his account of the distress, he arrives at statements which correspond neither to Jonah's special situation nor to the utterances of traditional psalms (cf. J. D. Magonet, *Form* [1973] 77-90). Sea-plants twisted round the drowning person's head perform the function of "deadly cords" (Ps. 18:4f.). The word סוף is otherwise used only for the reeds on the banks of the Nile (Exod. 2:3, 5; Isa. 19:6). But here we have to think of huge algae growing in the depths of the sea, for the קצבי הרים are probably the "anchorages" of the mountains which let them stand firm above the primeval waters (cf. Ps. 24:2). They correspond to what Deut. 32:22 calls "the foundations" of the mountains (מוֹסְדֵי הָרִים) and Job 28:9 their "roots" (שֹׁרֶשׁ); cf. also 1QH 3.31. That the Jonah of the psalm was in this way delivered up to death is made unmistakably clear by the last sentence in the description of his distress. In the psalter, the dead person is often described as someone who "descends" into the dust (עָפָר, 22:29), into the pit (בּוֹר 28:1; 30:3) into the grave (שַׁחַת, 30:9) or into the underworld (שְׁאוֹל, 55:15). But on this one occasion the destination is called "the land which closed its bars behind me for ever." That the writer deliberately wanted to build up the triple use of ירד (descend) in 1:3 and 5 (see p. 112 above), as J. D. Magonet considers (*Form* 13f.) is improbable. The idea of the world of the dead as the land of no return is a common one, both in the Old Testament and its surrounding cultures (cf. Job 7:9f. and F. Horst, *Hiob,* BK 16/1 [1960] 117). But the Old Testament offers no other example of this particular expression. The word אַרְץ ("land"), which also means the innermost parts of the earth (Ps. 139:15) means here the underworld, like the Akkadian *erṣetu* (W. von Soden, *Akkadisches Handwörterbuch* [1965ff.] 245). The word is in no way used in antithesis to the idea of the primeval waters (vv. 4, 6), for Ps. 71:20 can also talk about the תְּהֹמוֹת הָאָרֶץ "the depths of the earth." The "bars" indicate that the world of the dead is conceived of as a fortified city (cf. Amos 1:3; Isa. 45:2 and H. W. Wolff, *Joel/Amos,* BK 14/2 [1975²] 189 [Eng., *Joel and Amos,* 1977, on Amos 1:5]). If these bars are closed "behind" (בעד) a human being, they remain "finally" shut; on לעולם as legal term for what is unalterable, see H. W. Wolff, *Hosea,* BK 14/1 (1976³); Eng., *Hosea* (1974) 52. Thus for the psalmist, Jonah's fate at the end of the voyage seemed to be an inescapable descent to death.

But he was able to perceive that the final word is spoken by Yahweh's mercy, and that this is so, not merely for the men on the ship and the people in

Nineveh, but for Jonah too, even though all that he wanted for himself was to die (1:12; 4:3, 8f.). The unexpected turn of events from the threat of death to new life is reported in v. 7b, in the form of a grateful address to Yahweh, his God; on יהוה אלהי, "Yahweh my God," cf. יהוה אלהיו, "Yahweh his God," in v. 2 and p. 130 above. For Yahweh to "lead out" the helpless is his very own, most characteristic act of salvation, ever since the Israelites were led out of Egypt (on עלה *hiph'il,* "bring up," cf. H. W. Wolff, *Joel/Amos,* BK 14/2, 206 [Eng., *Joel and Amos*], on Amos 2:10). Psalms 30:3 and 71:20 also use the word for a rescue from death. Now the familiar language of the Psalms breaks through again — in חיי משחת, "out of the pit," as well, as Ps. 103:4 shows. Now that Jonah's life has been saved, the unusual phrase about the grave of the sea (vv. 4, 6-7) is replaced by the usual word for the grave, שחת (as in Ps. 16:10; 49:9; 103:4; Isa. 38:17; and frequently elsewhere).

[2:8] In v. 8, in a similar way to v. 3, the whole path of distress, prayer, and the granting of the petition is traced once more. Here again it can be shown that the poet falls back on familiar phraseology. Perhaps this is the reason why Yahweh is talked about in the third person in v. 8a, but is spoken to directly in 8b, as he is earlier, in v. 7b. Where עטף *hithpa'el,* "faint," is applied to the subject נפש, "life" (Ps. 107:5), and where זכר, "remember," appears in the immediate context (Ps. 77:3) Yahweh is also referred to in the third person. He is addressed directly in Ps. 142:3; 143:4, where the verbal form follows עלי, as it does here. That the author has drawn from the treasury of the psalms for his language may count as certain. What is less clear is *which* texts he had in mind. עטף *hithpa'el,* "languish," describes the subjective feeling of distress that has been endured; cf. textual note to v. 8a. The endangered person feels completely impotent and despondent. In himself there was nothing in which he could find comfort, or through which he could save himself. Then "he thought of Yahweh." זכר, perfect, means the remembering of Yahweh which is the presupposition for turning to him (cf. textual note to v. 8b) — indeed זכר means this "turning," this approach, itself (so W. Schottroff, *Gedenken,* WMANT 15 [1967²] 177f.). So the distress and the prayer are again mentioned in order to stress with particular force in 8b the fact that the prayer was heard. For it is this that the writer wants to declare here in all solemnity: that the imploring lament to Yahweh "found admittance" (ותבוא) at the place of his presence, in his holy temple. His prayer succeeded in achieving what was still denied to the petitioner himself — to enter the sanctuary (v. 5; cf. Ps. 5:7a). What the petitioner still implored in the songs of lament Ps. 88:2; 102:1, is reported here, in very similar words, as having taken place. The power of Yahweh's presence in the sanctuary allows even the cry from the far-off depths of the sea to arrive at its goal.

[2:9] After this experience, the petitioner whose prayer has been heard becomes the teacher of his fellows. His teaching, like no other passage in the interpolated psalm, allows us to identify the listeners to whom he is speaking. They are people who worship something different, instead of Yahweh. The construct chain

הבלי־שׁוא intensifies the meaning of the individual, almost synonymous nouns into a powerful superlative (cf. Joüon, *Gr* §141m): הבל, "what is emptily null and transitory," is nothing other than שׁוא, "uselessly worthless deceit." The compound is known to us from Ps. 31:6, where it means "idols," as it does in Deut. 32:21. But whereas the petitioner of Ps. 31:6 declares that he hates the worshipers of idols, here these worshipers are told about the other side of the coin: "they forsake the one who is faithful to them." Here חסד, "steadfast love," does not mean human faithfulness. It means the divine attitude which in the Psalter is continually extolled as God's faithfulness, goodness, and graciousness, which is the one true help for human beings. The third person plural suffix does not refer to the subject of the faithfulness; it means its object (cf. Ps. 59:17; 144:2), i.e., those to whom the dependable help is given. In 4:2 חסד, as almost always, is one of the divine attributes. These can sometimes be talked about "almost as if they were personalities" (W. Zimmerli, *ThWNT* 9:375, 23ff.; cf. Ps. 23:6; 57:3; 85:10, 11, 13). But here the word is used directly as synonym for God (cf. Ps. 144:2 and N. Glueck, *Das Wort ḥesed,* BZAW 47 [1927] 61f.). The teaching is unambiguous: anyone who respects idols and deserts Yahweh exchanges reliable goodness for what is empty and useless. This shows that the listeners whom the psalmist is addressing are not heathen; they are Israelites. Otherwise יעזבו would not fit: they "forsake" Yahweh, "fall away" from the One whose name is "help" (cf. Jer. 1:16; 2:13). Thus the interpolator shows readers of the book of Jonah the repulsive picture of the old Jonah over against a new picture — the picture of Jonah the man of prayer and the teacher, who recognizes the foolishness of his backsliding — not least in contrast with the counterpicture of the heathen in chaps. 1 and 3 — and who allows the stubbornness of chap. 4 to be overcome by Yahweh's persistent goodness. But what taught him most of all was his rescue from the sea.

[2:10]   So the new Jonah comes to make his sacrifice of thanksgiving. At last he does what the heathen sailors did before him. The poet can deliberately link up with 1:16 (thus G. H. Cohn, *Jonah* [1969] 93) by quite obviously taking over the repertoire of the songs of thanksgiving in the psalter. The first thing that belongs to the celebration of the thank offering is "the voice of the song of gratitude" (קול תודה), with its loud jubilation (Ps. 118:15; cf. 26:7; 42:4). This ushers in the thanksgiving meal for Yahweh in the group of fellow celebrants. The cohortative (אזבחה "I will sacrifice," like אשׁלמה afterwards   "I will fulfill") indicates the declaration of intent ("I will"). The fulfillment of the vow is promised in the same way. What is vowed in the song of lament can be the feast of thanksgiving itself. But over and above that, the vow may promise continual praise of Yahweh and lasting trust in him; cf. comments on 1:16 above. The parallel statement about sacrifice and vow is frequent in the individual song of thanksgiving, where the phraseology used is very closely related to our passage here; cf. Ps. 66:13; 116:14, 17f.; also 50:14. The final sentence again passes over from a grateful address to Yahweh to a confession of faith made in the presence of the congregation. It corresponds to Ps. 3:8a but moves the name of Yahweh into an emphatic position at the end, thereby once more underlining the teaching of v. 9. With this the psalmist succinctly shows the way in which he has interpreted the book of Jonah, in the form in which he found it: Yahweh's will to save can be wholly and unconditionally relied upon, even in the case of an intractable Jonah.

[2:11]   The ancient storyteller does not even now give expression to these ideas (see comments on 2:1 above). His stress is rather on Yahweh's grandiose power of disposal. It is this which makes the fish vomit Jonah up. The theme may have been inspired by the Jason saga and other similar material (see p. 132 above). But the reader will detect a bitter humor and a mocking note in these undignified dealings with Jonah. The word קיא is only used in the Old Testament in images that rouse disgust (Isa. 19:14; 28:8; Jer. 48:26; Job 20:15; Lev. 18:28); it is a coarse word which we might translate as "to throw up." Cf. on the other hand Jer. 51:44 and the comment below. So the man who is on the run from the Lord of sea and land finds himself grotesquely "high and dry" again. The satirist is not interested in any precise designation of the landing place. Instead he gives scope for the rude laughter of his readers. What a figure Jonah makes, over there on dry land! He wanted to run away and to die — we have been told as much, at considerable length. And now, in the tersest words: swallowed up by the fish at Yahweh's command, three days in its belly, and then vomited up onto land again, as if he were something intolerably indigestible. This is the storyteller's ironic view of the person who thinks he can escape Yahweh. And yet this irony, with all its exaggeration, is slyly absurd rather than bitter.

It would be impermissible for us to interpret this satirical sketch as an allegory of the Babylonian exile, in the light of Jer. 51:34, 44 (cf. J. D. Smart, "Jonah," *IB* 6 [1956] 888). Only the "devouring" and the "vomiting up" link the two texts; indeed in actual wording, it is only the "devouring" (בלע) which they have in common. Instead of the great fish, the writer talks about a dragon (תַּנִּין), the word used for his belly is different (כָּרֵשׂ), and the vomiting is described in much politer terminology. Yahweh brings the person who has been devoured out of the monster's mouth (מִפִּיו . . . וְהֹצֵאתִי). Babylon is described as monster. But in the present scene of our novella too, the satirist is interested solely in Yahweh's relationship to Jonah.

[3:1-3a]   After the unusual narrative climax of 2:11, the writer can only intensify into effect through the almost chilly recapitulation in 3:1f. of 1:1f. Through Yahweh's power and his humor (Ps. 2:4) Jonah has been brought back to the very beginning of his story. With relaxed patience, Yahweh now begins all over again — "a second time." The charge to go to Nineveh is repeated word for word (3:2a = 1:2a). But the command to preach is not this time supported by the reason, as in 1:2b; now Jonah is given the message itself (3:2b). The change of prepositions, from עַל to אֶל may be connected with this modification: the wickedness of Nineveh is the reason why Jonah is to speak "against" the city (עַל); the message itself has to be carried "into it" (אֶל). What the message is to be, is not expounded. In the light of the book's theme, the only important thing at this point is that Jonah's preaching should reproduce exactly what Yahweh now says to him (on the relative clause, see textual note to 3:2c). The relative clause is a reminiscence of Exod. 6:29b, where the charge to Pharoah which Moses is given is also entrusted to a reluctant messenger (cf. v. 30). The expectation of obedience is underlined in both cases. The reader's suspense (how will Jonah behave this time?) is immediately relieved by the scene's final sentence. This picks up the first two words in 1:3, but goes on to indicate that Jonah's actions now accord exactly with the commission which has been repeated in 3:2a. The writer explicitly adds that Jonah's new beginning was "in accordance with Yahweh's word." This brings the third scene in the book to the conclusion to which it has been tending.

Purpose

Yahweh's actions and his word have certainly not made Jonah any less taciturn. He has not a single word to say to Yahweh, let alone an admission of guilt or a declaration of his willingness to obey. He has no more to say to Yahweh than he had in the first and second scenes (see p. 123 above). It is only in 4:2ff. that he will turn to his God, for the final reckoning.

Now the narrator has much more to say about Yahweh than he has about Jonah. God's silent action by way of the fish makes it possible for God's utterance to lead to Jonah's silent obedience. The way through death becomes a preparation for service. The hurling into the sea delivers Jonah up to the powers of annihilation (1:15a). This threat of death is implemented through the great fish, since he has been appointed "to devour" Jonah (cf. p. 133 above; also C. A. Keller, *Joël, Abdias, Jonas,* CAT 11 [1965] 277: "The fish signifies hell"). The length of the period spent in the fish puts the seal on the hopelessness of the situation (cf. p. 133 above). But when Jonah is vomited up onto dry land, all at once the death for which he has been destined, and which has been confirmed three separate times, proves after all to be Yahweh's preserving act — an act described in highly grotesque terms. He patiently begins a second time with his escapee. Everything is designed to serve the one purpose: that Jonah, who in 1:3 wanted "to get away from Yahweh," should now act "according to Yahweh's word." So *Yahweh* is the first and last word in this third scene, just as it was, essentially speaking, in the very first scene of all (1:1-3). But the end has been transformed. In spite of everything, Yahweh brings Jonah on the way to Nineveh.

This Jonah becomes the subject of the later interpolation: "Behold he is praying" (Acts 9:11). Did the interpolator not thoroughly understand the satire which exposed Jonah to ridicule and glorified God's mighty goodness and graciousness? Was he afraid that the reader might mistakenly draw a fatalistic conclusion? Was it at all conceivable that the seamen and the Ninevites should be saved after their petition (1:14f.; 3:8ff.), and that Jonah should escape judgment without a single word of prayer? At all events, in the introduction to the psalm (v. 2), as well as in the psalm itself (vv. 3ab, 5ab, 8ab) the writer stresses the importance of calling on God before liberation. And here references to the particular features of the Jonah story are very sketchy (see p. 129 above). We saw how "the confines of the individual biography are thrown open in the direction of what is common to all humanity" (G. Bader, "Das Gebet Jonas"[1973] 188; also p. 134 above). The congregation can enter into this psalm, as thanksgiving for rescue from different kinds of danger. But it is particularly appropriate for people who are in danger of forsaking Yahweh, who is goodness in person (see comments on 2:9 above). Jonah in the story was a person of this kind. All he could bring himself to utter were petitions of protest and longings to die (4:3f., 8b, 9b). In the context of the final chapter, the redactor could not well interpolate a totally different prayer without destroying the narrative. The best place, relatively speaking, for a psalm in which a new Jonah could find expression was in his extremist necessity (i.e., immediately after 2:1). The Jonah of the psalm shows that he has grasped the sarcastic teaching of the prose text, since he acknowledges Yahweh's will to save for himself as well as for all others (10b). Chapter 2:2-10 introduces a legendary element into the satiric novella, for legends deal with what can be emulated (A. Jolles, *Einfache Formen* [1968[4]] 34ff.). Here as nowhere else Jonah becomes a model, in the abyss of his forlornness. So the psalm became a paradigm prayer — a model both for the synagogue in ancient times and for early Christian art, very strongly influencing the themes with which it dealt; cf. E. Dinkler, *RGG[3]* 1:179; E. Stommel, "Zum Problem der frühchristlichen Jonadarstellungen," *Jahrbuch für Antike und Christentum* 1 (1958) 112-115; U. Steffen, *Mysterium* (1963) 108f. The prayer is generally interpreted as an act of repentance; for Jonah is shown in the process of being devoured, head first, and then in the process of being vomited up, also head first. A marginal miniature illustrating the psalm of Jonah in the 9th-century Mount Athos Psalter Pantokratoros 61 shows Jonah inside a monster which has front paws and a furled dragon's tail; he is kneeling upright, so that the monster's belly is arched and dilated (cf. P. Huber, *Athos* [1969] 172, no. 54). In the whale pulpits in Silesia and Bohemia, the preacher had to climb up right through the fish's body, in order to address the congregation out of the beast's open mouth; cf. U. Steffen, *Mysterium* 135f., and G. Grundmann, *Schlesische Barockkirchen und Klöster* (1958), 20f. and Pl. 38: "Walfischkanzel der Kath. Kirche Reinerz 1730" (whale pulpit in the Catholic church in Reinerz, 1730).

Where the ancient story stresses what Yahweh does with Jonah and for him, the later addition depicts Jonah's prayer as repentance in the framework of Yahweh's work. But neither stratum suggests that we should here look for an allegory, depicting Israel's history in Babylonian exile, parallel to Jer. 51:34, 44 (see p. 139 above) — an allegory in which Jonah would represent the people and the fish Babylon, and in which the exile would be interpreted to mean that Israel should fulfill its office as witness in the Gentile world; cf. A. D. Martin, *The Prophet Jonah: The Book and the Sign* (1926); A. R. Johnson, "Jon. 2.3-10" (1950); P. R. Ackroyd, *Exile and Restoration* (1968). M. Burrows rightly maintains a contrary view; cf. his "Category" (1970), 80-107, esp. 89f. The story would like to prepare its readers to discover in many new situations Yahweh's mighty goodness — the goodness which works on Jonah and through him, in spite of all that this refractory messenger can do.

In Matt. 12:38-40 Jesus rejects the demand of the scribes and Pharisees for a sign: the only sign they are to be given is the σημεῖον Ἰωνᾶ, "the sign of Jonah.'' What this sign is, we are told in the quotation from 2:1b, according to which ''Jonah was three days and three nights in the belly of the whale.'' Curiously enough, Jonah's rescue is not mentioned; nor does the interpretation make any reference to Jesus' resurrection. The only feature referred to is the sojourn of ''three days and three nights in the heart of the earth,'' in accordance with the period spent by Jonah in the fish's belly. It sounds as if this logion was originally intended merely to emphasize the words in which Jesus refuses a sign, by pointing to the vexatious and troublesome sequestration of the prophet. This would be quite possible in the context of an ''atomistic'' handling of Scripture. But Matthew was probably already thinking of both Jesus' resurrection and Jonah's rescue as being ''a legitimation of the one sent by God'' (J. Jeremias, *ThWNT* 3:413; cf. also E. Schweizer, NTD 2¹³ [1973] 190). At all events, in the book of Jonah the fish is the deadly abyss of the person who has been rejected (cf. 1:12ff. with 2:1, 5); and yet the narrator testifies that God is at work and that his deliverance is near even in this rejection. So Jonah's fate became a ''type'' or prefiguration of the fate of Jesus. Cf. K. H. Rengstorf, *ThWNT* 7:231.

Through Jonah, our narrator addresses the whole of his Israel; and in the same way the Christian church should look at itself in the mirror of this grotesque third scene. Very many groups within the church deserve no more than to be devoured and spat out; and yet that church must not forget the playful triumph of her God who, in spite of all, still makes her serviceable and ready to set out at long last on the way to Nineveh. Cf. K. H. Miskotte, *When the Gods Are Silent* (Eng., 1967).

Even the Cattle Repent

Literature

H. Winckler, "Zum buche Jona," *Altorientalische Forschungen* 2, 2 (1900) 260-265. I. B. Schaumberger, "Das Bussedikt des Königs von Nineve bei Jona 3,7.8 in keilschriftlicher Beleuchtung," *Miscellanea Biblica edita a Pontificio Instituto Biblico ad celebrandum annum XXV ex quo conditum est Institutum (1909 — VII Maii — 1934)* 123-134. A. Feuillet, "Les sources du livre de Jonas," *RB* 54 (1947) 161-186. D. W. Thomas, "A Consideration of Some Unusual Ways of Expressing the Superlative in Hebrew," *VT* 3 (1953) 210-224: A. Parrot, *Nineve et l'Ancien Testament*, CAB (1953) (page numbers below are cited from the German translation, *Ninive und das Alte Testament*, BiAr [1955]). H. Bardtke, *Der Erweckungsgedanke in der exilisch-nachexilischen Literatur des Alten Testaments*, ZAW Beiheft 77 (1958) 9-24, esp. 21-23. N. Lohfink, "Jona ging zur Stadt hinaus (Jona 4,5)," *BZ* NF 5 (1961) 185-203. E. Kutsch, " 'Trauerbräuche' und 'Selbstminderungsriten' im Alten Testament," ThSt (B) 78 (1965) 25-42. M. Wagner, *Die lexikalischen und grammatischen Aramaismen im alttestamentlichen Hebräisch*, ZAW Beiheft 96 (1966). G. H. Cohn, *Das Buch Jona im Lichte der biblischen Erzählkunst* (1969). A Jepsen, "Anmerkungen zum Buche Jona: Wort-Gebot-Glaube," *Fests. W. Eichrodt* (1970) 297-305. A. Fáj, "The Stoic Features of the Book of Jonah," *AION* 34 (1974) 309-345. J. Jeremias, "Die Reue Gottes," *BST* 65 (1975) 98-109.

Text

3:3b   Now Nineveh was then (even) for God[a] a great city; to cross it on foot required three days.[b]

4   Then Jonah hastened to go into the city. He went for a whole day.[a] Then he preached and said, "Another forty[b] days, and Nineveh shall be destroyed."[c]

5   But the men of Nineveh put their trust in[a] God. They proclaimed a fast and put on sackcloth, (all of them)[b] from the greatest to the least.[b]

6   [For] the saying had (meanwhile)[a] reached the king of Nineveh. He had risen from his throne, thrown aside his robe of state, put on sackcloth, [b] and sat down in the dust.

7   Then he had proclaimed in Nineveh as[a] an edict[b] of the king and his great men: "Men and beasts, cattle and flocks shall not taste anything

at all; they shall not feed, they shall not drink any water.

8   But they shall put on sackcloth, [a] men and beasts,[a] and shall cry mightily to God. And they shall return every one of them from his wicked ways and from the deed of violence which clings to their hands.

9   Perhaps[a] the God will yet be sorry[b] and will turn away from his burning anger, so that we do not perish."

10   And the[a] God saw their deeds, how they turned from their evil ways. Then the[a] God was sorry for the evil which he had announced he would do to them. And he did not do it.

3a   What is totally unusual among human beings is frequently expressed in the Old Testament like this, or in similar ways; cf. Gen. 10:9; Pss. 36:6; 80:10; also D. W. Thomas, "Consideration" 210f., 216f., on ways of expressing the superlative.

3b   The Hebrew defines the size by way of a nominative: "a distance of three days."

4a   The distance of the preaching place in the center of the city from the city boundary is also merely described by way of a nominative: "a day's distance"; cf. textual note to v. 3b.

4b   Gk τρεῖς, "three," can hardly go back to the original text; for MT is supported by α', σ', and θ' (τεσσαρακοντα, "forty," and also Targ ארבעין); the number *three* must be explained as a scribal error, due to the fact that the number occurs immediately beforehand in 3:3 and twice in 2:1 (1:17). Duhm, Bewer, Jepsen, and others have decided in favor of Gk for factual reasons; see the commentary below.

4c   Again the participle describes the immediately impending future; cf. textual note to 3:2c and BrSynt §44d; Ges-K §116p.

5a   Targ במימרא דיוי is more explicit: "in God's Word."

5b-b   Literally, "from their greatest to their least"; cf. 1 Sam. 30:19 and Joüon, *Gr* §141j.

6a   Compared with the broad, overall account in v. 5, vv. 6-9 are a kind of flashback, which develop in more detail the activities triggered off by Jonah's preaching in v. 4; cf. textual note to 2:1a (1:17a).

6b   Targ ואתכסי presupposes the *hithpaʿel* וַיִּתְכַּס, as in v. 8. The change from *piʿel* to *hithpaʿel* in MT probably goes back to the original text.

7a   Gk and Vg interpret MT in such a way that the wording of the edict begins only after לאמר, i.e., with v. 7b. But then המלך in v. 7a is discordant, since the king is the subject, according to v. 6. Gk therefore interprets the verbs in a passive sense (ἐκηρύχθη καὶ ἐρρέθη, "It has been proclaimed and you have been told"). Vg does not, reading *clamavit et dixit* ("he cried out and said"). To let the wording of the edict begin after בנינוה with מטעם, without לאמר (Rudolph's view, among recent commentators) seems unclear. מן denotes author (2 Sam. 3:37) and cause (2 Chron. 36:12), introduced here by the narrator with the official-sounding phrase "through the edict of the king and his great men," instead of the pronominal form ("through his edict"), which would here sound too weak; moreover, the postulated suffix to טעם would collide with that in גדליו. In Ezra 7:13 the king talks about himself in the first person at the beginning of the edict. This also suggests that the wording of the edict should be seen as beginning after לאמר.

7b   It is only in this one passage that the word טעם is used in the Old Testament in the sense of "command," "edict." It is obviously an Aramaism; cf. Ezra 6:14; 7:23; and M. Wagner, *Aramaismen* [1966] 61.

8a - a   To omit the repetition of the phrase used at the opening of the edict (v. 7b) either entirely (Wellhausen) or in part (omitting והבהמה, Bewer, Rudolph) finds no support through the transmitted text.

9a Literally: "Who knows?"; cf. Joel 2:14; 2 Sam. 12:22; and H. W. Wolff, *Joel/Amos*, BK 14/2, 59 (Eng., *Joel and Amos* on Joel 2:14).

9b ישוב is passed over entirely by Gk. Here it is used as *verbum relativum* with adverbial meaning; cf. Ges-K §120d. For Hebrew ears the idea of God's "repentance" developed in 9b is a complete echo and analogy of the repentance of the Ninevites in v. 8b.

10a The narrator continues to use the language which accords with the thinking of the Ninevites (cf. v. 9a).

Form

The fourth scene is entirely bounded and determined by events in Nineveh. The action moves forward with all the narrative tension proper to the novella form. At the beginning the vast arena is spread out before the reader (v. 3b). Stories beginning with similar circumstantial clauses occur elsewhere as well (cf. 1 Kings 1:1; Gen. 13:2; 37:3). Then Jonah enters the stage briefly (v. 4). Everything that follows undoubtedly results from what he says; but the Ninevites have no further concern with him. They have to do only with God himself (vv. 5-10). From H. Winckler onwards (his commentary dates from 1900), commentators have frequently inclined to shift the picture of the waiting Jonah in 4:5, inserting it immediately after 3:4. But N. Lohfink has shown (1961) that this proposal (which is based on literary criteria) fails to grasp the guiding concern of our narrator. For more detail cf. H. W. Wolff, *Studien* (1964, 1975²) 40-48.

After 3:4 the narrative divides, rather as it does after 1:15a. Jonah disappears from the stage. It is only later, in a new scene, that he is confronted with his God (4:1ff.). First of all the reader has to learn how the threatening oracle stirs up Nineveh to its depths. Here the scenic development resembles that of 1:4-16. First of all the central, overall effect is reported — individual acts afterwards (cf. 3:5 with 1:5, 10, 16). In the context of this method, we are already told in 3:5b that the rites of repentance have been performed by the whole people, even though the order goes forth only in vv. 6ff. This means that vv. 6-9 should probably be understood as a "flashback" explanation, which catches up with events that have already taken place; we came across a similar method in 1:5b, 10b (cf. 2:1). The people affected are mentioned as a whole before their leader (cf. 3:6 with 1:6). If we interpret vv. 6f. as being in the pluperfect, this would explain why (after v. 9) nothing more is said about the implementation of the edict: this was anticipated in v. 5. (Verse 5bβ should especially be noticed; see pp. 150f. below. But even the report about the "believing" in v. 5 already includes the hope only actually expressed later, in v. 9; see pp. 150f. below.) In this way, the report that God withdraws his proclamation of disaster (v. 10) can be skillfully linked with the close of the royal edict, in which this expectation is voiced in open suspense (v. 9: "who knows . . .?). The construction of the scene is in fact masterly.

In this construction, historical interest totally recedes behind the *didactic* concern. The king of Nineveh is neither given a name nor assigned to any particular period. He seems rather to be portrayed as antitype to Jehoiakim, as we know

him from Jeremiah 36 (A. Feuillet's view). In Jerusalem there is no king who is
prepared to rise from his throne in response to Jeremiah's prediction of disaster.
Jehoiakim stays sitting in order to throw the prophet's words into the fire (Jer.
36:22ff.). He does not cast off his royal robes (v. 24), nor does he order any fast.
The disaster falls on "man and beast" (v. 29; cf. Jonah 3:7f.). Jeremiah's hope
that the people would listen afresh and repent, and that God would withdraw his
word of judgment (vv. 3, 7) is not fulfilled. But all this is precisely what actually
takes place in Nineveh, and it is described in vv. 8-10 in the same words. Jeremiah
18:7f. proclaims the doctrine that the message of judgment will be withdrawn
from the Gentiles too, if it brings about repentance. The passage is unique in the
Old Testament; and it is in our present scene alone that this message is shown as
reaching fulfillment. In presenting this the narrator does not merely take over
Jeremian-Deuteronomistic doctrinal tenets; by doing so he also offers a critical
challenge to life in Jerusalem as it was really lived. In this way the narrator introduces into his story an unheard-of hope for the Gentile world.

      The satiric tone cannot be overlooked in this antithetical picture to
Jerusalem. But a number of exaggerations soften its acridity, bringing it close to
the grotesque. This exaggeration already begins with the description of the city's
size (v. 3b) and the general participation in the fast "from the greatest of them to
the least" (v. 5b). But it reaches its climax when even the animals are included in
the full fast and, more than that, are actually supposed to put on the fasting garment and to cry mightily to God (v. 7b). Remembering fanatics on the other side,
the author reckons that "by treating the matter like this, with his tongue in his
cheek, he will rob it of its virulence, and that the criticism will be more disarming
than a serious attack bringing up the heavy guns of theological argument" (B.
Duhm, *ZAW* 31 [1911] 202).

Setting

The narrative construction gives the impression that this is an independent work of
art. Yet the fourth scene shows with equal clarity the narrator's *theological "location" and provenance*. This is obviously within the context of the Jeremian-
Deuteronomistic traditions, as the adoption of leading phrases from Jer. 18:7ff.
and Jeremiah 36 shows (see p. 154 below). We must also ask whether our scene
does not have to be distinguished from the scenes at sea in its *literary pedigree* as
well. For it is noticeable that the name of Yahweh is not used in a single sentence.
Of course, this is quite understandable in the context of the edict (vv. 8f.), just as
it was understandable when it was the sea captain who was speaking (1:6). But the
superlative expression in v. 3b could quite well have been constructed with יהוה,
"Yahweh" (cf. Gen. 10:9; 1 Sam. 26:12), even though compounds with אלהים,
"Elohim," are more frequent (see p. 148 below), and the name for God used in
the superlative is by no means bound to conform to the phraseology of the context
(cf. Ps. 36:5f.). The point becomes really noticeable in v. 5, when the text talks
about faith in "God," whereas 1:16 has talked about fear before "Yahweh";
above all, in v. 10 the narrator himself says *"the God* saw their works," just as the

heathen edict does earlier. This raises the question whether we cannot here detect the self- contained complex of an earlier literary unit which has been used as foundation for the present text — a stratum which came into being independently of chap. 1 and which was incorporated in the present narrative only in a later literary process (L. Schmidt's view; cf. *De Deo* [1976] 23f., 102f.; also 79f. above). And yet in v. 5 "God" as the object of faith is almost required, since the Ninevites have been told nothing about Yahweh (as were the sailors in 1:9). And it is with conscious artistry that 3:10 picks up האלהים from 3:9 (see textual note to v. 10a). Moreover, the fourth scene shows a narrative relationship to the second (see pp. 144f. above). This may be said of important individual features: the sailors pray like the Ninevites (קרא, "cry," is the word used in both 1:14 and 3:8); and in both groups the "leaders" take the initiative (1:6 and 3:6f.). But above all *the purpose* in both passages is the same: "that we do not perish" (1:6 [14]; 3:9 ולא נאבד). All that we can really say with certainty is that the narrator readily absorbs traditional material into his scenes; this is obvious from the Jeremian-Deuteronomistic material (cf. vv. 8-10). Whether this material was already part of the Jonah story in some earlier literary form must remain an open question. At all events, the material has been so firmly welded together in the text as we have it, that it is impossible to arrive at any sound reconstruction of the writer's source through the methods of literary criticism.

Commentary

[3:3b-4]   At the beginning the narrator explains to his reader the way in which he is supposed to imagine Nineveh (see p. 144 above). He takes him back to "time immemorial," making it clear that he is beginning to tell part of a saga, a saga containing a lesson, as it were (on היתה cf. Gen. 1:2; 3:20; also L. Schmidt, *De Deo* [1976] 37f.). This is also the way that Nineveh is presented in the Yahwist's Table of the Nations, as "the great city" (Gen. 10:12) — though in a later interpolation, which was incorporated into the present text at an unsuitable point (H. Gunkel, *Genesis* [1966⁷] 88). The saga-like character of Nineveh is clearer still in vv. 6f., when the title "king of Nineveh" conveys the impression of a vast city-state. This is not in line with archeological findings, but it reflects the writer's intention to create an antitype to Jerusalem (see pp. 145f. above).

Nineveh lay on the left bank of the Tigris, opposite what is today the city of Mosul, at the confluence of the Tigris and the Khosr (north of the Great Zab). Archeologists have been able to excavate the ancient ruins from the *Tell Kuyunjik,* but not from the neighboring *Tell Nebi Yunus* (Tell of the prophet Jonah), which is populated (A. Parrot, "Nineve" [1955] 118ff.).[1] The archeological findings

---

1. F. Sarre and E. Herzfeld (*Archäologische Reise im Euphrat- und Tigris-Gebiet* 2 [1920] 206f.) report that, according to Islamic legend, Jonah's grave is venerated here at "the hill of repentance" (*Tell el-Taubah,* where the Ninevites are supposed to have destroyed their temple and to have broken the idol worshiped in it). Seven pilgrimages to the Jonah sanctuary are the equivalent of one pilgrimage to Mecca. A tooth belonging to the whale is displayed in the sanctuary. A Christian Jonah monastery was incorporated in the Islamic sanctuary round about A.D. 1000.

show that 70 feet of debris represent one of the oldest cities in Mesopotamia, with beginnings going back to the 5th and 4th centuries. Inscriptions record its existence from the end of the 3rd century, designating it one of the cultic places dedicated to the goddess Ishtar. Assyrian kings belonging to the Old, Middle, and Late periods contributed to the building of Nineveh, but it was Sennacherib (704-681) who expanded the city for the first time into what was for a quarter of a century the capital of the neo-Assyrian empire, with palaces, temples, fortifications, and aqueducts (Herodotus 1.193), residing there as "king of Assyria." It was here that Ashurbanipal (668–631) founded the most famous of cuneiform libraries. In 612 the Medes and the neo-Babylonians destroyed the city forever.

For our narrator and his readers, therefore, Nineveh was a power belonging to the remote past—"time out of mind." Notions about the great neo-Assyrian capital mingle with the idea of an ancient city-state. This means that it would be pointless to try to find any basis in historical fact for Nineveh's "fairytale" size. עיר גדולה לאלהים, "a great city even for God," is an ultimate superlative (D. W. Thomas, "Consideration" [1953] 210, 216). The compound with ל is reminiscent of the reference to Nimrod, "the mightiest hunter *before* Yahweh" (לִפְנֵי יהוה) Gen. 10:9 = as far as Yahweh's eyes look upon the whole earth; cf. Gen. 6:11). This parallel is closer to our passage than references to unusually large phenomena, such as "the princes of God" ("mighty prince," Gen. 23:6), "the struggles of God" ("mighty wrestlings," Gen. 30:8), "the terrors of God" ("a very great panic," 1 Sam. 14:15), "the sleep of Yahweh" (1 Sam. 26:12), "the mountains of God" (Ps. 36:6) and "the cedars of God" (Ps. 80:10). Nineveh's size, that is to say, is measured against the incomparable yardstick of God. This superlative too fits in well with the sagalike character.[1] The narrator lends the city specific form by giving it dimensions which were completely unheard-of in the world of the time: "the extent of a three days' march." This means that the city had a diameter of about 40 to 50 miles. Sennacherib's Nineveh was 3 miles wide at its greatest extent (from north to south). Attempts to verify these dimensions historically miss the point of what the writer is trying to say. This is equally true of the proposal that we should think of the "Assyrian triangle" — the ca. 25-mile area between the Tigris and the Great Zab, in which, between Khorsabad and Nimrud, one settlement bordered on another (A. Parrot, 167). It is also useless to work out the extent of the walls, let alone the total length of all the streets in Nineveh, for v. 4a unquestionably suggests diameter. The reader is not supposed to do arithmetic. He is supposed to be lost in astonishment, so that he can take in the events that follow in an appropriate way. He catches a brief but sharply delineated glimpse of Jonah as "he begins" to make his way into the uncannily vast and wicked city, and then continues his march: לבוא following on ויחל cannot mean the entry at a particular moment or point in time; it has to be understood here in a durative sense (cf. Joüon, *Gr* §111d). Jonah pursues his way

---

1. When M. Luther translated the phrase "eyne stad Gotts" ("a city of God"), thereby thinking of God's beloved city (*LW* 19:84), Calvin, even at that date, found the explanation ingenious but in fact childish (*Opera omnia* 43, 250; cf. A. Fáj, "Stoic Features" [1974] 312).

further into the city "a day's walk." Why does the narrator make the point that Jonah had covered a third of the city's diameter when he began to speak? He is now in the center of the city; from here the message can spread like wildfire in every direction. But the consequences are going to be of much greater interest to the writer (vv. 5ff.) than Jonah's appearance on the stage itself. His account of Jonah's message is as taciturn as the taciturn messenger himself — the messenger who has been forced to obedience: "Another forty days and Nineveh shall be destroyed."

Since this is an ironically didactic novella and not a historical account, it is not surprising that the Ninevites — and even their animals — should understand Hebrew and speak it too (cf. vv. 7ff.). In the concise brevity of Jonah's message every word has weight. Heavy stress lies on the last word of all which, being a participle, confronts listeners with Nineveh as a city that *has already been destroyed* (see textual note to v. 4c). For Israelite ears, Nineveh's fate is the fate of Sodom and Gomorrah (cf. הפך in Gen. 19:25, 29; Deut. 29:23; Isa. 13:19; Jer. 20:16; 49:18; 50:40; Amos 4:11; Lam. 4:6) — that is to say, complete annihilation. The word הפך can certainly also have the neutral meaning "alter" or "transform" and can even bear the positive sense of a change of disposition (1 Sam. 10:6, 9; Jer. 31:13; Neh. 13:2; Exod. 14:5; Hos. 11:8; Esther 9:22; cf. Seybold, *ThWAT* 2:458f.). But it would be impermissible to turn Jonah's saying into the equivocal oracle: "another forty days and Nineveh is transformed" — either into a field of ruins or into a repentant city. This would be neither Jonah's own view nor the opinion of the narrator (cf. E. M. Good, *Irony* [1965] 48f.). For the sequel (vv. 9f.) clearly shows that the only way of understanding Jonah's message correctly is as an unambiguous announcement of judgment made by the divine wrath.

But why does the saying talk about 40 days? The word עוד, "yet" or "another," shows that what the writer has in mind is "the extent" of the intervening time (Gk ἔτι = "still") rather than the final point (אחר, μετά, the words for "after"). Between the announcement and the event of the destruction there is still a waiting space. So the confronting event of the threat acquires a profound significance of its own, without any special word being wasted on the fact. No conditions are attached to the judgment; nothing is said about what could be done, or should be done, in the interim. But a space is conceded. We shall see that the delay does not prolong the agony; it makes the change possible — a transformation through the unqualified word of judgment. It becomes clear later on that the messenger's word, which hastens ahead of events, is as such a gift of the divine patience, even if all it promises is disaster; cf. Amos 3:7 and A. Fáj, *Stoic Features* [1974] 313f. Fáj interprets Jonah's saying in the light of the conditional logic of the Stoics: if 40 days pass without repentance, Nineveh will be destroyed. But the narrator does not indicate in the slightest what could possibly happen within the 40 days.

Forty days are a long time. It is the time conceded for a comprehensive world judgment (Gen. 7:4, 12); it is the time Yahweh needs to instruct Moses fully (Exod. 24:18; 34:28; Deut. 9:9) and the time required for Moses' great vicarious repentance, which he took on himself in order to turn away Yahweh's wrath from his people (Deut. 9:18). These 40 days are granted to Nineveh. According to the narrator's intention, the time is required, first, so that the message may reach all the inhabitants of the huge city; also, and especially, that it may be brought to the notice of the king and his great men, and may bring about the necessary decisions (v. 6f.); and, finally, to make possible the ritual of repentance, and a new way of life for every individual in the metropolis (vv. 8, 10). When the Septuagint talks about only three days instead of 40 — and if this is more than a scribal error (cf. textual note to v. 4b) — the underlying idea may have been that, in view of the city's size as given in v. 3b, three days would have been needed to spread the news throughout the city. The rapidity of the repentance that follows so immediately on the message would at the same time be grotesquely accelerated. But the number 40 remains more probable than the three: 40 does not occur anywhere else in the context, whereas three can be more easily explained as a secondary reading due to an assimilation of the "three" mentioned in 2:1 and 3:3b. The definitely fixed period is a challenge to reflection: What can be done?

[3:5] The narrator answers this indirect question first of all by again (as in 1:5, 10, 16) describing the fundamental and decisive attitude of all concerned, before he goes on to outline individual acts or allows individual persons to take center stage. Here the text says: "they put their trust in God" (on the meaning of הֶאֱמִין בְּ cf. Gen. 15:6; Exod. 14:31; Ps. 106:12; also H. Wildberger, *THAT* 1:187ff.; A. Jepsen, *ThWAT* 1:327f.). Just as in Exod. 14:31 so here וַיַּאֲמִינוּ (בֵּאלֹהִים) is a synonymous parallel to אֶת־יְהוָה . . . לַיִּרְאוּ in 1:16 (cf. J. Magonet, *Form* [1973] 134). If the meaning differs at all, it does so only by a nuance: ירא may perhaps lay more emphasis on the relationship of obedience (cf. 1:16 with 1:10), while הֶאֱמִין rather stresses the relationship of trust (Ps. 78:22). But both words aim to stress the complete reliance on God. We are not told that the Ninevites believed "the word" (as Ps. 106:12; 119:66). But the messenger's word is the releasing factor which makes them cling to God (cf. Exod. 14:31; Isa. 7:9; 2 Chron. 20:20). "Believing" means trusting because of the word that has been testified to. Here the hope expressed first of all in the king's edict (v. 9) is already efficacious. We again see how important it is to perceive that vv. 6-9 are to be interpreted as subsequent explication of v. 5 (see pp. 145f. above). Otherwise הֶאֱמִין בְּ is used only in connection with Israel, as all the references cited show; at the same time, the sense is often that this kind of faith is not to be found in Israel (Num. 14:11; 20:12; Deut. 1:32; 2 Kings 17:14; Ps. 78:22). Against this background it is "almost as if the narrator wanted to say: 'Not even in Israel have I found such faith' " (A. Jepsen, 328; cf. Matt. 8:10 with 12:41 and John 1:9f.; 4:1ff.). Jonah's saying did not mention God, let alone Yahweh (note the difference compared with 1:9). But for the narrator, the only person who takes the messenger's word seriously is the person who sees his whole future destiny as lying in the will of the God who sends that messenger. This is what "the men of Nineveh" do (for the people of Nineveh the narrator uses the same word as in 1:10, 13, 16, הָאֲנָשִׁים, "the men").

The Ninevites show their faith in the God who sends Jonah by taking the threatened danger just as seriously as if disaster had already struck: a "fast" is proclaimed (cf. 1 Kings 21:9ff.; 2 Chron. 20:3; Joel 1:8ff., 13f.). Here צוֹם does not merely mean abstention from food. It is a comprehensive word for the period of mourning and repentance that is to be spent. The first immediately visible sign of the ritual that has begun is the donning of coarse, hairy mourning garments — the external sign of humility and a token that the person concerned has turned his back on his previous life; cf. H. W. Wolff, *Joel/Amos*, BK 14/2, 34, 37f. (Eng., *Joel and Amos*, on Joel 1:8, 13). That everyone participated "from the greatest to the least" is a proleptic comment. It runs ahead of the event, showing that the popular movement in Nineveh took in everybody (see p. 145 above). The reader is supposed to grasp, even at this early point, that it is not only a limited number who came to believe. (This was the chance open to Sodom, where at the end even ten righteous men would have been enough to save the whole city [Gen. 18:23-33].) Nineveh's comprehensive repentance made Luther say that "das eytel heyligen sind ynn der stad gewesen" ("none but saints inhabited the city"; *LW* 19:85).

[3:6]   How this came about is explained in vv.6-9 (on the "flashback" see textual note to v. 6a and p. 145 above). For the saying had (also) reached the ears of the king of the great city, and had deeply affected and moved him (נגע). Here הדבר, "the word," does not mean the news of the people's conversion. If that were meant we should expect to find הַדְּבָרִים הָאֵלֶּה, "these things" (Gen. 15:1; 1 Kings 17:17; 21:1; and frequently). It is precisely "the word" which Jonah proclaimed, דבר being the specific term for the prophetic word (Jer. 18:18; Amos 3:1; Ezek. 33:30, and frequently).

It is useless to try to identify "the king of Nineveh" with any neo-Assyrian king belonging to the 8th century, the period of the historical Jonah (2 Kings 14:25); this is obvious from the history of the city of Nineveh itself (see pp. 147f. above) and in the light of the literary genre with which we have to do here (see p. 145 above). What the novella tells us about this king and his city is not borne out by anything in neo-Assyrian annals. We have to find its foundation in the antithetical picture of Jehoiakim, as Jeremiah 36 presents him (see pp. 145-146 above), and in the hope which Old Testament prophecy had in different ways thrown open to the Gentile nations (cf. for example Isa. 2:2-4; 19:23-25; 45:14f., 20-25; Jer. 18:7f.). This has empowered our satirist to draw the picture of a Ninevite antitype to Israel's obduracy. Before ever he fulfills the functions of a ruler, the heathen king shows himself to be the model of humble, repentant faith. By rising from his throne, he is stripping himself of his insignia as ruler and judge (cf. Jer. 36:22; 1 Kings 1:46). He throws aside his royal robe, the token of his sovereignty; עבר *hiph'il* is a powerful word for "put away," and is used especially for things which are offensive to Yahweh; cf. 1 Kings 15:12; Zech. 3:4; 13:2. He wraps himself in the hairy garment of repentance which everyone else in Nineveh then wears too (vv. 5, 8); but his act is described, not with the usual word for "putting on clothes" (לבשׁ, v. 5; Esther 4:1), but with the rarer word "cover," "hide" (כסה *pi'el* with accusative "cover oneself with," Ezek. 16:18). Finally the king sits down "in the dust" instead of on his throne. The king's edict (vv.

7f.) does not exact from any of his subjects this part of the ritual of repentance and mourning (cf. Jer. 6:26; Ezek. 27:30; Isa. 47:1; 58:5; Job 2:8). But stress is laid on the fact that he takes this self-humiliation upon himself — a change of place that puts him at the side of the least of all; cf. 1 Sam. 2:8; Ps. 113:7. So in the consistency of his faith, the heathen ruler becomes the model of a king. This is in fact the king as he should really be in Israel, according to Deut. 17:20 — a king who "does not lift his heart" above the men and women of his people ("his brethren") but is exemplary in his fear of God.

[3:7]   A reigning prince like this, in the dust of the streets, has full authority to issue a decree. On the problem of where the edict actually begins, cf. textual note to v. 7a. It is only on this one occasion that the word טעם is used in the Old Testament to mean "edict" or "command," but we have several instances in Aramaic; cf. Jean and Hoftijzer, *DIS* 102 and Cowley, *ArPap* 26: 22.23,25. The Assyrians were already familiar with "the great men" (*rabûtu/rabâni*) who were at the king's side; the phrase is used for the princes, the civil servants who were in charge of administrative affairs, and the king's advisers (P. Gavelli, *RLA* 4 [1975] 448f.; W. von Soden, *Akkadisches Handwörterbuch* [1965ff.], 938a; cf. Micah 7:3b). But we have no example in either Assyria or Israel to suggest that ordinances were ever issued by "the king and his great men" simultaneously. We do have evidence of this in the Persian empire, however: for example, Ezra 7:14 (cf. Esther 1:13) and Herodotus (3. 31, 84, 118: seven legal advisers to the king); cf. E. Bickermann, *RHPhR* 45 (1965) 250. The formulation of the decree seems to have given the writer particular pleasure. He obviously enjoys the hyperbole, as "men and beasts" are given their instructions. To make quite sure that "the beasts" are not overlooked, he soon underlines the point again: "cattle and flocks." "They are not to taste anything at all!" As if this were not clear enough, he tells the cattle particularly: Do not graze! Do not drink any water! טעם is not the word used for just everyday eating (2 Sam. 3:25; 1 Sam. 14:24). It refers especially to the epicure's luxurious appreciation, where it is always a matter of little "tastes," rolled round the palate (Job 12:11; 34:3; 1 Sam. 14:29, 43; 2 Sam. 19:36). So the command אל יטעמו, "do not enjoy," includes the smallest morsels. But in this case what is meant are not samples of the delicacies of a king's table (2 Sam. 19:36) or thimblefuls of honey (1 Sam. 14:29, 43); the edict means tastes of the simplest, most basic forms of nourishment, such as water or "anything at all." The word מאומה may be derived etymologically from the Akkadian *min-ma* (W. von Soden, *Akkadisches Handwörterbuch* [1965ff.] 653); but Israelite ears will have heard in it a doubling of the interrogative pronoun מָה, "What?" (cf. Latin *quidquid*); cf. R. North, *Exégèse pratique des petits prophètes postexiliens* (English summary, 1969) 141. Not the tiniest crumb and not the smallest drop are permitted. The Gentiles could not possibly be described to Israel in more pious terms than these. How Jonah's word has transformed this "bloody city" (Nah. 3:1)!

[3:8]   The satiric tones which the Israelites must have detected here are intensified even further. Not only the people, but the animals too, are to cover themselves (כסה, now in *hithpaʿel*) with the garments of mourning (haircloth aprons worn round the loins). We find this also in Jdt. 4:10; and according to Herodotus 9.24, a Persian cavalry unit shaved their horses and their draught animals out of grief over the death of their leader. The animals are included in the requirement to cry to God, as if this were a matter of course; the cattle especially could see to it that this cry was "mighty"; cf. Joel 1:18, 20, parallel to 19. On the solidarity of human beings and animals, cf. Eccles. 3:18-21; on the "responsibility" of animals, cf. Exod. 21:28; on their praying, Job 38:41.

      It is only in 8b that the edict turns to human beings, the individual especially being stressed (איש, "a [single] man"). "Every one of them shall turn away from his wicked behavior." With this injunction the narrator picks up for the first time an expression common in the Jeremian traditions (Jer. 18:11bα; 25:5aα; 26:3aβ; 35:15aα; 36:3bα, 7aβ; cf. also Jer. 23:14, 22 and A. Feuillet, "Sources" [1947] 169ff.). דרך, "way," means here a human being's whole behavior. To turn away from *evil* ways would at the same time be to turn away from the way of *disaster*; to establish the inner connection between evil and disaster is, after v. 10, quite deliberate on the narrator's part. What links the two aspects of רעה, wickedness and disaster, is that they are both harmful: it is here that we have to see the fundamental meaning of רעה (cf. H. J. Stoebe, *THAT* 1:659). This is already implicit in the royal edict as we see from this verse, but here the point is initially the turning away from harmful behavior. This is more precisely defined as an "act of violence." In the story of the Flood, the "wickedness" (רעה) which has brought about the universal judgment according to Gen. 6:5 (J) is described in 6:11, 13 (P) as חמס. This word can be "a comprehensive expression for sin in general" (H. J. Stoebe, *THAT* 1:587). But here, as most often, it probably means the attack on a person's life, so that it is the equivalent of "shedding blood." The addition that חמס "sticks to their hands" also points to this; for this is also said about blood in Isa. 1:15 (cf. Joel 3:19; Obad. 9f.; Isa. 59:6; Job 16:17; 1 Chron. 12:18 and H. W. Wolff, *Joel/Amos*, BK 14/2,232 [Eng., *Joel and Amos*, on Amos 3:10]. Nineveh was notorious for deeds of violence, like Assyria in general (Nah. 3:1ff.). So the narrator has presented Nineveh as a city which is aware of the need for radical and comprehensive repentance.

[3:9] But it knows also that repentance does not necessarily mean that it has been saved. Its new behavior does not do away with the consequences of the old. That lies with "the God," at whose behest Jonah has threatened the city's destruction. האלהים, "the God," is just as understandable here, in the context of the court edict, as it was on the lips of the captain in 1:6. מי־יודע, "who knows?" is an expression of hope, which pays tribute to God's liberty of final decision; cf. textual note to v. 9a. It has the same force as אולי, "perhaps," "it may be" in Exod. 32:30; Amos 5:15; Zeph. 2:3; Lam. 3:29 (1:6b; see p. 113 above; cf. also 1:14bβ), but here it is an obvious link with the text of Joel 2:14a. This is shown by the wording of the continuation (as well as by the verbal borrowing from Joel 2:13b in Jonah 4:2; see p. 168 below). According to the prophet Joel, Jerusalem is ripe for judgment; the chance to repent which he offers her is a chance which

Nineveh here accepts. On the basis of its own resolute repentance, the city then hopes for the ''repentance'' of God. שוב in v. 8b, ''turn about,'' ''be converted,'' is picked up twice in v. 9; but whereas in 8b the subject of the verb is the Ninevites, in v. 9 the subject is God; cf. textual note to v. 9b.

The first clause, like Joel 2:14a, expects a turn to נחם. In terms of actual fact, what is meant is the withdrawal of the threat of destruction (v. 4b). The root נחם means an emotional act of spiritual relief; cf. J. Jeremias, ''Die Reue Gottes,'' *BSt* 65 (1975) 16. In the Old Testament, נחם *niph'al* signifies regret over an act already committed or — in the vast majority of cases — disapprobation of a judgment either planned or announced (examples in Jeremias, 15-18). Here it is expected that God will allow himself to be sorry for the word he has proclaimed in v. 4b (this even more precisely expressed in v. 10b). נחם *niph'al* therefore (here as generally) means ''a revoking out of compassion.'' It is what Jeremias calls an act of divine''self-command'' (40ff.). This hope that God will recall his judgment out of pity is the last term in a threefold theological progression: the first term speaks of the proclamation and hearing of the divine word of judgment; the second term mentions the repentance of the listeners which thereupon follows; the third tells of the revoking of the word of judgment. This threefold progression can be found in the Jeremiah traditions to which v. 8b already pointed us (see above), especially in Jer. 18:7f.; 26:2f.; 36:2f. There they are accompanied by the most important of the concepts that recur here: word of judgment — repentance — retraction (vv. 4b,6-8b-9). The Deuteronomistic nature of these Jeremian traditions is evident in the case of our theologoumenon if we compare it with Judg. 2:18; 2 Sam. 24:16.

The second שוב clause (v. 9b) hopes that God will turn away from his fierce anger. The 40 days in the threat (v. 4b) is, as we have seen, a reminiscence of traditions about Moses' intercession in Deut. 9:18f. (see p. 149 above); and here we can clearly hear the echo of a similar tradition: Exod. 32:12 combines the request of Moses that Yahweh may turn from his fierce anger (שוב מחרון אפך) with the desire that he will retract the disaster he has proclaimed (על־הרעה והנחם). This combination is found only in Exod. 32:12 and Jonah 3:9. But in Exodus it is applied to Israel — here to Gentile Nineveh (cf. J. D. Magonet, *Form* [1973] 129). The only text in which the three-term progression — word of judgment, repentance, and retraction — is applied to non-Israelite nations is Jer. 18:7f. That conditional promise made to an unspecified nation and kingdom has contributed essentially to the theological shaping of the Nineveh scene. The goal of the expectation is here ultimately formulated exactly as it is in the scene on board ship: ''that we do not perish'' (cf. 1:6, 14). It would be impossible to sum the matter up by saying that Nineveh is saved solely through its moral amendment. Apart from the rites of repentance and the cry to God (vv. 6-8), the substance of v. 9 shows confidence in leading assertions of the prophetic proclamation about Yahweh's abandonment of his wrath, even though the name of the God of Israel is never mentioned here at all. The statement about the ''faith'' of the men of Nineveh in God (v. 5a) makes sense only in the light of v. 9.

[3:10]   After Nineveh's attitude to the king's edict has been described ahead of time (v. 5; see p. 150 above), God's reaction to the hope in him expressed at the end of the edict can be reported immediately. By picking up in v. 10 the wording already used in vv. 8b-9a the narrator brings out the fact that God's behavior exactly corresponds to Nineveh's expectation. The repetition goes so far that, instead of the "Yahweh" which would be expected in the light of chap. 1, האלהים, "the God," is taken over into the account (v. 10) from the language of the Ninevite edict (v. 9). (On the literary problem, cf. p. 147 above.) In spite of this, the narrator is of course thinking only of the prophet's God (cf. vv. 4f.), even when he is incorporating this Ninevite turn of speech into his novella. At no point do the Ninevites have to do with any other god. This is made particularly evident, since the disaster did not strike before they were confronted with Yahweh's messenger (see in contrast 1:4ff.). What is in question here is in no sense knowledge of *the true* God; the point at issue is the proper relationship to *the one* God. (The main stress in 1:4-16 was similar; but cf. L. Schmidt, *De Deo* [1976] 102f.)

What "the God" saw in Nineveh (v. 10a) and the view he took of it (v. 10b) is brought out through the exact parallelism of the two statements in which the nouns are chiastically placed עשׂה — הרעה: הרעה — מעשׂיהם; cf. J. D. Magonet, *Form* [1973] 25f.). Here, in the center of the two statements, the great turning point is marked by the two key expressions out of the triple theological progression known to us from vv. 8b-9 (Jer. 18:7f.; see p. 154 above): Nineveh's "turn" is marked by the word שׁוב (10a), God's by the word נחם (10b). In this way the completion of the events that have to do with Nineveh, and which take place in the city, finds its documentation in the language. God sees from Nineveh's *deeds* that the people are *turning away* from their *harmful* (evil) way; so God *is sorry* for the *harmful* (evil) thing that he had announced he would *do* to them, and he did not *do* it. God does not explicitly take notice of any good work — neither the fasting observances nor the prayers of hope nor ethical behavior. All he regards is the turning away from evil (what is harmful, רעה). This renunciation on Nineveh's part is matched on the other side by God's revocation of the threat of his act of disaster (what is harmful, רעה). Whereas v. 9b was a reminiscence of the wording of Moses' petition in Exod. 32:12b, it is worth noting that 10b corresponds almost exactly to the account of the hearing of his prayer in Exod. 32:14, where the wording is: וַיִּנָּחֶם יהוה עַל־הָרָעָה אֲשֶׁר דִּבֶּר לַעֲשׂוֹת לְעַמּוֹ, "and Yahweh repented of the evil which he thought to do to his people." What Israel in her early days experienced then, Nineveh — hitherto so brutal — experiences now. Our writer paints the promise of Jer. 18:7f. (cf. 26:3, 13, 19) as having now been fulfilled. For many Israelites it must have sounded like bitter mockery that through this fulfillment Israel's last privilege loses its force. The catchword that God was sorry for Nineveh (נחם, vv. 9a, 10b) and the second catchword about the רעה ("evil," "harmful thing") of the people in the city (v. 10a) as well as the רעה of God (v. 10b) also sound the leitmotif for chap. 4 (cf. v. 2bγ; also v. 1). In this way it also presents the most important presupposition for the narrator's conversation with his contemporaries.

Purpose

In the context of the Jonah novella as a whole, the Nineveh scene (like the scene on board ship) really has a subordinate importance. On the one hand, it shows that Jonah cannot escape the will of his God (1:1-3; 2:1—3:3a); on the other, it delineates the situation in which Yahweh is striving to win Jonah's assent (4:1-11). And yet, in its reference to the final chapter especially, and hence to the story as a whole, this scene has its own message — a message in which it goes far beyond the second scene (1:4-16), theologically speaking.

Taking the brutal metropolis as example (on חמס in v. 8b, see p. 153 above), this scene is an exposition of what it means to arrive at belief in God—an exposition designed to shock its readers. The sentence: "the men of Nineveh won trust in God" (v. 5a) describes the effect of Jonah's threat (v. 4b) by summing up the conclusions these believers drew for themselves (vv.5b-8), and what they expected of God (v. 9) and then experienced (v. 10).

The precondition for the faith is the messenger's word that has gone forth. It announced Nineveh's downfall unconditionally and without any qualification. But it is equally clear that this is an "advance notice" allowing a certain space, though with a time limit, "an ultimatum but not as an ultimum," as K. H. Miskotte puts it (*When the Gods Are Silent* [1967] 431). The destruction of the bloody city is not the result of laws inherent in the evil acts of human beings themselves; it is an act of free disposal on the part of the Lord who uttered his purpose through the messenger's word. So his word, sent ahead of the disaster (cf. Amos 3:7) creates a space in which faith becomes possible.

The first consequence of faith is acceptance of the judgment as deserved. This is shown through rites of self-humiliation: the renunciation of everyday food and drink, and the exchange of normal clothing for the mourning garment (the haircloth apron; cf. v. 5b). The completeness of Nineveh's repentance is brought out in a number of different ways. The king is a pattern in his behavior — an extreme example, since (in contrast to Jehoiakim of Jerusalem) he exchanges his throne for a seat in the dust shared with the poorest (v. 6; cf. p. 151 above). The fact that even the beasts participate in the rites of repentance (vv. 7b-8a) may be a reminder to the reader that among these strangers even ox and ass (Isa. 1:2f., like the stork and the swallow, Jer. 8:7) know more about repentance than do men and women in Israel.

As far as the people in heathen Nineveh are concerned, we are specifically told that every single one of them, from the greatest to the least (vv. 5b, 8b), turned away from acts of violence. So the cultic rites of humiliation, as the second consequence of faith, are bound up with the reformation of day-to-day behavior towards other human beings. But even a combination of these things is not as yet sufficient to bring about deliverance from judgment.

The third, quite specific consequence of faith is already evident in the cry to God (v. 8a), and finds its concrete form in v. 9. It glorifies God's liberty (מי יודע "who knows?"; see p. 153 above), which is the sole context of the divine decision to save; but it dares to hope, on the foundation of what Israel has come to know about God (Exod. 32:12-14; Jer. 18:7f.; see also p. 154 above). Nineveh's consistent belief shows itself as audacious *dis*belief in the inescapable link between deed and destiny; at the same time it proclaims that God's grace is truly free grace.

This faith comes to experience the divine alterability which acts in its favor: that is the end of the story. Since the word of judgment has given its hearers a new direction, it no longer needs to find fulfillment in the implementation of that judgment. The Deuteronomic assertion that the prophetic word shows itself to be Yahweh's word only through its fulfillment (Deut. 18:18-22) may govern Jonah as he reveals himself in chap. 4 (see pp. 167f. below on 4:2), and this may be true of the word of salvation (Jer. 28:8f.). But the word of judgment has to be understood in its living relationship to the people who hear it (Ezek. 3:16-21; 18:21-23; Jer. 18:7-10; cf. J. Jeremias, "Reue," 83ff., 109ff.). It leads to the triumph of God's compassion with the world, violent and brutal though it is.

What gave our narrator the boldness to make Nineveh, of all places, the setting for his story of the reprieve granted to faith? Did he sense that, ever since the prophets of the exilic and postexilic period, at least (see pp. 151f. above), the laughter of a great hope was in the air? Is his story a way of documenting the great anticipatory joy over a new world in the midst of a still evil environment? Especially with his grotesquely exaggerated picture of Nineveh's repentance, what he probably wished to do was to provoke his fellow countrymen, who were far from any similar repentance and who yet claimed God's election for themselves alone, without hope for the world.

For ancient Israel, the scene in Nineveh may have been an almost unendurable satire. But in Jesus' proclamation it turns into a pattern of the faith which comes about in repentance (Matt. 12:41); and through the proclamation of the risen Christ it presently becomes realized hope. The world of today, whose days are numbered, and the churches in that world, will have to search their hearts anew, to see whether their faith and hope can compete with Nineveh's.

Jonah Complains
of God's Compassion

Literature

H. Winckler, "Zum buche Jona," *Altorientalische Forschungen* 2, 2 (1900) 260-265. H. Schmidt, "Die Komposition des Buches Jona," *ZAW* 25 (1905) 285-310. T. Boman, "Jahve og Elohim i Jonaboken," *NTT* 37 (1936) 159-168. A. Feuillet, "Les sources du livre de Jonas," *RB* 54 (1947) 161-186; "Le sens du livre de Jonas," ibid., 340-361. G. von Rad, "Der Prophet Jona," (1950) in *Gottes Wirken in Israel* (1974) 65-78; Eng., *God at Work in Israel* (1980). H. Rosin, *The Lord Is God* (1956) 6-33. R. Martin-Achard, "Israël et les nations," *CTh* 42 (1959) 45-48. N. Lohfink, "Jona ging zur Stadt hinaus (Jona 4,5)," *BZ* NF 5 (1961) 185-203. K. Heinrich, *Parmenides und Jona* (1966) 61-128. O. Kaiser, "Wirklichkeit, Möglichkeit und Vorurteil: Ein Beitrag zum Verständnis des Buches Jona," *EvTh* 33 (1973) 91-103. L. Schmidt, *De Deo: Studien zur Literarkritik und Theologie des Buches Jona, des Gesprächs zwischen Abraham und Jahwe in Gen 18,22ff. und von Hi 1, ZAW* Beiheft 143 (1976). G. H. Davies, "The Uses of רעע *Qal* and the Meaning of Jonah 4:1" (manuscript). T. E. Fretheim, "Jonah and Theodicy," *ZAW* 90 (1978) 227-237.

Text

4:1 But this brought a great displeasure[a] over Jonah and he became angry.

2 He cried out to Yahweh and said: "O Yahweh! Was not just this my thought, when I was still[a] in my own country? That is why I wanted to flee to Tarshish the first time.[b] For I knew that you are a gracious and a merciful God, slow to anger and abounding in clemency, who deplores disaster.

3 So now, [a]Yahweh, take my life from me! For death is better for me than life.[b]

4 But Yahweh said:[a] "Is it right[b] for you to be angry?"

5 (For) Jonah had gone out of the city[a] and had sat down east of the city. There he made a (leafy) booth for himself and sat down in its shade,[b] until he should see what would happen in the city.

6 Then Yahweh[a]-God appointed a castor oil plant. It grew up over Jonah, in order to give his head shade, [b]so as to wrest him out of his displeasure.[b] Then Jonah had great joy[c] because of the castor oil plant.

7   But the God appointed a worm, when the first light dawned on the following day. The worm pierced the castor oil plant, and it withered away.

8   But when the sun rose, God appointed a scorching[a] east wind. Then the sun beat on Jonah's head and he became quite faint. So he begged to die and said: "Death is better for me than life."[b]

9   But God said to Jonah: "Is it right that you are angry because of the castor oil plant?" He said: "It is right that I am angry enough to die."

10   Then Yahweh said: "You have compassion with the castor oil plant, which gave you no trouble and which you did not make grow, which sprang up in[a] a single night and perished in[a] a single night.

11   And I[a] may not have compassion with Nineveh, the great city, in which there are more than[b] a hundred and twenty thousand[c] people who do not know how to distinguish between right and left, and many animals?"

1a   Here we have another example of the narrator's favorite stylistic device (cf. 1:10, 16; 4:6b), the *figura etymologica*, the internal or absolute object (cf. Ges-K §117p, q and p. 116 above on 1:10). In this case he takes over, as this internal object, the keyword רעה out of chap. 3, which in 3:8, 10b is the term used for the Ninevites' wicked behavior, from which they turn away, and is in 3:10 the word for the disaster which God had threatened but did not implement. The subject of the sentence is the whole of 3:10, which explains that God withdrew the word of judgment (cf. G. H. Davies). Chapter 4 is now shaped and determined by the question whether Jonah's רעה can be overcome like the רעה of the Ninevites and the רעה of God (cf. 4:2b) (see esp. v. 6aβ). In v. 1 the phrase specifically means disapproval of God's decision (3:10); similarly Neh. 2:10; but cf. p. 165 below.

2a   It is not necessary (as A. B. Ehrlich thinks) to read עוֹד, following Gk (ἔτι "still") since עַד with the infinitive means "as long as"; cf. Judges 3:26 and L. Koehler and W. Baumgartner, *Lexicon in Vetus Testamenti Libros* (1953; 1967ff.[3], 680).

2b   קדם *pi'el* with infinitive with ל must be understood here as *verbum relativum* with an adverbial meaning ("to do something first"; cf. Ges-K §§114n, 120a).

3a   Gk δέσποτα κύριε, "master Lord," presupposes אדוני יהוה. Targ יוי and Vg *Domine*, "Lord," support MT.

3b   Literally, "Better is my dying than my living."

4a   Gk supplements by πρὸς Ιωναν, "to Jonah."

4b   היטב is here an infinitive absolute with adverbial meaning (BrSynt §93d); σ' δικαιως, "just," α' θ' and others, καλως, Vg. *bene*, "well," all bring out the sense better than Gk σφοδρα ("passionately," "violently") = Targ לַחְדָּא, as the context of v. 9 (cf. also vv. 10f.) shows especially.

5a   On the "flashback" style, cf. N. Lohfink, "Jona" (1961); also textual notes to 2:1a; 3:6a; and p. 169 below.

5b   The Septuagint tradition reads ἐν σκιᾷ ("in the shade") throughout; (cf. Ziegler). This does not permit us to view בצל as secondary (K. Marti's view), making this the solution of the doublet of 6bα; cf. G. H. Cohn, *Jona* (1969) 18f.

6a   Note the different names for God as subject of the same verb in 2:1; 4:6, 7, 8; on this point see also p. 164 below.

6b-b   The second infinitive clause, which is joined to the first without copula, has frequently been viewed as a secondary interpolation, ever since Wellhausen; but in fact it links up quite significantly with v. 1. If the first infinitive clause were deleted, the doublet to the "shade" in v. 5 would be eliminated (H. Winckler's suggestion). But v. 8 shows that

160

the clause is indispensable. The Septuagint assimilates the two infinitive clauses, translating להציל by τοῦ σκιάζειν, which probably indicates that it is reading לְהָצֵל (III צלל).

6c The *figura etymologica* (see textual note to 4:1a) brings out the contrast between "displeasure" (vv. 6b, 1a) and "joy."

8a The meaning of the word is probably more correctly rendered by Gk, συγκαίοντι, than by Targ, שְׁתִיקתא, "gentle," "sultry." In 1QH 7:4f. the word is used to describe "a wild, stormy wind" (בְּזַעַף חֲרִישִׁית), which endangers a ship (on זַעַף cf. 1:15). It is therefore best to derive the word from חרשׁ, "to plough," "cut," "stab."

8b See textual note to v. 3b.

10a On the relative pronoun שֶׁ see textual note to 1:7a; בִּן is a rarer construct form of בֵּן (cf. also Exod. 33:11; Deut. 25:2 and Ges-K §96; Eng., p. 285); "son of a night" here describes the "belonging together" of the growing up and the fading away on two successive nights, rather than the "age" of a single night; cf. vv. 6f. and Koehler and Baumgartner (1967ff.[3]) בֵּן no. 7 and 8; also H. Haag, *ThWAT* 1:676.

11a The interrogative pronoun can be omitted in rhetorical questions; the context, the link with the previous sentence by way of the ו, and the speech modulation make it clear that the sentence is a question; cf. Meyer 3[3] §111,2c.

11b הַרְבֵּה infinitive absolute *hiph'il* of רבה has here a substantive function as subject (cf. 2 Sam. 1:4, "a multitude"); the following מִן before the numeral points comparatively to the difference ("more than"; cf. Judges 18:26b; 1 Kings 5:10, Ges-K §133a and BrSynt §111g).

11c On the formation of the numerals, cf. Meyer 2[3] §59, 1.5 and W. Rudolph's comment on this passage.

Form

After 3:10 *the scene changes abruptly*. We have heard nothing about Jonah since 3:4. Now he suddenly appears on the stage again. From now until the end, he is the sole partner to whom God talks and with whom he negotiates. But the scene of the action is now different. When the reader lost sight of Jonah, he was right in the middle of Nineveh. Now he is outside the city, in a leafy hut, keeping an eye on events (v. 5).

The scene is therefore new. But it is clearly related to what has gone before, and is the final part of what shows itself to be a most skillfully constructed novella. Nineveh still determines Jonah's location and his concern, as it did earlier, both when he averted his face from the city (1:22ff.) and when he turned towards it again (3:1ff.). But more than that: Nineveh is also the sole subject of Jonah's conversation with Yahweh. For just as the final question in v. 11 is related explicitly to Nineveh or, to be more precise, to Yahweh's attitude towards Nineveh, so this same divine attitude of mind is the logical subject of the first sentence in the scene (see textual note to v. 1a); for this sentence is exactly related to the substance of 3:10. In addition, the dialog in v. 2a casts back to the scene of Jonah's flight (1:3ff.), and for the first time explains the fundamental reason for Jonah's behavior. By these retrospective glances, which link up different scenes and hold them together, the writer throws the climax of his story into high relief. The triple link between the catchword used both at the beginning of the new scene and at the close of the scene immediately preceding it, is particularly significant for a discernment of the problem which is at the heart of the story. The רעה (harmful thing) from which both Nineveh (3:8b, 10a) and Yahweh (3:10b) have withdrawn, now shifts to Jonah (v. 1a, cf. v. 6a); the anger from which Yahweh has turned away (3:9b, חֲרוֹן אַפּוֹ) flames up in Jonah (v. 1b, ויחר cf. 4:9); God's regret (compassion; נחם, 3:9a, 10b) becomes the main theme of the dialog between Jonah and Yahweh (v. 2b; cf. 10f., חוס).

If we examine *the build-up* of the scene, we can discern the structure of the dialog first of all in the five changes of subject, from Jonah to Yahweh and back again (vv.1-3 + 4; 5 + 6a; 6b + 7-8a; 8b + 9a; 9b + 10f.). In the first, fourth, and fifth of these alternations, we have speech and counterspeech, while in the second and third, silent action alternates with silent reaction. So three formally different phases emerge. But the first interchange between Jonah and Yahweh after the action phase (vv. 8b+9a) is exclusively related to this action (vv. 5-8a). Since it closes with Yahweh's question in v. 9b, which picks up and modifies the wording of v. 4, the scene can in fact be divided into three parts: vv. 1-4; 5-9a; 9b-11. The first phase points the problem; the second phase develops a paradigm, or example; the third tries to solve the problem with the help of the paradigm.

But to say this is to do no more than to indicate the formal basis of the narrator's true artistry. In the decisive closing scene, the novella's *didactic* trend can be discerned most of all in the circumstance that Jonah, who attacks his problem merely in anger, has nothing but questions put to him by Yahweh in the dialog sections (vv. 4, 9a, 10f.). In the action phase Yahweh brings Jonah to the point when he himself is forced to offer an instructive paradigm that is almost inescapable in its cogency (vv. 6-8 with 9 and 10). Since the final question (v. 11) is left open, the reader sees himself in the end challenged to think about the problem and to find his own answers.

The answer is made easy for him, since the example which Jonah is forced to present, linked with Yahweh's repeated question about the justness of his vexation, is full of racy *satire*. The ironic note is already sounded when Jonah is resentful and wants to die, even though his preaching has achieved the greatest possible effect. The story then pours scorn on the deadly seriousness of the religious hero. For, after brief rejoicing, he sinks back into self-pity, tired of living, just because the shade cast by a shrub disappears; yet at the same time he is unwilling to understand why Yahweh should feel pity for the great city of Nineveh. In the detailed exposition, we shall see how here the irony of the narrative art guides the reader towards theological wisdom.

Setting

However, we are still faced with the question whether the final scene was a literary unit from the very beginning, or whether certain sentences have not been introduced into the present context from some other literary source, either in error or intentionally.

Ever since H. Winckler (see p. 144 above), scholars have inclined to detach v. 5 from the complex of the final scene. It has seemed to many of them that these sentences as they stand come far too late on in the story. For "what happens in the city" (bβ) has been reported already, in 3:5-10; while — according to this view — 4:5 fits perfectly immediately before this passage, following directly on the account of Jonah's preaching (3:4). As evidence that the sentences have been moved to a position after 4:4 at some later moment, and in error, these scholars point to the fact that in v. 5 Jonah is already sitting in his leafy "booth," enjoying the shade which according to v. 6 he only receives by way of the castor oil plant. During the time presumed to elapse between 3:4 and 3:5, the shadow of the fresh leafy booth had a point; after all, a space of 40 days was at the disposal of the Ninevites for the complicated events described in 3:5-10, and after that the withered foliage would no longer have offered sufficient protection against the sun.

In the first place, however, it is questionable whether it is permissible for us to attribute to our narrator unexpressed trains of thought like this (about fresh and withered foliage). For him, צל ("shade") is צל, and it would present just as much of a problem for 4:6 in the light of chap. 3 as it does in its present position. The only important question that remains is the point about the temporal sequence of events. But this must be clearly distinguished from the *narrative* sequence (cf. N. Lohfink, "Jonah" [1961]). We saw in connection with 3:4 (see p. 146 above) that it is our writer's narrative method to follow the decisive events and speeches first of all with an account of the "inward" reaction; this was the case in 3:5 (after 3:4), just as it was in 1:10 (after 1:9), in 1:16 (after 1:15), and also in 4:1 (after 3:10). Other, "external" facts, on the other hand, were reported in a flashback, at the point where the progress of the narrative permitted no further delay, or where this flashback seemed to serve a useful explanatory function; 1:5b, 10b; 2:1 and 3:6 were all obviously cast-backs in time of this kind. Accordingly, the logic of the narrative method in the final scene is completely consistent with the particular character of the novella. Jonah's mental reaction to the events in Nineveh is reported first of all (v. 1); it is made explicit through his complaint to Yahweh (vv. 2f.). After the question with which Yahweh counters the complaint (v. 4) and — especially — before the introduction of the castor oil plant "parable," it is impossible to delay any further the deferred mention of Jonah's departure from the city (v. 5). By adding the purpose of this departure (to see "what would happen in the city"), the narrator gives this its useful function in the context. Verse 5 now takes the place of an answer to Yahweh's question in v. 4; cf. H. Gunkel, *RGG*[2] 3:367; J. D. Magonet, *Form* (1973) 105f.; L. Schmidt, *De Deo* (1976) 29f., 106. In this way a literary understanding of the significance of v. 5 in the narrative context replaces a textual intervention impelled by "literary" criteria for which the justification is all too feeble.

Another literary problem emerges from our observation of the remarkable changes in the names used for God in chap. 4. This problem was first considered by W. Böhme, "Die Composition des Buches Jona," *ZAW* 7 (1887) 224-284, then by H. Schmidt, *ZAW* 25 (1905) 285-310, and others, and most recently by L. Schmidt, *De Deo*. Whereas vv. 2, 4, 10 talk about Yahweh, just like 1:1-3, 3a, the term used in v. 6 is יהוה אלהים, "Yahweh God," in v. 7 האלהים, "the God" (as in 3:9f; cf. 1:6), in v. 8 and 9 אלהים, "God" (as in 3:3b, 5, 8). In addition we have the doublet of vv. 3 and 4 in vv. 8b and 9, as well as the double statement about the shade in vv. 5b and 6a. These points, combined with a number of observations about the content, lead L. Schmidt to postulate that what we have before us in chaps. 3 and 4 especially is a "basic stratum." He assigns to this stratum: "1:2; 3:3a (without 'in accordance with Yahweh's word'); 3:3b-10; 4:1, 5a, 6aα (without 'Yahweh'); 4:6b-11 (with 'Elohim' instead of 'Yahweh' in v. 10)" (*De Deo* 32; cf. 47). The rest must largely be assigned to a "reworking" of the material: "1:1, 3-16 (without vv. 8aβ, 10bβ); 2:1, 11; in 3:3a: 'in accordance with Yahweh's word'; 4:2-4, 5b; in 4:6aα 'Yahweh' and 4:6aβ" (125). It is certainly true that particularly the striking change in the names for God in chap. 4 is an indication that the present text has absorbed already firmly established phraseology. Is it possible to go even further, and to talk about a literary source ("basic stratum") which we can reconstruct and from which we can separate out the material that has been reworked? On this question see §3 of the Introduction.

The demarcation line between these assumed literary strata and their wording seems to be too uncertain. This is true above all of the beginning of the basic stratum, which is supposed to be found in 1:2 and 3:3a, and its assumed end in 4:10f., passages which are now closely linked with the name *Yahweh*. Here "basic stratum," "reworking," and redaction flow into one another, just as they do in 4:6, so that it is impossible to separate out the different strands. Moreover, within the sections assigned to the "basic stratum" in chaps. 3 and 4, there is material which has been variously molded at some earlier stage. Traditions about Elijah have exerted an obvious influence on 4:6-9 (see p. 168 below), whereas in 3:8-10 we found material that is indubitably Jeremian-Deuteronomistic. Theological tensions also emerge. Not only is Yahweh's mercy described in a different keyword (חוס) in 4:11 from the one used in 3:10 (נחם); more importantly, the reason given for this compassion is now the idea of creation, whereas the Ninevites' repentance in the wake of the word of judgment proclaimed to them is now no longer given as reason at all, although this was so emphatically stressed in chap. 3. The connection between 3:3b-10 and 4:6ff. is not comprehensible without the explication of 4:1 in 4:2ff. The internal thematic differences in chaps. 3f. and differences in their transmission history are no less important than the differences compared with chap. 1 (cf. L. Schmidt, *De Deo* 124ff.). Finally, the recapitulation of v. 4 in v. 9 can no more be pressed into service for a literary dissection of the text than the relationship of 3:1f. to 1:1f. (see p. 131 above), especially since here the intensifying element is even more marked; cf. H. W. Wolff, *Studien* (1964, 1975²) 59-64. We must therefore see also 4:1-11 as a whole as being the work of the same narrator, who has introduced highly varying material into his novella — material whose phraseology had already taken form at some earlier stage. In this final scene too, hypotheses based on literary criteria are too uncertain — very much more so than was the case in 2:1-9; (cf. pp. 129f. above). We shall have to try to interpret the individual utterances in the light of the single writer who at this particular point gathers up all the scenes that have gone before, bringing them to their appointed goal.

Commentary

[4:1] Syntactically, the first sentence is more closely linked with the sentence that precedes it than is the case at the beginning of any other scene. For the subject of the sentence can be neither Jonah, nor the רעה; we have to look for it in the event of 3:10b, in Yahweh's revocation of his prediction of disaster; cf. textual note to v. 1a. What does this subject have to say? רעע *qal* means "to be bad, harmful, useless." Without an explicit subject it generally means "to appear harmful," "to displease." This is the way in which it is also generally rendered in our passage; the internal object that is added, רעה גדולה, "the great harm," is then interpreted merely as intensification of this displeasure. But this hardly does justice to the narrator's choice of words. For the preposition אל is in itself a unique usage in combination with רעע *qal*. "Displease" is always expressed as רעע בְּעֵינֵי (Gen. 48:17; Isa. 59:15; 1 Chron. 21:7; and frequently), in two cases רעע ל (Neh. 2:10, also with internal object, and 13:8). On the other hand, אֶל underlines the purpose of a movement (BrSynt §108a). If we also remember that רעע, as well as meaning "to be evil" and "to appear evil," can also mean "to bring evil" (with ל in 2 Sam. 20:6; Ps. 106:32), this meaning will most readily suggest itself in conjunction with אֶל. It is only this interpretation which brings out the fact that the internal object רעה גדולה picks up the catchword רעה which was stressed three times in 3:8b, 10a and b. Although the literal sense varies in its triple combination with Nineveh, God, and Jonah (as wickedness, disaster, and ill-will), the meaning "will to harm" (see p. 153 above) is shared by all the compounds. Nineveh's violence and God's threat of disaster aimed to do harm. Now — since both Nineveh and God have turned away from their intention — this will to do harm overcomes Jonah. He is especially obsessed by the thought of Nineveh's wickedness, now that God has withdrawn his threat of disaster. Thus the repeated catchword does not merely accentuate Jonah's opposition to God's judgment; it also stresses that Jonah and Nineveh have actually exchanged roles. That it should be God's very mercy that brings "great wickedness on Jonah" is both dramatic and satiric. Verse 1b describes the result of 1a. The elliptical expression says only that "he became hot"; but this is an implicit recollection of [וֹ]אַף as subject of חרה (imperfect consecutive): "his (nose = snorting =) anger flared up in him." So this sentence too links up with the previous scene — i.e., with the expectation in v. 9b, fulfilled in v. 10, that God would turn away from the glowing embers (חָרוֹן) of his anger. This emphasized revolt of Jonah's against the outcome of the scene in Nineveh immediately rouses the reader's expectancy, even though the main problem is as yet no more than touched upon.

[4:2] In the prayer that follows, Jonah reveals what this problem is. The prayer is introduced as imploring lament (פלל *hithpaʿel*, as in the interpolation 2:1) and begins with the cry of someone distraught. The prayer of the heathen sailors in 1:14 began in exactly the same way; on אנה see textual note to 1:14b and p. 119 above. With an amazing stroke of narrative artistry, the writer shows that what is now under discussion is the general question underlying the novella as a whole. He introduces a flashback, to the first scene of all, to the hour when Jonah received his call ("when I was still in my own country"); Jonah reminds God of his plan "to flee to Tarshish." In that first scene the writer presented a rigidly silent Jonah (1:3). His thoughts remain completely hidden from the reader. Now that the vain flight and the result of the preaching in Nineveh have been related, Jonah divulges what he said to himself at the moment when he set off on his journey. Now the flashback to that moment has the dramatic effect of calling in question everything that God has done with Jonah (cf. G. M. Landes, *Interp* 21 [1967] 13).

The question "Was not this what I said when I was still in my own country?" is not merely the "I told you so" of the arrogant dogmatist. At the same time it reveals the fact that the know-all ends up in hopeless despair. Whether (as J. D. Magonet thinks; cf. *Form and Meaning* [1973] 137) the narrator realized it, or whether he did not, the question הלוא־זה דברי is reminiscent of Exod. 14:12; it is the very question put to Moses in the wilderness by the Israelites, after their earlier persecution by the Egyptians: הֲלֹא־זֶה הַדָּבָר, "Is not this what we said to you in Egypt, 'Let us alone and let us serve the Egyptians'? For it would have been better for us to serve the Egyptians than to die in the wilderness." "Were there no graves in Egypt?" (v. 11; cf. p. 150 above on the reminiscence of Exod. 14:31 in the language of 1:16a and 3:5a). In Jonah's case too the question is death, sooner or later, on his flight (1:12) or outside Nineveh (4:4). In Exodus 14 Israel despairs as to whether the exodus has any point. Our Jonah despairs about the point of his calling and his mission in the world.

It is Jonah himself who discloses the special reason (כי, "because") for his despair, when he cites his "knowledge." "For I knew. . . ." How different this ידעתי, "I knew," as the assertion of someone totally sure of himself, from the venturesome, hopeful מִי־יוֹדֵעַ, "Who knows?" of 3:9! Jonah knew what Nineveh did not know. But since he did not want to admit his knowledge — any more than he did earlier, when he fled over the sea from the very Yahweh whom he acknowledged to be the sea's Creator (1:9f.) — for all that he knows, he has stopped listening and stopped hearing; all that is left to him is the wish to die.

What, then, does this repudiated knowledge and this known repudiation really know? Simply what Israel had been able to confess from time immemorial — and what she can be shown to have confessed in postexilic times in largely these very words. In liturgical usage the confession of faith took on increasingly fixed form; cf. Ps. 86:15; 103:8; (111:4); 145:8; Exod. 34:6; (Num. 14:18; Nah. 1:3); Neh. 9:17, 31; Joel 2:13; also J. Scharbert, "Formgeschichte und Exegese von Ex 34,6f., "*Bibl* 38 (1957) 130-150; W. Zimmerli, *ThWNT* 9:368f.; L Schmidt, *De Deo* 89ff. Although the sequence of epithets describes God's attributes rather than his acts, according to the evidence of the various contexts, it nonetheless serves the condensed acknowledgment of what God has done. Its character cannot therefore be specifically designated as wisdom. It belongs typically within the context of worship; cf. — contrary to R. C. Dentan, "The Literary Affinities of Exodus XXXIV 6f.," *VT* 13 (1963) 34-51—L. Perlitt, *Bundestheologie im Alten Testament*, WMANT 36 (1969) 213f. Thus in addition to the confessional style (Ps. 103:8; 145:8 Exod. 34:6; Joel 2:13), the "address" style of the prayer with introductory אתה, as here, can also be found in Ps. 86:15 and Neh. 9:17.

Jonah's citation of the praise of God used in worship sounds cynical from the very outset, since it is bound to serve as declaration of his anger against God. This becomes clearer with every predicate. חנון means the God who inclines graciously to the humble and needy, and who exercises his supremacy on behalf of the inferior (cf. W. Zimmerli, *ThWNT* 9:367f.); רחום means the kindly, solicitous providence, that protects and sustains endangered life like a mother (רֶחֶם = womb); cf. also A. Jepsen *KuD* 7 [1961] 261-271). The rhymed word-pair חנון ורחום can be found in similar long sentences of praise, more often in the reverse order (Ps. 86:15; 103:8; Exod. 34:6), but in later literature generally in the form found here as well (Ps. 145:8; Neh. 9:17, 31; 2 Chron. 30:9; Joel 2:13; Ps. 111:4; about a person, Ps. 112:4). ארך אפים ("slow to anger") makes it more evident why for Jonah the praise of God is turned into an accusation. Here, for the narrator, the wording of the liturgical formula (cf. Exod. 34:6; Ps. 86:15; 103:8; 145:8; Neh. 9:17; Joel 2:13) touches the narrative context for the first time. The "hot embers of God's anger" (3:9) are replaced in the liturgical formula by the "delay of his anger," his "forbearance" (ארך = "protract for a long time"; cf. G. Sauer, *THAT* 1:220-224, esp. 222). The phrase means the patient deferment of the wrath that has been deserved, in which God does not destroy the guilty (Isa. 48:9). Even earlier, Yahweh's forbearance with Jeremiah's persecutors was a trial with which the prophet had to struggle (15:15). In the context of these ideas, the praise of the divine patience on Jonah's lips becomes a reproach. A shadow is also cast even on the phrase רב חסד, "the abundance of steadfast love." חסד is one of the commonest titles of praise applied to Yahweh (W. Zimmerli, *ThWNT* 9:374). It is the predicate through which Yahweh confers and sustains fellowship with his people. But the "abundance" (רב) or the "greatness" (גְדָל־חֶסֶד, "great in steadfast love," Ps. 145:8) exceeds all limits and is directed towards all created beings (cf. Ps. 145:9). It is characteristic of the whole liturgical formula not to include any limiting element which would confine Yahweh's behavior to Israel.

This is also true particularly of the final component in the "knowledge" to which Jonah points: "he is sorry for the disaster." This picks up the statement of 3:(9), 10 which was the essential reason for Jonah's rebellion and which reported Yahweh's revocation of his announcement of Nineveh's impending downfall. This consequently meant the withdrawal of the saying which Jonah proclaimed, according to 3:4 (for an explanation of the words see p. 154 above); נחם meant the compassionate revocation; רעה the destruction that was proclaimed. We should note that among the doxologies which include the previous four elements (Exod. 34:6; Neh. 9:17; Ps. 86:15; 103:8; 145:8), this final component is to be found only in Joel 2:13 (for its occurrence in postbiblical writing, cf. Pr. Man. 7); but what is proclaimed to Jerusalem in the book of Joel now applies to Nineveh (see pp. 153f.

above). In Exod. 34:6 and Ps. 86:15 the fifth element in the series is אֱמֶת; in Joel and Jonah this pointer to God's reliable faithfulness is interpreted in the same sense as in Ps. 103:8f. ("He does not sit in judgment for ever") and Ps. 145:8f. ("Yahweh is good to all"; cf. Neh. 9:17b "thou hast not forsaken them"). But in Joel and Jonah it is precisely related to the threatening oracle that has been previously proclaimed, but which God, out of compassion, refrains from implementing (cf. the anticipatory interpretation in 3:10b).

This exposes the essential reason for Jonah's despair. He makes the epithets which Israel uses in her praise of God a ground for reproach. God does not abide by his word of judgment. On the contrary, through his mercy he puts himself on the side of Israel's merciless enemies. In this way Jonah chimes in with the voices of the people with whom Malachi quarrels: "It is pointless to serve God" (3:14f.). What difference is there "between the person who serves God and the person who does not serve him" (3:18)? "Where is the God of judgment" (2:17)? The last little clause in v. 2 precisely delineates the problem on which Jonah thinks he must founder.

[4:3] "The loss of destructive certainty has a self-destructive result: he would rather die than live" (K. Heinrich, *Parmenides und Jona* [1966] 108). E. Bickermann, *RHPhR* 45 (1965) 239, quotes Jerome on Jonah 1:3: "scit propheta. . .quod poenitentia gentium ruina sit Judaeorum" ("the prophet knows. . .that the penitence of the Gentiles would be disaster for the Jews"). ועתה, "now therefore," introduces the result (cf. Gen. 3:22; 47:4; Amos 7:16; Mal. 3:15; and frequently): he begs to die. There is no mistaking the fact that the narrator is putting words into Jonah's mouth taken from the Elijah tradition (1 Kings 19:4bβ: עַתָּה יהוה קַח נַפְשִׁי, "Now, Yahweh, take away my life. . ."), especially since later v. 8b takes up 1 Kings 19:4bα. Is it chance that in the case of Elijah too we hear about the day's march (1 Kings 19:4a; cf. Jonah 3:4a) and about 40 days (and nights, 1 Kings 19:8; cf. Jonah 3:4b) and that in 1 Kings 19:9ff. a great dialog follows, as it does here? Cf. A. Feuillet, "Sources," *RB* 54 (1947) 168f., and J. D. Magonet, *Form* (1973) 124, 201. נפש, initially, the organ that makes life possible, here means life itself; cf. חיי ("my life") in 3b; Ps. 7:5; 26:9; and pp. 119f. above on 1:14. It is not without irony when Elijah's prayer is picked up here. Elijah is suffering from persecution; Jonah suffers from success he did not want. Elijah views himself as being "no better than his fathers"; Jonah suffers from God's incalculable vacillation. He despairs of God's justice and the point of his service (cf. vv. 4, 9b). The declaration "dying is better for me than life" is once more a reminiscence of the despairing Israel of Exod. 14:12 (see p. 166 above), which finds that slavery and death (v. 11) in Egypt was better than to die in the desert. So for Jonah the problem of the validity of God's word and God's justice has become an existential problem. And yet we can observe a remarkable shift here: on the one hand, the fact of Nineveh's repentance, as the precondition for God's mercy (3:8-10), does not enter Jonah's orbit; on the other hand, his own ego ("I" occurs 9 times in vv. 2f.) moves into the foreground in an access of self-torment.

[4:4]   The shameless accusation of the otherwise so taciturn Jonah is blown up
into inflated proportions. The narrator makes Yahweh reply in tersest brevity. He
interprets the torrent of words as ''anger,'' in line with v. 1b (''you became hot'';
on the ellipsis see p. 165 above) and inquires shortly whether anger like this is appropriate, called for, right (on יטב *hiph'il* infinitive absolute see textual note to v.
4b). The particle הַ does not necessarily have an interrogative meaning; it can occasionally be exclamatory; Joüon, *Gr* §161b translates: ''Tu es bien en colère''
— ''you are in a proper rage!'' However, this interpretation surely depends on the
assumption that v. 4 is not countered by the words of v. 5. But the precise parallel
to v. 4 in v. 9 must certainly be seen as a question, which also receives an answer.
Accordingly we shall surely do better to understand v. 4 too as a question, and to
see v. 5 as substitute for an answer (see below). Whether Yahweh's question is intended to echo the formulation used to Cain in Gen. 4:6f. (thus W. Rudolph, KAT
13/2 [1971] 328, and J. D. Magonet, *Form* 192), and is therefore a play on Cain's
envy of Abel, is not entirely clear. At all events, Yahweh's initial reaction to Jonah's rebellious resignation is a positively tender kindness, which sets about
bringing the sulky Jonah to a proper self-examination.

[4:5]   In order that he can bring in God's direct lesson to Jonah, the narrator has
first of all to interpolate the fact (see p. 163 above) that Jonah had long since left
the city — it would seem immediately after he had fulfilled his assignment there
in 3:4—and that he had sat down east of the city in a leafy booth which he had
made for himself; whereas Nineveh's king had sat down in the dust (cf. וישׁב ''sat
down,'' in aβ and bα, with 3:6bβ). The purpose of Jonah's action is now stressed:
so that he could wait ''in the shade,'' i.e., without any hurry, ''until he saw what
would happen in the city''; and, in the light of v. 4, this allows us to perceive here
an answer to Yahweh's question. Without using any words, his very attitude is a
defiant reply: we shall see whether my anger is justifiable or not! He shows his
scorn of Yahweh by waiting for a change ''in the city'' instead of examining himself. Verse 5bγ is the third mention of ''the city'' (after aα and β). In his self-
opinionated dogmatism, it is on the city that all Jonah's attention is concentrated.
Will it soon relapse into its old wickedness? And will Yahweh then intervene after
all? He is determined to ''see'' something different from what Yahweh ''saw''
(cf. bβ with 3:10aα). In the flow of the narrative, it is not merely v. 5a which is indispensable as a preparation for vv. 6ff.; v. 5b is equally important as a reaction to
v. 4. But the links are so subtle and so tenuous that it is impossible to assign the
material to different literary strata with any conviction (see p. 164 above; for a different view cf. L. Schmidt, *De Deo* 27ff.). According to the story as we have it,
up to the end of v. 5 Jonah in his obduracy responds to Yahweh's kindly admon-
ishment (v. 4) only with the very opposite of an assent to the sparing of Nineveh.

[4:6]   But Yahweh does not leave Jonah to himself, with his scowling glare in
the direction of Nineveh; nor does he follow his gaze. He does, however, cease to
reply to him in words. The Creator of all things begins a game with him, just as

Wisdom, God's delight, plays a game before the Creator on the inhabited globe (see p. 132 above on 2:1 [1:17]).[1] Just as in 1:17 God "appointed" the great fish (see p. 132 above), so he now appoints a castor oil plant. The transition to this educative action goes along with departure from the use of the simple name "Yahweh" (vv. 2, 4; cf. 1:17). The subject of וימן, "appointed," in v. 6 is יהוה אלהים, "Yahweh Elohim"; in v. 7 האלהים "the Elohim" (or "the God"), in v. 8 אלהים "Elohim" (and again in v. 9). There is a compelling presumption here that the narrator was working from a model (see p. 164 above). It is impossible to counter this supposition by the assertion that the change in the name for God is prompted by a particular theological intention, and that [ה]אלהים, "[the] Elohim," points to the hidden God, in the form in which he acts on the Gentiles (cf. T. Boman, *NTT* 37 1936; H. Rosin, *The Lord* [1956]; H. W. Wolff, *Studien* [1964 1975²] 81f.). Chapter 1 clearly speaks against this view. It is more plausible to suppose that the narrator has taken up already formed material, as he often does (see p. 165 above). In doing so he makes no perceptible distinction between אלהים "Elohim," and האלהים, "the Elohim." The name יהוה־אלהים, "Yahweh Elohim," has a transitional significance (between vv. 4 and 7; cf. Gen. 2:4b—3:24 and the comment by C. Westermann, *Genesis 1-11*, 198-199, and 1 Chron. 17:16f.). It should also be remembered at the first mention of the divine subject of וימן, "appoint," in the final scene, that the formula in 1:17 is וימן יהוה, "Yahweh appointed." Whether the castor oil plant has been chosen as counterpart to the broom tree under which Elijah sat and wished for death (1 Kings 19:4) is worth consideration, in view of the link between v. 8b (v. 3a) and the same text (cf. A. Feuillet, *Sources* 168f., who also views the story of Jonah's booth in v. 5 as being inspired by Elijah's cave in 1 Kings 19:9).

In all probability קיקיון is the *ricinus communis* (thus α'θ'κικεών), although Gk (κολοκύνθα)[2] and S have in mind the bottle gourd, and σ'(κισσός) and Vg (*hedera*) ivy. For the castor oil plant grows rapidly, gives abundant shade through its great plate-like leaves, but also dies easily (cf. vv. 7, 10). Dalman (*AuS* 1:65) saw plants 10 to 15 feet high at the Jordan. This is the form in which

---

1. M. Luther: "In order to dispel Jonah's scruples and also to supply him with an answer to give to his angry fellow Jews, God toys with him and gives him a sign, just as He did to Peter in Acts 10:11ff., when Peter labored under a similar illusion as Jonah here. God showed him a vision from heaven, a linen cloth containing all kinds of animals, and told him that everything was pure, although he saw nothing but heathen without the laws of Moses" (*Luther's Works*, vol. 19 [St. Louis: Concordia, 1974], p. 94).

2. The early Roman representations of Jonah on sarcophagi which date from the second half of the 3rd century show a naked Jonah in a gourd arbor; they combine 4:5 and 4:6 (Gk). Jonah is by no means displaying any tense expectancy ("what would happen in the city"); he is lying in a state of prostration, like someone who — after having gone through the experience of death inside the fish — has just awaked to new life. The gourd booth represents the house which God himself builds for the person who had been rescued from death (2 Cor. 5:1ff.). Iconographically, the influence of Dionysius lying in an arbor of vines is unmistakable. Cf. the illustrations in *RGG*³ 4, pl. 52, illustrations 1 and 2; E. Stommel, "Zum Problem der frühchristlichen Jonasdarstellungen," *Jahrbuch für Antike und Christentum* 1 (1958) 112-115; H. Rohden, *Architektonische römische Reliefs der Kaiserzeit* (1911) pl. 8a.

this unusual plant will have been known in postexilic times too. Yahweh lets it grow up over Jonah in order to give him shade. The fact that the shade of the castor oil plant is mentioned so soon after the shade of the booth (v. 5b) may be due to the combination of different traditional material. At all events, in what follows, the narrator is now thinking only of the shade that Yahweh has conferred. It is meant for Jonah's head, which is in particular need of it. There is no suggestion that the shade cast by the booth would have been insufficient, especially when it was no longer new (cf. G. Dalman, *AuS* 2, pl. 13-16, and 6, pl. 15). Of the two infinitive clauses, which are set asyndectically side by side (i.e., without any connecting conjunction), the first is quite indispensable for the sequel in vv. 7-9. But the second should not be too hastily deleted either, since it goes back to v. 1a, thus linking Yahweh's illustrative, didactic game with the occasion which made the instruction necessary — Jonah's spiteful ill-will. The doublet may again go back to the absorption of material that had already taken on a fixed form. The asyndesis can be explained by our narrator's pleasure in the alliteration (להיות צל ‏להציל. . .); cf. also BrSynt §133c: "Asyndesis in the sequence of cause and effect." When the intention behind the gift of the shade is explained (to extricate Jonah from his deep resentment), the rapid success of God's experiment with Jonah's psyche is all the more dazzling: Jonah is overcome by "great joy" over the castor oil plant. The sentence construction, with internal, absolute object from the same verbal root (see p. 116 on 1:10 and textual note to 4:1a), is formally reminiscent of v. 1; but Jonah is now the subject; it is a construction which allows the reader thoroughly to enjoy the turn of events. The irony is unmistakable: the change has nothing to do with Nineveh, and the problem of God's word and God's justice. It is due solely to Jonah's own trivial sense of well-being.

[4:7]   God's game continues. After the mighty, miraculous plant, "he appoints" the tiny worm, the maggot which already spoilt the manna (Exod. 16:20ff.). From earliest dawn onwards, this new creature of God's determines the whole of the following day: the worm pierces through the castor oil plant so that it withers away; we find נכה *hiph'il* for a deadly wounding in 2 Sam. 10:18, for example; cf. also Lev. 24:18. So the reason for the "great joy" is very soon snatched away.

[4:8]   What happens now? The reader is eager to hear the effect on Jonah. But the slow-motion technique retards the account. Hardly an hour elapses between the first glimmer of light in the eastern sky and the rising of the sun; cf. Dalman, *AuS* 1:601. Then God orders up the next creature for his service: the east wind, which is described by the word חרישית (see textual note to v. 8a) and is probably intended to be the scorching sirocco, with which Israel was familiar and which comes from the desert (M. Noth, *Die Welt des Alten Testaments* [1962⁴] 29f. [Eng., *Old Testament World*, 1966]; E. M. Good, *Irony* [1965] 52, believes — probably rightly — that our author had never actually been in Mesopotamia). So two attacks are mounted against Jonah's "great joy": through the worm and through the wind. Does this correspond to the double shade of vv.

5b and 6a? H. Winckler "Jona" (1900) 265, thought that the east wind knocked down the leafy booth. The text says nothing about this. But it is true that the effect of the double attack is also reported in two sentences. First, the sun beats down on Jonah's head. ותך is a repetition of v. 7b (see above); נכה *hiph'il*, with the sun as subject, means a sunstroke, as in Ps. 121:6; Isa. 49:10; the sun "hits" the person's head like the well-aimed arrow from a bow (1 Kings 22:34; 2 Kings 9:24). The special mention of Jonah's head reminds us of the purpose of the castor oil plant's shadow in v. 6a. Secondly, we are told that Jonah "felt quite faint"; here the writer will be thinking of the combination of a sunstroke (cf. 2 Kings 4:18-20) and the sirocco; cf. Amos 8:13 and H. W. Wolff, *Joel/Amos* BK 14/2, 380f. (Eng., *Joel and Amos*, on Amos 8:13). So Jonah's great joy is quickly swallowed up in complete exhaustion. This brings the silent dialog in vv. 5-8a (see p. 162 above) to an end. Again, as in v. 3 (see p. 168 above), the narrator picks up words taken from the Elijah story (1 Kings 19:4bα, וַיִּשְׁאַל אֶת־נַפְשׁוֹ לָמוּת וַיֹּאמֶר) and, with the little clause out of v. 3b, makes Jonah ask for death. So the Creator's purposeful game has taken him back precisely to the point of his accusation.

[4:9]   But when God also takes up again, word for word, his question in v. 4, he can now — after the entr'acte with the plant — relate that question to something different: it is now prompted by Jonah's anger over the castor oil plant. (The unaltered recapitulation of Yahweh's question to Elijah in 1 Kings 19:9, 13 must be evaluated differently; cf. L. Schmidt, *De Deo* 32, on F. Feuillet. *RB* 54 [1947] 168f.) Now insight can be required of him by way of the wisdom paradigm. Earlier, Jonah was indignant because Yahweh took pity on Nineveh. Now it is self-pity that incites his indignation. By showing Jonah as ready to die because there is no more shade, the satirist exposes the fact that his first expression of unwillingness was also deeply rooted in self-pity, not in genuine concern about the validity of God's word and his justice. Earlier he was asked whether "he did right to be angry" in the face of God's goodness towards the city of Nineveh; he is now asked the same question, in the context of God's destruction of what had given him personal pleasure.

How will Jonah respond to this new question? To say "no" would be to admit the injustice of his anger. For, after all, he had no claim to the shade cast by the castor oil plant: the joy it gave him was a free gift. But in granting this he would have simultaneously to admit that God was free to pardon Nineveh. On the other hand, if he insisted on his right to be angry because of the castor oil plant, he would then be claiming God's enduring kindness towards himself, and could hardly deny it to Nineveh. Thus, in his wisdom game with the rebel, the Creator has become Jonah's irrefutable preceptor, whether his answer to the question is a "yes" or a "no" (cf. T. E. Fretheim, "Jonah and Theodicy," *ZAW* 90 [1978]).

Jonah maintains that his anger is quite right "to the point of death." עד־מות as a superlative says more than "the extremest" (so KBL[3]; cf. D. W. Thomas, *VT* 3 [1953] 220, and W. Rudolph's comment on the passage, KAT 13/2 [1971]); as Jonah's final word, it again points to his wish to die (vv. 3b, 8b). Yahweh's last question, however he answered it, forced him to admit God's free compassion; and with this God he does not want to live. Paradoxically enough, he neither wished to live under the government of free grace (vv. 1-3), nor is he now prepared to live under a government without grace (vv. 7-9). If to live means living with a God who is free to pity, then he chooses the final separation from him: death. He thinks that in the land of oblivion the confession of faith he mockingly cites in v. 2b would no longer be known (Ps. 88:10-12), although Yahweh has already caught up with him in death once (1:17ff.). This is the unreasonable impasse in which Jonah is involved through his protest against God's sovereign right to compassion.

[4:10]   But Yahweh does not let his Jonah go, even though Jonah himself sees no way out. He returns a second time to his didactic parable in vv. 6-8, stating the fact of the matter to Jonah, on the basis of his reaction in vv. 8b and 9b. Here the narrator uses the word חוס, "to pity," which acquires a decisive significance in v. 11 also. The word occurs 24 times in the Old Testament. On 15 of these occasions the eye is the subject: Gen. 45:20; 5 times in Deuteronomy (e.g., 7:16); Isa. 13:18; and 8 times in Ezekiel (e.g., 5:11). The notion of the "flowing" = "weeping" of the eye (cf. KBL³) no longer emerges very distinctly, but the clouded, sad glance can still be read in the word. On 7 occasions, the reason for this clouded glance is not directly stated (although in the context it is always Israelites who are meant); in 17 cases the reason is additionally put forward with על; in 15 the word touches on human beings (e.g., Ps. 72:13; Jer. 21:7), so that the meaning "to have pity" is also implicit. Only twice does it refer to things (in Gen. 45:20 to household goods that have been left behind; in Jonah 4:10 to the withered castor oil plant), so that we might assume the meaning "to be sad," "to suffer." But in the case we are considering it is more probable that the storyteller means "to grieve pityingly." For here he deliberately uses חוס parallel to v. 11, where it is clearly related to people. In this way he is in line with the almost exclusive use of חוס in connection with human beings (Gen. 45:20 is the exception). The fact that the word generally expresses a distress which also means pity is shown by the fact that in Deuteronomy חוס would also bring about a less severe judgment (19:13, 21; 25:12), so that it must mean not merely "to look distressfully" but also "to regard pityingly." Moreover, the synonymous parallel to חוס is often חמל, "to feel compassion," "to spare" (Deut. 13:9; Ezek. 7:4, 9; 8:18; 9:5, 10; 16:5) or רחם *pi'el* ("have mercy," Isa. 13:18), or both (Jer. 13:14; 21:7).

The narrator, that is to say, makes Yahweh define Jonah's behavior as a compassionate grief for the castor oil plant. In this way he once more displays his skillful use of irony. For he actually means the very opposite of what Yahweh says: Jonah is not really suffering with the withered plant at all; he is simply missing his own comfort, just as, earlier, it was not because of Nineveh that he suffered; it was because of his own theological prestige (cf. M. Burrows, "Category" 99). But it was the castor oil plant that triggered off his self-pity. Here Yahweh points out that he had not "exerted himself" personally on the plant's behalf. The verb עמל occurs only in late usage for troublesome work, for either physical (Prov. 16:26; Eccles. 2:11; Ps. 127:1, building) or mental (Eccles. 2:19-21) labor (apart from the passages cited, only in Ecclesiastes, eight times in all). The castor oil plant grew up on Jonah's behalf, as a pure gift of Yahweh's. The continuation: "you did not make it grow" stresses the same point. גדל *pi'el* is used elsewhere as well not merely for the upbringing of children (Isa. 1:2; 49:21) but also for the cultivation of plants (Isa. 44:14; Ezek. 31:3f.). But in the case of this castor oil plant, Jonah was not involved in the genesis and growth of the plant in any way at all. Finally, the ephemeral nature of the plant is emphasized — the ostensible reason for Jonah's grief. It sprang up in a night and perished in a night. On שֶׁ see textual note to 1:7a; on the form and meaning of the double בֶּן see textual note to v. 10a; on the fact itself cf. vv. 6a and 7; at the first light, i.e., before dawn (v. 8a) and therefore still during the night following the day of great joy, the plant withered. Here the word used is אבד, "it perished." It is therefore an echo of the catchword with which in 1:6, 14; 3:9 the heathen hope and pray that "they may not perish." What a rejection of this hope means, Jonah has been able to learn from the example of the castor oil plant. He laments it for his own sake, and so should no longer wish any such rejection for Nineveh. And yet the final clause indicates how trivial a matter it is that is suddenly causing Jonah such violent distress. But this very fact ought to make him understand the great matter which is occupying Yahweh (cf. the rejection of the complaints of Jeremiah and Baruch in Jer. 12:1-5; 45:3-5; cf. here S. H. Blank, "Doest Thou Well to Be Angry? A Study in Self-Pity," *HUCA* 26 [1955] 29-41).

[4:11]   A final question is designed to bring about Jonah's assent at long last. As a rhetorical question (cf. textual note to v. 11a) it is an intensified assertion, but one that calls for reflection and agreement. It picks up v. 10 with the keyword: "You have compassion with the castor oil plant. . .and I may not have compassion with Nineveh. . .?" As it is here, חוס is used in connection with Yahweh on 10 other occasions (out of a total of 24), 7 of them negative: Yahweh shows himself to be the Lord by not allowing himself to be moved by pity (Jer. 13:14; Ezek. 5:11; 7:4, 9; 8:18; 9:10; 24:14). It is also said about the great military conquerors that they will not look mercifully on their victims (חוס Isa. 13:18; Jer. 21:7). Israel's judges are not to do so either (Deut. 13:9; 19:13, 21; 25:12). But in one case we find a prayer, with our word, that the king of Israel may have pity on the poor (Ps. 72:13). Only on one single occasion does the Old Testament report that Yahweh has had חוס (Ezek. 20:17); twice he is implored to do so. These two texts are close to the end of the Jonah story, both in content and period. In Neh. 13:22, Nehemiah asks of his God compassion (חוּסָה), in accordance with his abundant steadfast love (כְּרֹב חַסְדֶּךָ); according to this, Yahweh's חוס corresponds to the great חֶסֶד cited by Jonah in v. 2. Jonah, that is to say, is being moved to take up a new attitude to that acknowledgment of faith. The plea חוּסָה can be found a second time in Joel 2:17. There it goes back to the prophetic promise in Joel 2:13f., which encourages Israel, on the one hand, with the same divine predicates (v. 13b) which we find repeated word for word in Jonah 4:2b and, on the other, with the hope for Yahweh's compassionate withdrawal of the threat of judgment (v. 14a) which we also find again, word for word, in Jonah 3:9. In both parallels, the decisive catchword is (עַל־הָרָעָה) נִחַם. It was this saying about the compassionate withdrawal of the threat (cf. 3:10) which particularly enraged Jonah in vv. 2f. It is this that the final question picks up, in the inquiry whether Yahweh may not exercise חוס. There is a tiny shift in the meaning of the word here. In theological usage נחם always refers to an earlier act, an earlier plan, or a saying of Yahweh's that has been uttered at some earlier point (see p. 154 above); חוס, on the other hand, is directed wholly to the exciter of compassion here and now. Thus in v. 10 it is also stimulated by the scene with the castor oil plant which has just been experienced, and in v. 11 it is only the Nineveh of the present moment which is under consideration. There is no recollection of the threat that has been withdrawn, or of the city's repentance (cf. 3:8-10), or even of the implicitly suggested fact that Nineveh is a creation of Yahweh's. It is only what excites Yahweh's compassion here and now that is mentioned.

Astonishingly enough, it is the city's size that is touched on first of all. This was mentioned at the beginning of the story, in 1:2, and was elaborated in 3:3b. Now the precise number of the city's inhabitants is given: 120,000 (see textual note to 11c); the writer keeps his readers in suspense through new details up to the last minute. The number may well be a more or less accurate estimate of the size of Nineveh as it is known to have been in the seventh century, in the period of the neo-Assyrian empire. For the Sennacherib period (704-681) the population has been estimated at about 300,000 (A.T. Olmstead, *History of Assyria* [1960] 326); according to a stele of Ashurnasirpal II (883-859) 69,574 people lived in Kalakh, which was only half the size of Nineveh (D. J. Wiseman, ''A New Stele of *Ashurnasirpal* II,'' *Iraq* 14 [1952] 28). Of course אדם means all the inhabitants. The relative clause does not permit us to think only in terms of children. The clause rather explains that a further reason for Yahweh's mercy is that the capacity for distinguishing and judging is not as fully developed among the Ninevites as Jonah would like to expect. For ידע בין. . .ל = ''distinguish,'' cf. 2 Sam. 19:36; Ezek. 22:26; 44:23. Again there is a tinge of irony here. What Jonah is inclined to despise is for Yahweh one more reason for compassion. This also applies, finally, to the great number of animals (cf. 3:7f.). Care and love for animals seldom finds any mention in the Old Testament: Deut. 22:6f.; 25:4; Prov. 12:10; cf. 1 Cor. 9:9; 1 Tim. 5:18. Here the cattle play a part in Yahweh's decision to have mercy on the city. Animals are closer to human beings than plants, as the Priestly writing shows in the clearest possible way; cf. Gen. 1:11f. with v. 24f. So, to the very end the final question proceeds from the lesser (pity for the castor oil plant) to the greater, trying to conquer Jonah's resistance through convincing arguments.

Jonah makes no further reply. The reader has to carry away the question, think about it, and decide rightly — or so our writer thinks.

Purpose

The problem of the final scene is Jonah's anger. This is introduced into the story in the first sentence (v. 1), with the description of ''the hero's'' state of mind; it is kept alive by way of Yahweh's reiterated question (vv. 4, 9a) and — through Yahweh's reply in v. 9 — is confirmed as being the decisive point at issue, right up to the last sentence of all. Yahweh's question and Jonah's answer define the problem more precisely: is Jonah's anger justified? The question became acute because Yahweh withdrew his anger from Nineveh after the city turned away from its wickedness (on the relationship between 4:1 and 3:8-10 see p. 165 above).

Why, in the narrator's view, is Jonah angry? It would seem that what is tormenting him is the problem of theodicy; but in fact his real concern is self-assertion. The satire shows how the theory is simply a pretext. When he looks back to Nineveh's cruel acts (חָמָס 3:8), the preacher of judgment (3:4) is outraged to learn that his threat of destruction has been revoked. In a process of hindsight, he excuses the flight described in chap. 1 (4:2a). For God's compassion came as no surprise to him: the theology of the confession of faith he quoted in v. 2b showed him that nothing else was to be expected. The way in which Jonah deals with Israel's experience of Yahweh's mercy is frightening and chilling. For him this confession of faith, with its consequences for the hostile Gentile world, completely calls in question Israel's beliefs and her ministry in the world. The narrator makes Jonah the spokesman of the sullen murmuring among ''the God-fearing'' of the postexilic era, who found it pointless to go on serving God and useless to inquire about his commandments (Mal. 3:14ff.) since — in the face of the happiness of the wicked — it seemed vain to ask: ''Where is the God of judgment?'' (Mal. 2:17; see p. 168 above). In just the same way, Jonah was on the lookout for Nineveh's well-deserved downfall (v. 5b) — but in vain. Since God's justice had come to nothing, Jonah's anger seems quite justified. All that is left to wish for is death — which means existence far from the incalculable God.

But the narrator exposes this mock theological battle for what it is. He does so with forcible conviction by way of the castor oil plant, whose shade rapidly transforms Jonah's rage to joy (v. 6), without anything having changed either with God or in Nineveh. What the harsh light of satire makes glaringly evident here is already indicated in the great accusation in vv. 2f., and finally through the relapse into anger in vv. 8f., after the plant has withered: what is of really decisive importance for him is his own mighty ego (see p. 172 above). His need for self-assertion clutches at a rigid theology and makes it impossible for him to follow the divine modulations and transformations. He is consequently also unable to assimilate the facts theologically — and above all the fact that Yahweh's pitying withdrawal of his pronouncement of judgment goes back to Nineveh's repentance (3:10). What he himself said in Nineveh is more important to him than what God thereby brought about. In total apathy, he cuts himself off from the efficacy of the word of God. In rigidly unyielding arrogance, he remains wrapped up entirely in himself. It is therefore Jonah and the justifiability of his anger which is in reality the problem.

The psychology of this dismally mulish theologian is masterly; but what is more important for the writer is the way in which Yahweh handles him. God reveals his purpose clearly enough in v. 6aβ: he wants to pluck Jonah out of his self-willed malignancy at all costs. He does so in two ways. First, he no less than three times urges questions upon him, questions designed solely to stimulate his own self-critical reflection, to move him to test his own reluctance (vv. 4, 9a), and to compare his own justice with God's (v. 10f.). In his demands (vv. 3, 8b), Jonah behaves as if he is finished with God; but Yahweh is by no means finished with Jonah; he shows him the same kindness that he shows to Nineveh. He emphasizes this through his silent action. In the effect it has on Jonah, the game with the castor oil plant is a practical joke. Just because Yahweh wants to free Jonah from his inward anger, just as he freed Nineveh, he does not take Jonah's spitefulness too seriously. What he does is not without its comic side. The narrator makes God avoid the theological vocabulary of his rebel. One point particularly worth noting is that in the questions God puts to Jonah God enters into the dissentient's position insofar as he too does not mention Nineveh's repentance as the precondition for his withdrawal of the disaster. What he does is to guide Jonah towards a comprehension of completely free grace. According to v. 11, the helplessness of the great city is a sufficient argument for the compassion (cf. Amos 7:2, 5 and H. W. Wolff, *Joel/Amos*, BK 14/2, 343f. [Eng., *Joel and Amos*, on Amos 7:2]; also p. 175 above). By rousing "pity" in Jonah himself, Yahweh seeks understanding for his pity with Nineveh; on the distinction in meaning between נחם and חוס see pp. 174f. above. God seeks to liberate the inhibited theologian through his own experience, at the same time laying bare his own heart to him, in his withdrawn self-confinement.

Yahweh's question is the narrator's final word to his reader. That reader is not spared the necessity of finding his own answer. What will Israel say, in a world in which she has to suffer herself, while the great empires flourish? What will her attitude be to God's unlimited mercy with the whole world? Nowhere in the Old Testament is this question put so stringently and yet so kindly as in the Jonah story.

The question takes on new life in the New Testament. How will those closest to Jesus feel about his goodness to those afar off? The parable of the laborers in the vineyard (Matt. 20:1-16) is, in content, a precise recapitulation of Jonah's problem. There the laborers who are hired in the first hour rebel against the equal treatment accorded to those who are hired only at the eleventh. The Lord counters their murmurings, too, with kindly questions: "Am I not allowed to do what I choose with what belongs to me? Or do you begrudge my generosity?" The final scene in the book of Jonah can show Jesus' disciples even a little more drastically still that, as K. H. Miskotte says, " 'church people,' when they are bad, are worse, more divided, more undependable, ignoble, and inhuman than ordinary people" (*When the Gods Are Silent* [1967] 434). But the scene also shows how their Master liberates them.

Abbreviations

ABR	*Australian Biblical Review*
AfO	*Archiv für Orientforschung*
AION	*Annali del' Istituto Universitario Orientale di Napoli*
AJA	*American Journal of Archeology*
AJSLL	*American Journal of Semitic Languages and Literature*
ANET	*Ancient Near Eastern Texts Relating to the Old Testament*, ed. J. Pritchard
AOAT	*Alter Orient und Altes Testament*
AOT	Altorientalische Texte zum Alten Testament
ArPap	*Aramaic Papyri of the Fifth Century B.C.*, ed. A. Cowley
ASTI	*Annual of the Swedish Theological Institute* (in Jerusalem)
ATD	Das Alte Testament Deutsch
AuS	G. Dalman, *Arbeit und Sitte in Palästina*, 6 vols. (1928-1942)
BA	*Biblical Archeologist*
BASOR	*Bulletin of the American Schools of Oriental Research*
BC	Biblischer Commentar
BeO	*Bibbia e Oriente*
BHH	*Biblisch-historisches Handwörterbuch*
Bibl	*Biblica*
BiblStud	Biblische Studien (Neukirchen)
BiKi	*Bibel und Kirche*
BiViChr	*Bible et Vie Chrétienne*
BK	Biblischer Kommentar
BRL	*Biblisches Reallexikon*
BS	*Bibliotheca Sacra*
BSt	*Biblische Studien*
BT	*Bibliothèque de théologie*
BVSAW.PH	Berichte über die Verhandlungen der sächsischen Akademie der Wissenschaften zu Leipzig, Philologisch-historische Klasse
BZAW	Beihefte zur *ZAW*

BZ NF	*Biblische Zeitschrift*, Neue Folge
CAB	*Cahiers d'archéologie biblique*
CBQ	*Catholic Biblical Quarterly*
CSCO	Corpus Scriptorum Christianorum Orientalium
CTh	Cahiers Théologiques
DB(H)	*Dictionary of the Bible*, ed. J. Hastings
DBS	*Dictionnaire de la Bible. Supplément*
DB(V)	*Dictionnaire de la Bible.* Vigouroux
DIS	*Dictionnaire des inscriptions sémitiques de l'ouest*
DLZ	*Deutsche Literaturzeitung*
DThC	*Dictionnaire de Theologie Catholique*
EB	*Encyclopaedia Biblica*
EJ	*Encyclopaedia Judaica*
EJ(D)	*Encyclopaedica Judaica*. Berlin
Est Bíb	*Estudios Bíblicos*
ÉtB	Études Bibliques
ÉtOr	Études Orientales
EvTh	*Evangelische Theologie*
EzAT	*Erläuterungen zum Alten Testament*
FRLANT	Forschungen zur Religion und Literatur des Alten und Neuen Testaments
Gk	The Septuagint
HAT	Handbuch zum Alten Testament
HIsl	*Handwörterbuch des Islam*
HLa	*Heilig Land*. Nijmegen
HThR	*Harvard Theological Review*
HTS	Hervormde Teologieses Studies
HUCA	*Hebrew Union College Annual*
IB	*Interpreter's Bible*
ICC	International Critical Commentary
IDB	*Interpreter's Dictionary of the Bible*
Interp	*Interpretation*
JbAC	*Jahrbuch für Antike und Christentum*
JBL	*Journal of Biblical Literature*
JE	*Jewish Encyclopedia*
JPOS	*Journal of the Palestine Oriental Society*
JTS	*Journal of Theological Studies*
KAI	*Kanaanäische und aramäische Inschriften*
KAT	Kommentar zum Alten Testament
Kath	*Der Katholik*
KBL	L. Köhler and W. Baumgartner, *Lexicon in Veteris Testamenti Libros*
KEH	*Kurzgefasstes exegetisches Handbuch*
KEK	Kritisch-exegetischer Kommentar über das Neue Testament
KlSchr	*Kleine Schriften zur Theologie*

Abbreviations

KrR	*Křesťanská Revue*
KuD	*Kerygma und Dogma*
LThK	*Lexikon für Theologie und Kirche*
LW	*Luther's Works*, American edition. 56 vols. St. Louis: Concordia, and Philadelphia: Fortress, 1955-.
LXX	The Septuagint
MEAH	*Miscelánea de estudies árabes y hebraicos*
MGWJ	*Monatsschrift für Geschichte und Wissenschaft des Judentums*
MPG	Migne, *Patrologiae. . .Graeca*
MPL	Migne, *Patrologiae. . .Latina*
MT	Masoretic text
NThT	*Nieuw Theologisch Tijdschrift*
NTT	*Norsk Teologisk Tidsskrift*
OuTWP	*Die Ou Testamentiese Werkgemeenskap in Suid-Afrika*, Pretoria
PastB	*Pastor Bonus*
PEQ	*Palestine Exploration Quarterly*
PrincThR	*Princeton Theological Review*
RB	*Revue Biblique*
RBíblArg	*Revista Bíblica* (Argentina)
RE	*Realencyklopädie für protestantische Theologie und Kirche*
REcL	*Revue ecclésiastique de Liège*
RÉJ	*Revue des Études Juives*
RGG	*Religion in Geschichte und Gegenwart*
RHPhR	*Revue d'Histoire et de Philosophie Religieuse*
RLA	*Reallexikon der Assyriologie*
RQ	*Römische Quartalschrift für christliche Altertumskunde*
RSEHA	*Revue Sémitique d'Épigraphie et d'Histoire Ancienne*
Scrip	*Scripture*
Sem	*Semitica*
SJTh	*Scottish Journal of Theology*
SSN	Studia Semitica Neerlandica
StD	Studies and Documents
Strom	*Stromata*
TDNT	*Theological Dictionary of the New Testament* (Eng. trans. of *ThWNT*)
THAT	*Theologisches Handwörterbuch zum Alten Testament*
ThB	Theologische Bücherei
ThL	*Theologische Literaturzeitung*
ThPQ	*Theologish-praktische Quartalschrift*
ThQ	*Theologische Quartalschrift*
ThR	*Theologische Rundschau*
ThST(B)	*Theologische Studien*, ed. Barth
ThStKr	*Theologische Studien und Kritiken*
ThWAT	*Theologische Wörterbuch zum Alten Testament*
ThWNT	*Theologische Wörterbuch zum Neuen Testament*

ThZ	*Theologische Zeitschrift*
UT	C. Gordon, *Ugaritic Textbook*
VT	*Vetus Testamentum*
*VT*Suppl	*VT* Supplement
WA	Weimarer Ausgabe of Luther's works
WAAFLNW	Wissenschaftliche Abhandlungen der Arbeitsgemeinschaft für Forschung und Lehre des Landes Nordrhein-Westfalen
WdF	Wege der Forschung
WMANT	Wissenschaftliche Monographien zum Alten und Neuen Testament
ZAW	*Zeitschrift für die alttestamentliche Wissenschaft*
ZDPV	*Zeitschrift des deutschen Palästina-Vereins*
ZKTh	*Zeitschrift für katholische Theologie*
ZLThK	*Zeitschrift für die (gesamte) lutherische Theologie und Kirche*
ZNW	*Zeitschrift für die neutestamentliche Wissenschaft*
ZRGG	*Zeitschrift für Religions- und Geistesgeschichte*
ZThK	*Zeitschrift für Theologie und Kirche*

Index of Hebrew Words

Index of Biblical References
(with Apocrypha
and Other Ancient Literature)

Index of Biblical References

Index of Biblical References

Index of Names and Subjects